CONTEMPORARY ISSUES
IN CULTURAL ANTHROPOLOGY

Betty A. Smith
Wayne Van Horne
Kennesaw State College

KENDALL/HUNT PUBLISHING COMPANY
2460 Kerper Boulevard P O Box 539 Dubuque, Iowa 52004-0539

CONTENTS

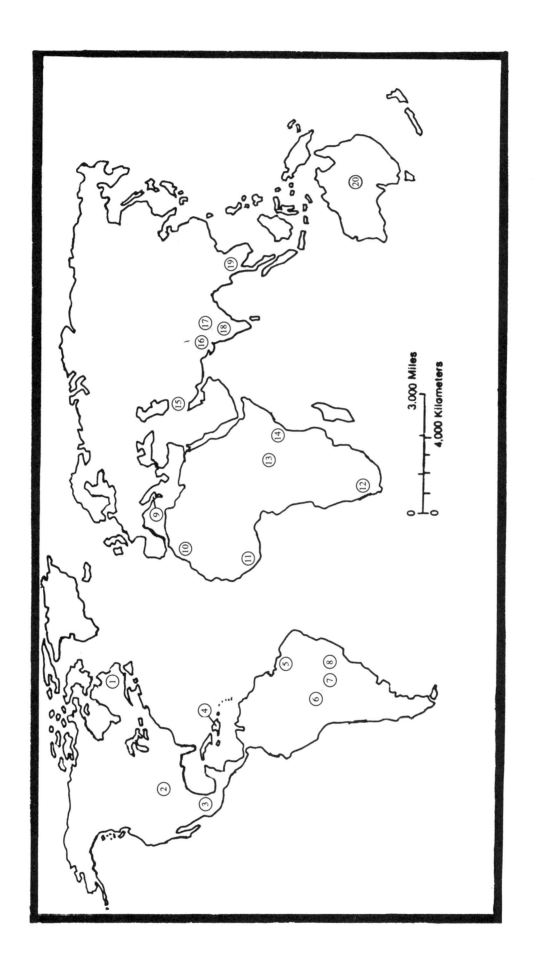

1. Montagnais - Naskapi
2. United States
3. Mexico
4. Haiti
5. Alto do Cruzeiro (Brazil)
6. Bolivia
7. Wauja
8. Kayapó
9. Naples, Italy
10. Morocco
11. Ashanti
12. San (Bushmen)
13. Mbuti Pygmies
14. Gusii
15. Iran
16. Pakistan
17. Nepal
18. India
19. Thailand
20. Australian Aborigines

INTRODUCTION

Humanity—An Endangered Species?

The numerous and complex problems of racial and ethnic conflict, poverty, gender issues, AIDS, population increase, and environmental degradation assault us daily in newspapers and news magazines, on television, and on radio. No one, it seems, whether here in America or in the global community, is immune to them; and many people feel overwhelmed, helpless, or hopeless. They often vaguely understand the causes of these problems but are unable to identify realistic solutions to them.

This book addresses these problems from the perspective of cultural anthropology. The approach of cultural anthropology emphasizes that each problem must be understood in the total context of the culture of which it is a part. Cultural anthropology provides global, cross-cultural comparisons of the behaviors contributing to these problems. It also examines the unique combinations of social, cultural, and environmental circumstances that create these problems in specific societies, since any solution must take these unique combinations into account. Cultural anthropology can help the reader to better understand our global problems through these insights, and understanding is the beginning of the solution.

Humanity—Shared Understanding

This book was developed for use in an undergraduate course designed to balance the increasing specialization needed in many fields of study with a broad, general education through which students gain a shared understanding of, among other things, contemporary social issues, cultural diversity, and the practical and academic connections between cultural anthropology and other disciplines. The course for which this text has been designed is not intended to be a traditional introductory anthropology course; it is, instead, an issues-oriented course. It emphasizes anthropological topics—such as cultural diversity, social change, and social conflict—which affect human survival and the place of anthropology among the social sciences. The text supports the goals of the course by examining cultural anthropology's contribution to researching and solving social problems affecting human survival around the world, by examining the variety of research methods and perspectives used by cultural anthropologists, and by showing the degree to which human culture affects contemporary social problems and how necessary it is to understand culture in order to arrive at a solution.

Each article has been chosen because of its relevance to an issues-oriented cultural anthropology course. Since most students come to the course with little or no background in cultural anthropology, articles were also selected for their potential to engage the reader's interest while presenting basic cultural anthropological concepts with a minimum of professional jargon. A brief glossary has been included to define those terms and concepts which are essential to the discipline, the meaning of which may not be familiar to the student.

Although the text has been designed to meet the needs of a specific nonintroductory course, it is also appropriate for use as a supplemental reader in a traditional introductory anthropology course. The anthology presents topics that are among those generally included in introductory courses; and since many of the articles present more than one topic, the individual instructor can alter the topic and article sequence to suit his/her own approach. For example, in "When Brothers Share a Wife," marriage and kinship roles are central themes; however, the article also illustrates related themes of gender roles, subsistence and economic systems, and cultural ecology.

Humanity—We Are One

To our students: as you read the following selections, may each of you experience the sadness and joy, the outrage and satisfaction, and the despair and hope that are the human condition.

CULTURAL ANTHROPOLOGISTS AND WHAT THEY STUDY

The goal of cultural anthropology is the study of human social behavior, and cultural anthropologists approach this study in a manner that is unique among the social sciences. The research focus and methods of anthropologists differ from those of sociology and psychology, which also specialize in the study of human behavior. Sociology focuses on sampling groups of people within complex societies in order to discern patterns of behavior. Sociologists analyze correlations between demographic attributes (such as age, gender, ethnicity, etc.) and aspects of behavior (such as political, religious, and consumer attitudes); and this process allows them to predict some aspects of people's behavior. Psychology focuses on the behavior of the individual, relying heavily on experimental research that can control variables that affect human behavior.

In contrast, cultural anthropology focuses on the study of people who identify themselves as a social group, whether it be a band of nomadic hunting and gathering people, a rural village, or a neighborhood in a large city. Cultural anthropologists also typically study people in their everyday setting by living with them, a process called fieldwork. Fieldwork is done in order to gain insight into the actual behavior of the group by observing their typical daily behavior, in contrast to studying them in an experimental setting or sampling some of the behavioral characteristics of a few individuals from the group. Fieldwork is also typically carried out for an extended period of time, usually for several months or a year or more, in order to gain more detailed information about the group's behavior.

Cultural anthropologists are also known for their unique methodological approach to studying people. This method, which is called participant observation, goes beyond merely observing and recording the behavior of the group being studied in that the anthropologist actually participates in the daily life of the community. This means that anthropologists live in the community with the people they are studying, eat the foods they eat, work and socialize with them, participate in their ceremonies and rituals, and involve themselves in their daily behavior as much as possible. By doing this, anthropologists hope to gain a deeper understanding of the thoughts, beliefs, values, customs, social interactions, and all of the subtle meanings embedded in the behavior of the people they are studying.

When anthropologists study a group of people, they are specifically interested in understanding their culture, the shared knowledge and behavior of a group of people which allows them to interact and survive as a society. Culture includes all the knowledge that is taught from one generation to the next about interacting with others in the society and about surviving in the world. Values, customs, beliefs, world views, ideology, and technology are all examples of the knowledge that is taught to each of us as part of our culture; and this cultural knowledge is different in each society. This process of teaching and learning culture is called enculturation. Cultural anthropologists attempt to describe and analyze the culture of people in a given society in order to understand how their culture affects their behavior. When anthropologists analyze cultural behavior, they pay particular attention to the way that all of the various aspects of social behavior interact, an approach called holism.

People in every society have a tendency to be ethnocentric, to believe that their culture is superior to all others. Everyone is enculturated to believe that the values, beliefs, customs, and behavior of people in their group are correct; and, when they observe people from other cultures acting differently, they ethnocentrically judge them as being incorrect and, therefore, inferior. Cultural anthropologists obviously cannot understand and explain the cultural behavior of people in various societies if they ethnocentrically judge this behavior as incorrect or inferior. Anthropologists, therefore, approach the study of people in various societies through the research perspective of cultural relativism. In the cultural relativistic approach, human behavior is understood as rational (people do the things they do for a reason); and the behavior of a group of people can be understood if it is analyzed within the context of their particular culture. In other words, the beliefs, customs, and actions of people make sense if one understands the culture of that particular group of people.

The ultimate reason for studying various human societies and their respective cultures is for the purpose of comparative research. Anthropologists attempt to discern which behaviors are universal to all humans in every society (innate behaviors) and those which are taught to people through their culture (culturally relative behaviors). A century of anthropological research has shown that, while all humans share certain innate behaviors, the majority of human behavior is learned and culturally determined. Indeed, it is the ability to develop and learn cultural behavior that is the hallmark of our species; and it is this capacity which has led to the present cultural diversity and success of humans as a species.

The articles that follow in this first section provide examples of how cultural anthropologists conduct their research and the insights they gain into cultural behavior. Andrew Cornish's humorous story, "Participant Observation on a Motorcycle," provides a memorable example of how much anthropologists can learn about the culture of a society by becoming involved in the everyday world of the people they are studying. Philippe Bourgois' "Just Another Night on Crack Street" illustrates the hazards of participant observation while demonstrating the value of using anthropological methods to understand people's behavior in our own society. It also shows that even behavior that is considered deviant by the majority of the people in our own society is rational and makes sense within the context of the culture of the people who have the behavior. In "Doctor, Lawyer, Indian Chief," Richard Kurin describes problems that he faced as an anthropologist trying to perform fieldwork and participant observation in a rural village in Pakistan. His research problems not only deepened his understanding of the culture of the people that he was studying; they also pointed out that anthropologists must realize that their relationship with the people they are studying is not just a scientific relationship, but also a personal relationship. Together, these articles provide a picture of cultural anthropologists and what they study.

Participant Observation on a Motorcycle

Andrew Cornish

As you read:
1. *Define participant observation.*
2. *What did Cornish learn about how disputes are settled in Thai culture? What would probably happen in a similar situation in the United States?*

A short while after arriving in the field in southern Thailand, I managed to acquire a motorcycle. While I did not actually possess a licence to ride it, some kind words to those in high places by patrons who had taken me under their wing had cleared the way for me to be turned loose on the roads of Thailand without hindrance unless, it was sharply stressed, I was foolish enough to get involved in an accident. At an early stage I had wondered whether I should mention that my licence at home had been repossessed by a couple of incredulous policemen who took a very dim view of creative driving, but I felt that to try and explain this in Thai would probably lead to misunderstandings, and might well have caused my hosts unnecessary anxiety.

Come St. David's Day, the inevitable accident occurred. I had been on an afternoon jaunt on my freshly cleaned motorcycle, merrily weaving through the traffic, and thinking how interesting it was that Thai motorists actually lived out the theory of loose structure in their driving. During this course of musing I decided to make a right-hand turn, and still being rather set in my Western ways, slowed down to do so. This was an ethnocentric mistake. As I

By Andrew Cornish. From *Anthropology Today*, 3 (6), pp. 15–16. Copyright © 1987 by the Royal Anthropological Institute of Great Britain and Ireland. Reprinted by permission.

began to turn, another motorcyclist, complete with an ice chest full of fish and a large basket of oranges on the pillion seat, decided that this was the ideal moment to overtake. I was much too slow, he was far too fast, and our subjective constructions of existence spectacularly collided with the limits of the material world.

What followed was actually quite pleasurable for the brief but slow-motion moments it lasted. A massive surge of metal, flesh, fish, and disintegrating oranges swept me from behind, then passed overhead in a surrealistic collage as my body easily performed a series of gymnastic stunts that I had been totally unable to master at school. As always in life, the brief pleasure had to be repaid with an extended flood of unwelcome pain, relieved only by the happy realization that I, and the other motorist who had flown so gracefully above me, had narrowly but successfully avoided truncating our skulls on a Burmese ebony tree.

Anxious to reassure myself that nothing was broken, I got quickly to my feet, dusted myself off, and walked over to switch off my motorcycle engine, which by now was making a maniacal noise without its exhaust pipe. Then I walked back to the other rider, who was still lying rigidly on his back and wondering whether he should believe what was happening. I politely asked him if he was all right, but the hypothesis that in a crisis everyone reverts to speaking English clearly required some revision. Months of Thai lessons began to trickle back, but far too slowly, and in the meantime he had also stood up. It was only then that I realized the pair of us had been surrounded by a rather large crowd of onlookers.

Television in Thailand does not commence broadcasting until 4:30 p.m. so our little accident had a good audience, with local residents coming out of their houses and shops, and cars, motorcycles, and trucks stopping to take in the scene. The other rider began talking to some people near him, and a shopkeeper who knew me came and asked if I was all right. From that moment, I never had a chance to speak to the other rider again. We were slowly but surely separated, each of us in the center of a group, the two groups gathering slightly apart from one another. I had a sudden and horrible realization that I was in the middle of one of those dispute settlement cases that I had intermittently dozed through as an undergraduate. With an abrupt and sickening shock, participant observation had become rather too much participation and too little cosy observation.

Some of the other rider's newly acquired entourage came over to ask the fringes of my group what exactly had happened. I pleaded my version to those standing close to me, and it was then relayed—and, I should add, suitably amended—back through the throng to be taken away and compared with the other rider's tale of woe. While this little contest was going on, a number of people from both groups were inspecting the rather forlorn wreckages of our motorcycles and debating over which one appeared to be more badly damaged. "Look at this!" someone cried, lifting a torn section of the seat and helpfully making the tear more ostentatious in the process. "But look at this!" came the reply, as someone else wrenched a limply hanging indicator light completely off its mounting. After a series of such exchanges, the two groups finally agreed that both motorcycles

were in an equally derelict state, though I could not help feeling, peering from the little prison within my group of supporters, that those judging the damage to the machines had played a more than passive role in ensuring a parity of demolition.

Physical injuries were the next to be subjected to this adjudication process. I found my shirt being lifted up, and a chorus of oohs and aahs issuing from the crowd, as someone with jolly animation prodded and pinched the large areas of my back which were now bravely attempting to stay in place without the aid of skin. My startled eyes began looking in opposite directions at the same time, while somewhat less than human groans gargled out of my mouth. From similar sounds in the distance I deduced that the other poor rider was being subjected to similar treatment. He frankly looked rather the worse for wear than I did, but whenever his group claimed this, my supporters would proceed to show just what excruciating pain I was suffering by prodding me in the back and indicating my randomly circumambulating eyes as if to say "see, we told you so."

On issues of damage, both mechanical and physical, we were adjudged by the two groups to be fairly evenly scored. Fault in relation to road rules had never been an issue. Then came a bit of a lull, as if something serious was about to happen. A senior person from the other group came over and spoke to me directly, asking if I wanted to call the police. A hush fell over everyone. I, of course, was totally terrified at the prospect—no license, visions of deportation, and so far only one meagre book of field notes to my name. I put on my best weak pathetic smile and mumbled that I thought it was not really necessary unless the other chap insisted. A culturally appropriate move: Everyone looked happily relieved, and the other rider's spokesman said generously that it would only be a waste of time and cause unnecessary bother to bring the police out on an errand like this. It was to be a few months before

I realized that, like many other motorcyclists, the other rider was also probably roaming the roads without a licence, and that in this part of the country calling the police was generally regarded as a last, and unsporting, resort.

The final agreement was that we should settle our own repairs—to both body and vehicle—and let the matter rest. A visible sigh of relief passed through the two groups that had gathered, and they slowly began to disperse. For the first time since the collision, I saw the other rider face to face, so I walked towards him to offer my apologies. I never managed to reach him. The dispersing groups froze in horror, then quickly regathered around me. "What is wrong now?" I was interrogated on all sides. Was I not happy with the result? I had clearly made a serious blunder, and it took a while to settle things down once more. A perceptive shopkeeper from nearby grabbed my arm and dragged me off to his shop for coffee, explaining to me that the matter had been settled and that further contact for any reason with the other rider or his group would only prolong an unpleasant situation that could now be forgotten by all involved.

So it was that later that evening I was able to start my second book of field notes with an entry on dispute settlement, though painful twinges up my back and throbbing between the ears made me wish I had relied on some other informant to provide the ethnographic details. I made a silent vow to myself to discontinue this idiosyncratic method of participant observation, and managed to some extent to keep the vow for the rest of my stay. Thereafter I successfully steered clear of motorcycle accidents, and instead got shot at, electrocuted, and innocently involved in scandal and otherwise abused. But all that, as they say, is another story.

Just Another Night on Crack Street

Philippe Bourgois

As you read:
1. *Why do people participate in the culture of cocaine dealing?*
2. *What is the value, if any, of studying the underground crack economy from the point of view of the participants?*

The heavyset undercover policeman pushed me across the ice-cream counter, spreading my legs and poking me around the groin. As he came dangerously close to the bulge in my right pocket I hissed in his ear, "It's a tape recorder." He snapped backward, releasing his grip on my neck, whispering a barely audible, "Sorry." Apparently he thought I was an undercover cop from another department. Before I could get a close look at him, he had left the bodega, a grocery store-cum-numbers joint.

After almost five years of living in a tenement apartment in East Harlem with my family, I have learned how to deal with the police officers who regularly stop me in the course of my work. I am an ethnographer conducting long-term, participant observation research on street culture in the underground economy. I spend long hours, night and day, in crack houses and on drug-copping corners, observing, befriending and interviewing street dealers, addicts and anyone else who will pause to talk with me. It is unusual work, to say the least, difficult for outsiders to appreciate, perhaps most particularly the police, who cannot fathom why anyone would immerse himself in the heart of the drug culture if not for the drugs.

Once I made the mistake of trying to explain my work to two patrolmen, both white, who stopped me late at night and angrily said, "Go buy your drugs in a white neighborhood, and get the hell off these streets, white boy." I had barely uttered, "No, you don't understand, I don't use drugs. I am a professor..." when I was called "dirty white scum," and threatened with a booking in the precinct if I didn't "shut up and get out of here right this minute."

The night in the bodega I did what I had learned to do when being frisked—stare at the ground, avoid eye contact and mumble obsequiously, "Yes, sir," whenever appropriate. This encounter was an easy one. I hadn't even had to say, "Thank you, sir," and I was not publicly cursed. As soon as the officer was out of earshot, I was able to focus back on my work.

In an effort to display trust and establish a better rapport, I told Jesus—the street dealer and crack addict I happened to be interviewing that night—to grab the change from my $10 bill from the cashier as I hurried to leave. At the doorway, however, I was blocked by a thin teen-ager named Bennie, who pushed me aside and lunged at the loose dollar bills in Jesus' hand.

"That's *my* money now, Jesus; give it to me," Bennie shouted. I started to shout back: "Hey! What are you talking about? That's my money!" But one look at Bennie's contorted face and narrowed eyes stopped me. Jesus muttered "Be careful—my man is dusted," but it was unnecessary. I was ready to give up the eight bills—and more if I had to—to avoid any out-of-control violence from an angry mugger high on angel dust.

Jesus went through the motions of confronting Bennie, to whom he really did owe money. First he was gentle. Staring into Bennie's face, which was two inches from his own, he pulled at the fistful of bills and said: "Yo, Bennie, chill out. I know how much I owe you. I'll take care of you tomorrow. This ain't my money. *Please* don't take this money." Then he tried a harsher tack: "I told you this ain't my money; Get off of it! It ain't my money!"

Bennie just got tougher. He knew Jesus was a coward. He yanked at the bills, hissing about the $60 still owed him. They had been selling marijuana together for several weeks on the corner next to the bodega, and during a bust a week earlier, the police had confiscated their supply. Bennie wanted Jesus to make good on his share. He knew that Jesus would not fight back. As the bills began to rip, Jesus finally let go, looking back at me sheepishly.

As we stepped out the door of the bodega, Bennie kept yelling at Jesus about the $60. Then he let out a whistle, and a dented Vega came roaring down the block. It careered to the curb and cut us off. A young man in the passenger seat tried to open his door and jump onto the sidewalk before the car stopped, but he fell on his face in the gutter. He jumped back to his feet, and stood, unsteadily. His nose was bleeding. He was waving a baseball bat in his right hand.

The driver, who was steadier—apparently not as high as his companion—had also rushed out of the car and was running at us. Bennie called out that all was "cool," that he already had the money; and they slowed down, walking toward us with puffed backs, the one with the baseball bat resting it on his shoulder.

Frightened, I jumped back to the bodega door, trying to figure out where to run and what to do, but Jesus had to stand firm.

This was the corner he worked; those were his former partners. They surrounded him, shouting about the money, and began kicking him and hitting him with the bat. Jesus still did not turn and run; instead he jumped up and down, prancing sideways along the sidewalk toward the corner on the main avenue. He was hoping his new colleagues at the bogus botanica, a shop that ostensibly sold herbal potions and spiritual items, around the corner, to whom he was steering crack customers, might catch sight of what was happening. He was knocked down twice before reaching the corner. Then the two men backed away, walking back to the Vega with deliberate slowness, pretending not to see me. They had not seen the policeman search me, and they evidently did not think it wise to pick a fight with an unknown "white boy" who was just the right age to be an undercover. Obviously nervous, they pulled at Bennie's elbow to hustle him into the car. Then they drove off, leaving rubber at the curb.

By the time I caught up with Jesus, half a block down the avenue, he was telling the story to his cousin. A woman in her late 20's, dressed "butch" in a long-sleeved jean jacket, she was on her way to the botanica crack house. Her emaciated face and long sleeves made it likely she was a coke mainliner. She was waving her skinny arms and stamping on the ground, whining hoarsely at Jesus, telling him he couldn't just run off like that; that he had to "go down swinging like a man"; that he couldn't just let people chase him around; that he had to show them who's who. Now what did he expect to do? Where was he going to work? Finally, she said she needed the money she had lent him the day before to buy a new supply of marijuana—he had spent it on crack instead—and that she was disgusted with him.

At the crack/botanica house, we told our story to Julio and Papito, who were on duty selling that night. Julio jumped up excitedly, calling out: "What street was that on? Come on, we can still catch them.

How many were they?" I said we should just forget about it; revenge wasn't worth it. And Papito looked at me disgustedly, sitting back down on the milk crate in front of the botanica's door. Julio, whom I knew better, jumped up in front of me, raising his voice to berate me. "Man, you still think like a *blanquito*," he said. A half-dozen spectators—some of them empty-pocketed, "thirsty" crack addicts, but most of them sharp-dressed teen-age girls competing for Papito's and Julio's attentions—snickered at me.

To regain some minimal respect, I turned on Jesus, telling him he owed me the $8 Bennie had stolen, and ordering him to empty his pockets. Grinning, he pulled out a dollar and promised he would come by tomorrow with seven more. He told me not to worry; he would pay me back first. Of course, I knew he would not. He knew that I was one of the few individuals on the street even softer than he.

At this point, seeing my feeble attempt, Julio, making sure I saw what he was doing, dropped a vial of crack in Jesus's shirt pocket in payment for the half dozen customers he had steered to the crack house that evening. I was supposed to grab the vial—worth $5—from Jesus's pocket as partial compensation for the seven he still owed me. But I could not bring myself to rip Jesus's shirt pocket open, knowing that Jesus was "thirsty" to smoke and might get violent with me.

A few minutes later, Papito and Julio told everyone it was time to close shop. It was 12:30, and they had to turn in the evening's receipts to their boss. They pulled down the metal gates over the botanica's entrance, eager to leave work and get on with an evening of partying.

Unlike the crack dealers and addicts that I hang out with and interview, the vast majority of the residents of East Harlem are honest and hard-working. It is a struggle to live there, and they struggle honorably. Nevertheless, to many, especially the young, the underground economy beckons seductively as the ultimate "equal opportunity employer." The rate of unemployment for Harlem youth is at least twice the citywide rate of 8.1 percent, and the economic incentive to participate in the burgeoning crack economy is overwhelming.

The individuals "successfully" pursuing careers in the "crack economy" or any other facet of the underground economy are no longer "exploitable" by legal society. They speak with anger at their former low wages and bad treatment. They make fun of friends and acquaintances—many of whom come to buy drugs from them—who are still employed in factories or in service jobs.

Most of the people I have met are proud that they are not being exploited by "the White Man." All of them have, at one time or another, held the jobs—delivery boys, supermarket baggers, hospital orderlies—that are objectively recognized as among the least desirable in American society. They see the illegal, underground economy as not only offering superior wages, but also a more dignified workplace.

For example, Julio's last legal job before selling crack was as a messenger for a magazine. He had become addicted to crack and began selling off his possessions to pay for his habit. Finally he was thrown out by his wife, who had just given birth to his son. He quit his 10-hour-a-day messenger job in favor of stealing car radios for a couple of hours at night in the same neighborhoods where he had been delivering messages. After a close encounter with the police, Julio, who is 26 years old, begged his cousin for a job in his crack house. The sense of responsibility, success, and prestige that selling crack gave him enabled him to kick his crack habit and substitute for it a considerably less expensive powder cocaine and alcohol habit.

Julio's girlfriend Jackie also sells crack. Her husband used to own the botanica crack site, but he is now "upstate," serving two to five years for his second conviction for selling cocaine and possessing firearms. Two nights before he was scheduled to go to jail, as he was closing down the botanica, Jackie, who was eight months' pregnant at the time, shot him in the stomach in front of all his workers. She was furious because instead of leaving money for her before beginning his jail sentence, he had been running around spending thousands of dollars on young women and bragging about it.

Ten months later, Jackie, at 32, was doing much better, especially following the problem-free delivery of her fifth daughter. Her husband's cousin, who had taken over the crack franchise at the botanica while her husband was in jail, had witnessed the shoot-out, and had been impressed by Jackie's aggressiveness; shortly after the birth of her daughter, he hired her to sell "twenties of rock"—$20 foils of cocaine—at his other sales point in the neighborhood, a candy store.

Not everyone shared his feelings, however. Shortly after her husband's hospitalization and jailing, Jackie took up with Julio, and she told Rose, a 15-year-old former girlfriend of his, to stop hanging around the crack house—or else. I was there one evening when Rose was discussing this threat with a crowd hanging around the crack house. Someone was warning Rose that Jackie meant business, when Aida, the seller on shift at the crack house that evening, looked up from the pink blanket she was knitting for the baby she was pregnant with and called out: "Big deal! Anybody can buy a gun. You just stay here, Rose. You can come visit me any time you want. That woman's just nasty. She can't tell me or you or anyone else what to do here. She don't own the place."

Rose did, indeed, keep coming back, even after another of her ex-boyfriends, who claimed he still loved her, threatened to kill Julio and then commit suicide if she kept hanging out at the crack house at night. He showed up a few days later with two big friends, but by then Julio had gathered a group of his own for protection, and the would-be assailants just kept walking. Julio was exasperated with the whole issue; he had lost interest in Rose after he had gotten her pregnant, and they had argued heatedly when he refused to pay for her abortion.

Regular displays of violence are necessary for success in the underground economy—especially the street-level drug-dealing world. Violence is essential for maintaining credibility and for preventing rip-offs by colleagues, customers, and intruders. Thus behavior that appears irrationally violent and self-destructive to the middle- or working-class outsider can be interpreted, according to the logic of the underground economy, as judicious public relations.

This can be clearly seen in the events described at the outset of this article. Jesus and I were mugged because he had a reputation for being a coward and because I had been publicly unmasked as not being an undercover cop—hence, safe to attack. Jesus had tried to minimize the damage to his ability to sell on that corner by not turning and running. Nevertheless, the admonishments of his cousin just minutes later could not have been clearer: Jesus was not going to be upwardly mobile in the underground economy. Where was he going to work after such a public humiliation?

Employers or new entrepreneurs in the underground economy are looking for people with experience that proves their capacity for effective violence—Jackie's being hired to sell cocaine by the man who witnessed her shooting her husband is an example. Papito had a "bionic leg." He had been shot through the thigh in a previous crack confrontation, and his leg had been successfully rebuilt, leaving him with a pronounced limp. He frequently referred to his rebuilt limb in conversation; it was a source of pride and credibility for him. He was considered an effective crack dealer.

For the owner of the crack house, the ability of his employees to face up the possibility of violence is crucial; stickups of dealing dens are common. During my time there, the botanica was held up twice. Julio was on duty both times. He admitted that he had been very nervous when robbers held a gun to his temple and asked for money and crack. Nevertheless, not only did he withhold some of the money and crack, kept hidden inside a hollowed-out statue of a saint, but he also later exaggerated to his boss the amount that had been stolen; he pocketed the difference himself.

The possibility of being held up was constantly on Julio's mind. When more than two people walked into the botanica at once, he would stiffen, as if expecting them to pull out weapons. Once he told me he was nervous about a cousin of his who had started hanging out at the crack house, feigning friendship. Julio suspected him of being in the process of casing the place for a future stickup.

Several times I asked crack dealers or robbers to explain how they were able to trust their partners in crime. In each case, I was told: "What do you mean how do I trust him? You should ask how does he trust me!"

They were claiming, I believe, that they are not dependent upon trust because they are tough enough to command respect and enforce all contracts they enter into. Ruthlessness is their security.

My failure to display a propensity for violence cost me, in several instances, the respect of the crack sellers. This was evident when I turned down Julio and Papito's offer to search out the three men who mugged Jesus and me. Julio was genuinely disappointed that I was not someone with common sense and self-respect.

His reaction was a setback for my research. In the few weeks prior to getting mugged, I had established a routine for tape recording life-history interviews. After Julio closed the botanica, we would go back to Jackie's apartment to babysit her children and her husband's grandfather, a 65-year-old alcoholic. Babysitting involved sending one of the children out for beer, keeping the grandfather from drinking any hard liquor, shouting at the young children if they quarreled, playing with the 9-month-old. Eventually I would follow Julio and whoever else had come with us from the crack house into the bedroom, to keep talking to them as they ground up and snorted cocaine. At this point I could comfortably take out my tape recorder, and they would dictate chapters for my book, competing for my attention and for space on the tape. By daybreak, Jackie had usually returned from work with fresh coke for Julio to snort. He would then sleep from mid-morning until mid-afternoon, careful to arrive on time for the evening shift— 3 P.M. to 12:30 A.M.—at the botanica crack house.

Inner-city street violence is not limited solely to drug sellers or to street criminals; to a certain extent, anyone living in the neighborhood who wants to maintain a sense of autonomy—i.e., who does not go outdoors during daylight hours only—finds it useful to participate, at least passively, in some corner of the culture of terror.

I overheard the story of a boy whose mother had told him never to fight. Not long into the school year a classmate mugged him, stealing his midafternoon snack and pocket money. The child quickly developed a reputation as a weakling. During the ensuing weeks, he lost his snack and money daily until finally he complained to his mother. Her response was to berate him: "What's the matter with you? Can't you fight back?"

Anyone who is frequently out on the street will be exposed to the violence of the underground economy, even if he does not participate in it. In the first 13 months I spent in Spanish Harlem I witnessed:

- A deadly shooting, outside my window, of the mother of a 3-year-old child, by an assailant wielding a sawed-off shotgun.
- A bombing and a machine-gunning of a numbers joint, once again within

view of my apartment window.

- A shoot-out and police-car chase in front of a pizza parlor where I happened to be eating a snack.
- The aftermath of the fire-bombing of a heroin house.
- A dozen screaming, clothes-ripping fights.
- Almost daily exposure to broken-down human beings, some of them in fits of crack-induced paranoia, some suffering from delirium tremens, and others in unidentifiable pathological fits of screaming and shouting insults to all around them.

Perhaps the most poignant expression of the pervasiveness of the culture of terror was the comment made to me by a 13-year-old boy in the course of an otherwise innocuous conversation about how his mother's pregnancy was going. He told me he hoped his mother would give birth to a boy "because girls are too easy to rape."

Based on my experience, I believe the assertion of the culture-of-poverty theorists that the poor have been badly socialized and do not share mainstream values is wrong. On the contrary, ambitious, energetic, inner-city youths are attracted to the underground economy precisely because they believe in the rags-to-riches American dream. Like many in the mainstream, they are frantically trying to get their piece of the pie as fast as possible. In fact, they follow the traditional model for upward mobility: aggressively setting themselves up as private entrepreneurs. Without stretching the point too much, they can be seen in conventional terms as rugged individualists on an unpredictable frontier where fortune, fame, and destruction are all just around the corner.

Consider the example of Indio, an ambitious young crack dealer who, while he was high on angel dust, shot his brother in the spine and paralyzed him for life in a battle over sales rights. His brother now works for him, selling on crutches. Meanwhile, the shooting has cemented Indio's reputation, and his workers are awesomely disciplined. Indio reaffirms this symbolically by periodically walking his turf with a $3,000 gold chain and nameplate hanging around his neck.

Many of the street dealers claim to be strictly utilitarian in their involvement with the drugs they sell, and disdain their clients despite the fact that usually, like Indio, they have alcohol and powder-cocaine habits themselves. They refer to their merchandise as "this garbage" and openly deride addicts as they arrive with fistfuls of money. Papito used to chant at his regular customers: "Keep on killing yourself. Bring me that money. Smoke yourself to death. Make me rich."

Though the average street seller is employed by the owner of a sales point for whom he has to maintain regular hours, meet sales quotas, and be subject to being fired, the street seller has a great deal of autonomy and power in his schedule. His boss comes once or twice a shift to drop off drugs and pick up money or else sends a young messenger. Because of the money and drugs passing through their hands, sellers are often surrounded by a bevy of "thirsty" friends and hangers-on—frequently teen-age girls—willing to run errands, pay attention to conversations, lend support in arguments and fights, and provide sexual favors upon demand. In fact, even youths who do not use drugs will hang out and try to befriend the dealer, just to be privy to the excitement of people coming and going, copping and hanging.

The ultimate expression of success is opulence without visible means of support. There is plenty of proof of this on the street as teen-age crack dealers drive by in white Suzuki jeeps and middle-aged cocaine tycoons speed around in well-waxed Lincoln Continentals or Mercedes-Benzes. Anyone can aspire to be one of the ubiquitous sellers, perched on mountain bikes with beepers on their belts. In fact, many youths not particularly active in the drug trade wear beepers, just pretending to be big time.

The feeling of self-worth that the street-level dealer's life style offers cannot be underestimated. A former manager of a coke-shooting gallery who had employed a network of a half-dozen sellers, lookouts, and security guards before he was jailed, explained to me that the best memories of his drug-dealing days were of the respect he received from people on the street. After his release, he became a clerk in a Wall Street brokerage concern, determined, he said, not to return to street life. But he recalled that, as a dealer, when he drove up in one his cars to pick up the day's receipts, a bevy of attentive men and women would run to open the door for him and engage him in polite small talk. Others would offer to clean his car. He would invite a half-dozen friends and acquaintances out to dinner in expensive restaurants almost every night. Jokingly, he also noted that his shooting gallery had enabled his wife and two children to get off welfare.

A casual stroll through Spanish Harlem exposes one to legions of emaciated coke and crack addicts. Many will be begging for their next vial; others will be "petro" or "bugging out"—i.e., high, intensely paranoid, shying from everyone around them—shivering, mumbling agitatedly to themselves, with their eyes wide open and jaws tense. If the stroller should happen upon a "copping corner" it will look like a street fair, especially late at night—cars driving by, people coming and going, doors of buildings opening and closing, people hanging out all over. Most likely a hail of whistles and shouts will accompany the stroller's arrival as the lookouts warn those "pitching" the drugs that a potential undercover is on the scene.

Anthropologists have developed a concept known as "conjugated oppression"— whereby ethnic discrimination interacts with class exploitation to produce a perception in its victims of inescapable oppression. I have come to believe that this begins to explain why hordes of crack heads continue to fry their brains and burn up their bodies.

Substance abuse in general, and crack in particular, offers the equivalent of a born-again metamorphosis. Instantaneously, the user is transformed from an unemployed, depressed high school dropout, despised by the world—and secretly convinced that his failure is due to his own inherent stupidity and disorganization. There is a rush of heart-palpitating pleasure, followed by a jaw-gnashing crash and wide-eyed alertness that provides his life with concrete purpose: Get more crack—fast!

After almost five years living in and out of that world, it is impossible not to get depressed, especially when some of the emaciated figures I see are women in advanced states of pregnancy, mothers dragging screeching toddlers behind them—or a former friend broken down on a binge.

Often, the day after an especially brutal night of fieldwork, I seek out the bright-eyed, cheery-faced schoolchildren who fill the streets of Harlem after 3:30 each afternoon. I've come to know a half dozen of them and have their mothers' permission to take them on outings. We'll play ball, take a walk to the East River, visit a fancy toy store or a museum downtown. The energy, love, and dreams of these children stand in stark contrast to the desperate substance-abuse and violence that goes on around them. I am suddenly filled with the hope that they might survive these mean streets—and, for a while at least, I feel better.

Doctor, Lawyer, Indian Chief

Richard Kurin

As you read:

1. *Why did the villagers initially consider Kurin to be "...a member of a species of subhuman beings, possessing little in the form of either common or moral sense?"*

2. *What evidence can you cite to demonstrate that Kurin was finally accepted by the villagers? Do you think they ever truly understood why he was in their village?*

3. *What did Kurin learn about Punjab culture from his fieldwork experience?*

I was full of confidence when—equipped with a scholarly proposal, blessings from my advisers, and generous research grants—I set out to study village social structure in the Punjab province of Pakistan. But after looking for an appropriate fieldwork site for several weeks without success, I began to think that my research project would never get off the ground. Daily I would seek out villagers aboard my puttering motor scooter, traversing the dusty dirt roads, footpaths, and irrigation ditches that crisscross the Punjab. But I couldn't seem to find a village amenable to study. The major problem was that the villagers I did approach were baffled by my presence. They could not understand why anyone would travel ten thousand miles from home to a foreign country in order to live in a poor village, interview illiterate peasants, and then write a book about it. Life, they were sure, was to be lived, not written about. Besides, they thought, what of any importance could they possibly tell me? Committed as I was to ethnographic research, I readily understood their viewpoint. I was a *babu log*—literally, a noble;

figuratively, a clerk; and simply, a person of the city. I rode a motor scooter, wore tight-fitting clothing, and spoke Urdu, a language associated with the urban literary elite. Obviously, I did not belong, and the villagers simply did not see me fitting into their society.

The Punjab, a region about the size of Colorado, straddles the northern border of India and Pakistan. Partitioned between the two countries in 1947, the Punjab now consists of a western province, inhabited by Muslims, and an eastern one, populated in the main by Sikhs and Hindus. As its name implies—*punj* meaning "five" and *ab* meaning "rivers"—the region is endowed with plentiful resources to support widespread agriculture and a large rural population. The Punjab has traditionally supplied grains, produce, and dairy products to the peoples of neighboring and considerably more arid states, earning it a reputation as the breadbasket of southern Asia.

Given this predilection for agriculture, Punjabis like to emphasize that they are earthy people, having values they see as consonant with rural life. These values include an appreciation of, and trust in, nature; simplicity and directness of expression; an awareness of the basic drives and desires that motivate men (namely, *zan, zar, zamin*—"women, wealth, land"); a concern with honor and shame as abiding principles of social organization; and for Muslims, a deep faith in Allah and the teachings of his prophet Mohammad.

Besides being known for its fertile soils, life-giving rivers, and superlative agriculturists, the Punjab is also perceived as a zone of transitional culture, a region that has experienced repeated invasions of peoples from western and central Asia into the Indian subcontinent. Over the last four thousand years, numerous groups, among them Scythians, Parthians, Huns, Greeks, Moguls, Persians, Afghans, and Turks, have entered the subcontinent through the Punjab in search of bountiful land, riches, or power. Although Punjabis—notably Rajputs, Sikhs, and Jats—have a reputation for courage and fortitude on the battlefield, their primary, self-professed strength has been their ability to incorporate new, exogenous elements into their society with a minimum of conflict. Punjabis are proud that theirs is a multiethnic society in which diverse groups have been largely unified by a common language and by common customs and traditions.

Given this background, I had not expected much difficulty in locating a village in which to settle and conduct my research. As an anthropologist, I viewed myself as an "earthy" social scientist who, being concerned with basics, would have a good deal in common with rural Punjabis. True, I might be looked on as an invader of a sort; but I was benevolent, and sensing this, villagers were sure to incorporate me into their society with even greater ease than was the case for the would-be conquering armies that had preceded me. Indeed, they would welcome me with open arms.

I was wrong. The villagers whom I approached attributed my desire to live with them either to neurotic delusions or nefarious ulterior motives. Perhaps, so the argu-

ments went, I was really after women, land, or wealth.

On the day I had decided would be my last in search of a village, I was driving along a road when I saw a farmer running through a rice field and waving me down. I stopped and he climbed on the scooter. Figuring I had nothing to lose, I began to explain why I wanted to live in a village. To my surprise and delight, he was very receptive, and after sharing a pomegranate milkshake at a roadside shop, he invited me to his home. His name was Allah Ditta, which means "God given," and I took this as a sign that I had indeed found my village.

"My" village turned out to be a settlement of about fifteen hundred people, mostly of the Nunari *qaum*, or "tribe." The Nunaris engage primarily in agriculture (wheat, rice, sugar cane, and cotton), and most families own small plots of land. Members of the Bhatti tribe constitute the largest minority in the village. Although traditionally a warrior tribe, the Bhattis serve in the main as the village artisans and craftsmen.

On my first day in the village I tried explaining in great detail the purposes of my study to the village elders and clan leaders. Despite my efforts, most of the elders were perplexed about why I wanted to live in their village. As a guest, I was entitled to the hospitality traditionally bestowed by Muslim peoples of Asia, and during the first evening I was assigned a place to stay. But I was an enigma, for guests leave, and I wanted to remain. I was perceived as being strange, for I was both a non-Muslim and a non-Punjabi, a type of person not heretofore encountered by most of the villagers. Although I tried to temper my behavior, there was little I could say or do to dissuade my hosts from the view that I embodied the antithesis of Punjabi values. While I was able to converse in their language, Jatki, a dialect of western Punjabi, I was only able to do so with the ability of a four year old. This achievement fell far short of speaking the *t'et'*, or "genuine form," of the villagers. Their idiom is rich with the terminology of agricultural operations and rural life. It is unpretentious, uninflected, and direct, and villagers hold high opinions of those who are good with words, who can speak to a point and be convincing. Needless to say, my infantile babble realized none of these characteristics and evoked no such respect.

Similarly, even though I wore indigenous dress, I was inept at tying my *lungi*, or pant cloth. The fact that my *lungi* occasionally fell off and revealed what was underneath gave my neighbors reason to believe that I indeed had no shame and could not control the passions of my *nafs*, or "libidinous nature."

This image of a doltish, shameless infidel barely capable of caring for himself lasted for the first week of my residence in the village. My inability to distinguish among the five varieties of rice and four varieties of lentil grown in the village illustrated that I knew or cared little about nature and agricultural enterprise. This display of ignorance only served to confirm the general consensus that the mysterious morsels I ate from tin cans labeled "Chef Boy-ar-Dee" were not really food at all. Additionally, I did not oil and henna my hair, shave my armpits, or perform ablutions, thereby convincing some commentators that I was a member of a species of subhuman beings, possessing little in the form of either common or moral sense. That the villagers did not quite grant me the status of a person was reflected by their not according me a proper name. In the Punjab, a person's name is equated with honor and respect and is symbolized by his turban. A man who does not have a name, or whose name is not recognized by his neighbors, is unworthy of respect. For such a man, his turban is said to be either nonexistent or to lie in the dust at the feet of others. To be given a name is to have one's head crowned by a turban, an acknowledgment that one leads a responsible and respectable life. Although I repeatedly introduced myself as "Rashid Karim," a fairly decent Pakistani rendering of Richard Kurin, just about all the villagers insisted on calling me *Angrez* ("Englishman"), thus denying me full personhood and implicitly refusing to grant me the right to wear a turban.

As I began to pick up the vernacular, to question villagers about their clan and kinship structure and trace out relationships between different families, my image began to change. My drawings of kinship diagrams and preliminary census mappings were looked upon not only with wonder but also suspicion. My neighbors now began to think there might be a method to my madness. And so there was. Now I had become a spy. Of course it took a week for people to figure out whom I was supposedly spying for. Located as they were at a crossroads of Asia, at a nexus of conflicting geopolitical interests, they had many possibilities to consider. There was a good deal of disagreement on the issue, with the vast majority maintaining that I was either an American, Russian, or Indian spy. A small, but nonetheless vocal, minority held steadfastly to the belief that I was a Chinese spy. I thought it all rather humorous until one day a group confronted me in the main square in front of the nine-by-nine-foot mud hut that I had rented. The leader spoke up and accused me of spying. The remainder of the group grumbled *jahsus! jahsus!* ("spy! spy!"), and I realized that this ad hoc committee of inquiry had the potential of becoming a mob.

To be sure, the villagers had good reason to be suspicious. For one, the times were tense in Pakistan—a national political crisis gripped the country and the populace had been anxious for months over the uncertainty of elections and effective governmental functions. Second, keenly aware of their history, some of the villagers did not have to go too far to imagine that I was at the vanguard of some invading group that had designs upon their land. Such intrigues, with far greater sophistication, had been played out before by nations seeking to expand their power into the Punjab. That I possessed a gold seal letter (which no one save myself could read) from the University of Chicago to the effect that I was pursuing legitimate studies was not enough to convince the crowd that I was indeed an innocent scholar.

I repeatedly denied the charge, but to no avail. The shouts of *jahsus! jahsus!* prevailed. Confronted with this I had no choice. "Okay," I said. "I admit it. I am a spy!"

The crowd quieted for my long-awaited confession.

"I am a spy and am here to study this village, so that when my country attacks you we will be prepared. You see, we will not bomb Lahore or Karachi or Islamabad. Why should we waste our bombs on millions of people, on factories, dams, airports, and harbors? No, it is far more advantageous to bomb this strategic small village replete with its mud huts, livestock, Persian wheels, and one light bulb. And when we bomb this village, it is imperative that we know how Allah Ditta is related to Abdullah, and who owns the land near the well, and what your marriage customs are."

Silence hung over the crowd, and then one by one the assemblage began to disperse. My sarcasm had worked. The spy charges were defused. But I was no hero in light of my performance, and so I was once again relegated to the status of a nonperson without an identity in the village.

I remained in limbo for the next week, and although I continued my attempts to collect information about village life, I had my doubts as to whether I would ever be accepted by the villagers. And then, through no effort of my own, there was a breakthrough, this time due to another Allah Ditta, a relative of the village headman and one of my leading accusers during my spying days.

I was sitting on my woven string bed on my porch when Allah Ditta approached, leading his son by the neck. "Oh, *Angrez!*"

he yelled, "this worthless son of mine is doing poorly in school. He is supposed to be learning English, but he is failing. He has a good mind, but he's lazy. And his teacher is no help, being more intent upon drinking tea and singing film songs than upon teaching English. Oh son of an Englishman, do you know English?"

"Yes, I know English," I replied, "after all, I am an *Angrez.*"

"Teach him," Allah Ditta blurted out, without any sense of making a tactful request.

And so, I spent the next hour with the boy, reviewing his lessons and correcting his pronunciation and grammar. As I did so, villagers stopped to watch and listen, and by the end of the hour, nearly one hundred people had gathered around, engrossed by this tutoring session. They were stupefied. I was an effective teacher, and I actually seemed to know English. The boy responded well, and the crowd reached a new consensus. I had a brain. And in recognition of this achievement I was given a name—"Ustad Rashid," or Richard the Teacher.

Achieving the status of a teacher was only the beginning of my success. The next morning I awoke to find the village sugar vendor at my door. He had a headache and wanted to know if I could cure him. "Why do you think I can help you?" I asked.

Bhai Khan answered, "Because you are a *ustad*, you have a great deal of knowledge."

The logic was certainly compelling. If I could teach English, I should be able to cure a headache. I gave him two aspirins.

An hour later, my fame had spread. Bhai Khan had been cured, and he did not hesitate to let others know that it was the *ustad* who had been responsible. By the next day, and in fact for the remainder of my stay, I was to see an average of twenty-five to thirty patients a day. I was asked to cure everything from coughs to colds to typhoid, elephantiasis, and impotency. Upon establishing a flourishing and free medical practice, I received another title, *hakim*, or "physician." I was not yet an anthropologist, but I was on my way.

A few days later I took on yet another role. One of my research interests involved tracing out patterns of land ownership and inheritance. While working on the problem of figuring out who owned what, I was approached by the village watchman. He claimed he had been swindled in a land deal and requested my help. As the accused was not another villager, I agreed to present the watchman's case to the local authorities.

Somehow, my efforts managed to achieve results. The plaintiff's grievance was redressed, and I was given yet another title in the village—*wakil*, or "lawyer." And in the weeks that followed, I was steadily called upon to read, translate, and advise upon various court orders that affected the lives of the villagers.

My roles as a teacher, doctor, and lawyer not only provided me with an identity but also facilitated my integration into the economic structure of the community. As my imputed skills offered my neighbors services not readily available in the village, I was drawn into exchange relationships known as *seipi. Seipi* refers to the barter system of goods and services among village farmers, craftsmen, artisans, and other specialists. Every morning Roshan the milkman would deliver fresh milk to my hut. Every other day Hajam Ali the barber would stop by and give me a shave. My next-door neighbor, Nura the cobbler, would repair my sandals when required. Ghulam the horse-cart driver would transport me to town when my motor scooter was in disrepair. The parents of my students would send me sweets and sometimes delicious meals. In return, none of my neighbors asked for direct payment for the specific actions performed. Rather, as they told me, they would call upon me when they had need of my services. And they did. Nura needed cough syrup for his children, the milkman's brother needed a job contact in the city, students wanted to continue their lessons, and so on. Through *seipi* relations, various neighbors gave goods and services to me, and I to them.

Even so, I knew that by Punjabi standards, I could never be truly accepted into the village life because I was not a member of either the Nunari or Bhatti tribe. As the villagers would say, "You never really know who a man is until you know who his grandfather and his ancestors were." And to know a person's grandfather or ancestors properly, you had to be a member of the same or a closely allied tribe.

The Nunari tribe is composed of a number of groups. The nucleus consists of four clans—Naul, Vadel, Saddan, and More—each named for one of the four brothers thought to have originally founded the tribe. Clan members are said to be related by blood ties, also called *pag da sak*, or "ties of the turban." In sharing the turban, members of each clan can share the same blood, the same honor, and the same name. Other clans, unrelated by ties of blood to these four, have become attached to this nucleus through a history of marital relations or of continuous political and economic interdependence. Marital relations, called *gag da sak*, "ties of the skirt," are conceived of as relations in which alienable turbans (skirts) in the form of women are exchanged with other, non-turban-sharing groups. Similarly, ties of political and economical domination and subordination are thought of as relations in which the turban of the client is given to that of the patron. A major part of my research work was concerned with reconstructing how the four brothers formed the Nunari tribe, how additional clans became associated with it, and how clan and tribal identity were defined by nomenclature, codes of honor, and the symbols of sharing and exchanging turbans.

To approach these issues I set out to reconstruct the genealogical relationships within the tribe and between the various clans. I elicited genealogies from many of the villagers and questioned older informants about the history of the Nunari tribe. Most knew only bits and pieces of this history, and after several months of interviews and research, I was directed to the tribal genealogists. These people, usually not Nunaris themselves, perform the service of memorizing and then orally relating the history of the tribe and the relationships among its members. The genealogist in the village was an aged and arthritic man named Hedayat, who in his later years was engaged in teaching the Nunari genealogy to his son, who would then carry out the traditional and hereditary duties of his position.

The villagers claimed that Hedayat knew every generation of the Nunari from the present to the founding brothers and even beyond. So I invited Hedayat to my hut and explained my purpose.

"Do you know Allah Ditta son of Rohm?" I asked.

"Yes, of course," he replied.

"Who was Rohm's father?" I continued.

"Shahadat Mohammad," he answered.

"And his father?" "Hamid."

"And his?"

"Chigatah," he snapped without hesitation.

I was now quite excited, for no one else in the village had been able to recall an ancestor of this generation. My estimate was that Chigatah had been born sometime between 1850 and 1870. But Hedayat went on.

"Chigatah's father was Kamal. And Kamal's father was Nanak. And Nanak's father was Sikhu. And before him was Dargai, and before him Maiy. And before him was Siddiq. And Siddiq's father was Nur. And Nur's Asmat. And Asmat was of Channa. And Channa of Nau. And Nau of Bhatta. And Bhatta was the son of Koduk."

Hedayat had now recounted sixteen generations of lineal ascendants related through the turban. Koduk was probably born in the sixteenth century. But still Hedayat continued.

"Sigun was the father of Koduk. And Man the father of Sigun. And before Man was his father Maneswar. And Maneswar's father was the founder of the clan, Naul."

This then was a line of the Naul clan of the Nunari tribe, ascending twenty-one generations from the present descendants (Allah Ditta's sons) to the founder, one of four brothers who lived perhaps in the fifteenth century. I asked Hedayat to recite genealogies of the other Nunari clans, and he did, with some blanks here and there, ending with Vadel, More, and Saddan, the other three brothers who formed the tribal nucleus. I then asked the obvious question, "Hedayat, who was the father of these four brothers? Who is the founding ancestor of the Nunari tribe?"

"The father of these brothers was not a Muslim. He was an Indian *rajput* [chief]. The tribe actually begins with the conversion of the four brothers," Hedayat explained.

"Well, then," I replied, "who was this Indian chief?"

"He was a famous and noble chief who fought against the Moguls. His name was Raja Kurin, who lived in a massive fort in Kurinnagar, about twenty-seven miles from Delhi."

"What!" I asked, both startled and unsure of what I had heard.

"Raja Kurin is the father of the brothers who make up—"

"But his name! It's the same as mine," I stammered. "Hedayat, my name is Richard Kurin. What a coincidence! Here I am living with your tribe thousands of miles from my home and it turns out that I have the same name as the founder of the tribe! Do you think I might be related to Raja Kurin and the Nunaris?"

Hedayat looked at me, but only for an instant. Redoing his turban, he tilted his head skyward, smiled, and asked, "What is the name of your father?"

I had come a long way. I now had a name

that could be recognized and respected, and as I answered Hedayat, I knew that I had finally and irrevocably fit into "my" village. Whether by fortuitous circumstance or by careful manipulation, my neighbors had found a way to take an invading city person intent on studying their life and transform him into one of their own, a full person entitled to wear a turban for participating in, and being identified with, that life. As has gone on for centuries in the region, once again the new and exogenous had been recast into something Punjabi.

Epilogue

There is no positive evidence linking the Nunaris to a historical Raja Kurin, although there are several famous personages identified by that name (also transcribed as Karan and Kurran). Estimated from the genealogy recited by Hedayat, the founding of the tribe by the four brothers appears to have occurred sometime between 440 and 640 years ago, depending on the interval assumed for each generation. On that basis, the most likely candidate for Nunari progenitor (actual or imputed) is Raja Karan, ruler of Anhilvara (Gujerat), who was defeated by the Khilji Ala-ud-Din in 1297 and again in 1307. Although this is slightly earlier than suggested by the genealogical data, such genealogies are often telescoped or otherwise unreliable.

Nevertheless, several aspects of Hedayat's account make this association doubtful. First, Hedayat clearly identifies Raja Kurin's conquerors as Moguls, whereas the Gujerati Raja Karan was defeated by the Khiljis. Second, Hedayat places the Nunari ancestor's kingdom only twenty-seven miles from Delhi. The Gujerati Raja Karan ruled several kingdoms, none closer than several hundred miles to Delhi.

Other circumstances, however, offer support for this identification of the Nunari ancestor. According to Hedayat, Raja Kurin's father was named Kam Deo. Although the historical figure was the son of Serung Deo, the use of "Deo," a popular title for the rajas of the Vaghela and Solonki dynasties, does seem to place the Nunari founder in the context of medieval Gujerat. Furthermore, Hedayat clearly identifies the saint (*pir*) said to have initiated the conversion of the Nunaris to Islam. This saint, Mukhdum-i-Jehaniyan, was a contemporary of the historical Raja Karan.

Also of interest, but as yet unexplained, is that several other groups living in Nunari settlement areas specifically claim to be descended from Raja Karan of Gujerat, who is said to have migrated northward into the Punjab after his defeat. Controverting this theory, the available evidence indicates that Raja Karan fled, not toward the Punjab, but rather southward to the Deccan, and that his patriline ended with him. It is his daughter Deval Devi who is remembered: she is the celebrated heroine of "Ashiqa," a famous Urdu poem written by Amir Khusrau in 1316. She was married to Khizr Khan, the son of Karan's conqueror; nothing is known of her progeny.

THE DIFFERENCES BETWEEN PEOPLE

As we saw in the previous section, cultural anthropologists focus on human behavior and the concept of culture; however, the discipline of anthropology is broader than simply cultural anthropology since human groups differ not only in terms of culture, but also in physical characteristics. Those anthropologists who are interested in the biological aspects of humanity are called physical anthropologists.

Early in the development of physical anthropology, the emphasis was on classification of humans into racial categories based upon body measurements and physical traits such as skin color, hair texture, stature, etc. Identifying a set number of racial groups within the human species proved to be no simple task, however; and different researchers classified humans into vastly different numbers of racial categories. Race was defined as a population within a species that differs genetically from other populations of the same spe-

cies. One problem, then, was the common reliance upon phenotype (outward physical features) rather than genotype (the shared genetic characteristics of a group) when creating racial categories. Also, physical anthropologists could not agree on how many physical differences were necessary to identify a separate race. These problems, and the social consequences of racism, have led modern physical anthropologists to abandon attempts to classify people into racial categories; instead, they focus on the study of specific genetically-based traits. Boyce Rensberger, in his article "Racial Odyssey," discusses the dynamic nature of the human species and the futility of trying to "define" pure races.

All too often the idea of racial differences among people results in prejudice and discrimination. "Are Blacks Natural Athletes?" addresses this point as James Peoples and Garrick Bailey describe how prejudice and discrimination play a larger role in athletic success among Blacks in America than does the simplistic explanation of natural physical talent.

The final article in this section, "Beyond the Melting Pot" by William A. Henry, III, explores the reality of contemporary America as a multiracial and multicultural society. Diversity offers America new ideas, new energies; but it also creates challenges and risks for *all* Americans.

Racial Odyssey

Boyce Rensberger

As you read:
1. *What is race?*
2. *Do races actually exist?*
3. *How are physical traits linked to environmental adaptation?*

The human species comes in an artist's palette of colors: sandy yellows, reddish tans, deep browns, light tans, creamy whites, pale pinks. It is a rare person who is not curious about the skin colors, hair textures, bodily structures and facial features associated with racial background. Why do some Africans have dark brown skin, while that of most Europeans is pale pink? Why do the eyes of most "white" people and "black" people look pretty much alike but differ so from the eyes of Orientals? Did one race evolve before the others? If so, is it more primitive or more advanced as a result? Can it be possible, as modern research suggests, that there is no such thing as a pure race? These are all honest, scientifically worthy questions. And they are central to current research on the evolution of our species on the planet Earth.

Broadly speaking, research on racial differences has led most scientists to three major conclusions. The first is that there are many more differences among people than skin color, hair texture and facial features. Dozens of other variations have been found, ranging from the shapes of bones to the consistency of ear wax to subtle variations in body chemistry.

The second conclusion is that the overwhelming evolutionary success of the human species is largely due to its great genetic variability. When migrating bands of our early ancestors reached a new environment, at least a few already had physical traits that gave them an edge in surviving there. If the coming centuries bring significant environmental changes, as many believe they will, our chances of surviving them will be immeasurably enhanced by our diversity as a species.

There is a third conclusion about race that is often misunderstood. Despite our wealth of variation and despite our constant, everyday references to race, no one has ever discovered a reliable way of distinguishing one race from another. While it is possible to classify a great many people on the basis of certain physical features, there are no known feature or groups of features that will do the job in all cases.

Skin color won't work. Yes, most Africans from south of the Sahara and their descendants around the world have skin that is darker than that of most Europeans. But there are millions of people in India, classified by some anthropologists as members of the Caucasoid, or "white," race who have darker skins than most Americans who call themselves black. And there are many Africans living in sub-Sahara Africa today whose skins are no darker than the skins of many Spaniards, Italians, Greeks or Lebanese.

What about stature as a racial trait? Because they are quite short, on the average, African Pygmies have been considered racially distinct from other dark-skinned Africans. If stature, then, is a racial criterion, would one include in the same race the tall African Watusi and the Scandinavians of similar stature?

The little web of skin that distinguishes Oriental eyes is said to be a particular feature of the Mongoloid race. How, then, can it be argued that the American Indian, who lacks this epicanthic fold, is Mongoloid?

Even more hopeless as racial markers are hair color, eye color, hair form, the shapes of noses and lips or any of the other traits put forth as typical of one race or another.

No Norms

Among the tall people of the world there are many black, many white and many in between. Among black people of the world there are many with kinky hair, many with straight or wavy hair, and many in between. Among the broad-nosed, full-lipped people of the world there are many with dark skins, many with light skins and many in between.

How did our modern perceptions of race arise? One of the first to attempt a scientific classification of peoples was Carl von Linné, better known as Linnaeus. In 1735, he published a classification that remains the standard today. As Linnaeus saw it there were four races, classifiable geographically and by skin color. The names Linnaeus gave them were *Homo sapiens Africanus nigrus* (black African human being), *H. sapiens Americanus rubescens* (red American human being), *H. sapiens Asiaticus fuscusens* (brownish Asian human being), and *H. sapiens Europaeus albescens* (white European human being). All, Linnaeus recognized, were members of a single human species.

A species includes all individuals that are biologically capable of interbreeding and producing fertile offspring. Most matings between species are fruitless, and even when they succeed, as when a horse and a donkey interbreed and produce a mule, the progeny are sterile. When a poodle mates with a collie, however, the offspring are fertile, showing that both dogs are members of the same species.

Even though Linnaeus's system of nomenclature survives, his classifications were discarded, especially after voyages of discovery revealed that there were many more kinds of people than could be pigeonholed into four categories. All over the world there are small populations that don't fit. Among the better known are:

- The so-called Bushmen of southern Africa, who look as much Mongoloid as Negroid.
- The Negritos of the South Pacific, who do look Negroid but are very far from Africa and have no known links to that continent.
- The Ainu of Japan, a hairy aboriginal people who look more Caucasoid than anything else.
- The Lapps of Scandinavia, who look as much like Eskimos as like Europeans.
- The aborigines of Australia, who often look Negroid but many of whom have straight or wavy hair and are often blond as children.
- The Polynesians, who seem to be a blend of many races, the proportions differing from island to island.

To accommodate such diversity, many different systems of classification have been proposed. Some set up two or three dozen races. None has ever satisfied all experts.

Classification System

Perhaps the most sweeping effort to impose a classification upon all the peoples of the world was made by the American anthropologist Carleton Coon. He concluded there are five basic races, two of which have major subdivisions: Caucasoids; Mongoloids; full-size Australoids (Australian aborigines); dwarf Australoids (Negritos—Andaman Islanders and similar peoples); full-size Congoids (African Negroids); dwarf Congoids (African Pygmies); and Capoids (the so-called Bushmen and Hottentots).

In his 1965 classic, *The Living Races of Man,* Coon hypothesized that before A.D. 1500 there were five pure races—five centers of human population that were so isolated that there was almost no mixing.

Each of these races evolved independently, Coon believed, diverging from a pre-*Homo sapiens* stock that was essentially the same everywhere. He speculated that the common ancestor evolved into *Homo sapiens* in five separate regions at five different times, beginning about 35,000 years ago. The populations that have been *Homo sapiens* for the shortest periods of time, Coon said, are the world's "less civilized" races.

The five pure races remained distinct until A.D. 1500; then Europeans started sailing the world, leaving their genes—as sailors always have—in every port and planting distant colonies. At about the same time, thousands of Africans were captured and forcibly settled in many parts of the New World.

That meant the end of the five pure races. But Coon and other experts held that this did not necessarily rule out the idea of distinct races. In this view, there *are* such things as races; people just don't fit into them very well anymore.

The truth is that there is really no hard evidence to suggest that five or any particular number of races evolved independently. The preponderance of evidence today suggests that as traits typical of fully modern people arose in any one place, they spread quickly to all human populations. Advances in intelligence were almost certainly the fastest to spread. Most an-

thropologists and geneticists now believe that human beings have always been subject to migrating and mixing. In other words, there probably never were any such things as pure races.

Race mixing has not only been a fact of human history but is, in this day of unprecedented global mobility, taking place at a more rapid rate than ever. It is not far-fetched to envision the day when, generations hence, the entire "complexion" of major population centers will be different. Meanwhile, we can see such changes taking place before our eyes, for they are a part of everyday reality.

Hybrid Vigor

Oddly, those who assert scientific validity for their notions of pure and distinct races seem oblivious of a basic genetic principle that plant and animal breeders know well: too much inbreeding can lead to proliferation of inferior traits. Crossbreeding with different strains often produces superior combinations and "hybrid vigor."

The striking differences among people may very well be a result of constant genetic mixing. And as geneticists and ecologists know, in diversity lies strength and resilience.

To understand the origin and proliferation of human differences, one must first know how Darwinian evolution works.

Evolution is a two-step process. Step one is mutation: somehow a gene in the ovary or testes of an individual is altered, changing the molecular configuration that stores instructions for forming a new individual. The children who inherit that gene will be different in some way from their ancestors.

Step two is selection: for a racial difference, or any other evolutionary change to arise, it must survive and be passed through several generations. If the mutation confers some disadvantage, the individual dies,

Disease Origins

The gene for sickle cell anemia, a disease found primarily among black people, appears to have evolved because its presence can render its bearer resistant to malaria. Such a trait would have obvious value in tropical Africa.

A person who has sickle cell anemia must have inherited genes for the disease from both parents. If a child inherits only one sickle cell gene, he or she will be resistant to malaria but will not have the anemia. Paradoxically, inheriting genes from both parents does not seem to affect resistance to malaria.

In the United States, where malaria is practically nonexistent, the sickle cell gene confers no survival advantage and is disappearing. Today only about 1 out of every 10 American blacks carries the gene.

Many other inherited diseases are found only in people from a particular area. Tay-Sachs disease, which often kills before the age of two, is almost entirely confined to Jews from parts of Eastern Europe and their descendants elsewhere. Paget's disease, a bone disorder, is found most often among those of English descent. Impacted wisdom teeth are a common problem among Asians and Europeans but not among Africans. Children of all races are able to digest milk because their bodies make lactase, the enzyme that breaks down lactose, or milk sugar. But the ability to digest lactose in adulthood is a racially distributed trait.

About 90 percent of Orientals and blacks lose this ability by the time they reach adulthood and become quite sick when they drink milk.

Even African and Asian herders who keep cattle or goats rarely drink fresh milk. Instead, they first treat the milk with fermentation bacteria that break down lactose, in a sense predigesting it. They can then ingest the milk in the form of yogurt or cheese without any problem.

About 90 percent of Europeans and their American descendants, on the other hand, continue to produce the enzyme throughout their lives and can drink milk with no ill effects.

often during embryonic development. But if the change is beneficial in some way, the individual should have a better chance of thriving than relatives lacking the advantage.

Natural Selection

If a new trait is beneficial, it will bring reproductive success to its bearer. After several generations of multiplication, bearers of the new trait may begin to outnumber nonbearers. Darwin called this natural selection to distinguish it from the artificial selection exercised by animal breeders.

Skin color is the human racial trait most generally thought to confer an evolutionary advantage of this sort. It has long been obvious in the Old World that the farther south one goes, the darker the skin color. Southern Europeans are usually somewhat darker than northern Europeans. In North Africa, skin colors are darker still, and, as one travels south, coloration reaches its maximum at the Equator. The same progression holds in Asia, with the lightest skins to the north. Again, as one moves south, skin color darkens, reaching in southern India a "blackness" equal to that of equatorial Africans.

This north-south spectrum of skin color derives from varying intensities of the same dark brown pigment called melanin. Skin cells simply have more or less melanin granules to be seen against a background that is pinkish because of the underlying blood vessels. All races can increase their melanin concentration by exposure to the sun.

What is it about northerly latitudes in the Northern Hemisphere that favors less pigmentation and about southerly latitudes that favors more? Exposure to intense sunlight is not the only reason why people living in southerly latitudes are dark. A person's susceptibility to rickets and skin cancer, his ability to withstand cold and to see in the dark may also be related to skin color.

The best-known explanation says the body can tolerate only a narrow range of intensities of sunlight. Too much causes sunburn and cancer, while too little deprives the body of vitamin D, which is synthesized in the skin under the influence of sunlight. A dark complexion protects the skin from the harmful effects of intense sunlight. Thus, albinos born in equatorial regions have a high rate of skin cancer. On the other hand, dark skin in northerly latitudes screens out sunlight needed for the synthesis of vitamin D. Thus, dark-skinned children living in northern latitudes had high rates of rickets—a bone-deforming disease caused by a lack of vitamin D—before their milk was routinely fortified. In the sunny tropics, dark skin admits enough light to produce the vitamin.

Recently, there has been some evidence that skin colors are linked to differences in the ability to avoid injury from the cold. Army researchers found that during the Korean War blacks were more susceptible to frostbite than were whites. Even among Norwegian soldiers in World War II, brunettes had a slightly higher incidence of frostbite than did blonds.

Eye Pigmentation

A third link between color and latitude involves the sensitivity of the eye to various wavelengths of light. It is known that dark-skinned people have more pigmentation in the iris of the eye and at the back of the eye where the image falls. It has been found that the less pigmented the eye, the more sensitive it is to colors at the red end of the spectrum. In situations illuminated with reddish light, the northern European can see more than a dark African sees.

It has been suggested that Europeans developed lighter eyes to adapt to the longer twilights of the North and their greater reliance on firelight to illuminate caves.

Although the skin cancer-vitamin D hypothesis enjoys wide acceptance, it may well be that resistance to cold, possession of good night vision and other yet unknown factors all played roles in the evolution of skin colors.

Most anthropologists agree that the original human skin color was dark brown, since it is fairly well established that human beings evolved in the tropics of Africa. This does not, however, mean that the first people were Negroids, whose descendants, as they moved north, evolved into light-skinned Caucasoids. It is more likely that the skin color of various populations changed several times from dark to light and back as people moved from one region to another.

Consider, for example, that long before modern people evolved, *Homo erectus* had spread throughout Africa, Europe and Asia. The immediate ancestor of *Homo sapiens*, *Homo erectus*, was living in Africa 1.5 million years ago and in Eurasia 750,000 years ago. The earliest known forms of *Homo sapiens* do not make their appearance until somewhere between 250,000 and 500,000 years ago. Although there is no evidence of the skin color of any hominid fossil, it is probable that the *Homo erectus* population in Africa had dark skin. As subgroups spread into northern latitudes, mutations that reduced pigmentation conferred survival advantages on them and lighter skins came to predominate. In other words, there were probably black *Homo erectus* peoples in Africa and white ones in Europe and Asia.

Did the black *Homo erectus* populations evolve into today's Negroids and the white ones in Europe into today's Caucasoids? By all the best evidence, nothing like this happened. More likely, wherever *Homo sapiens* arose it proved so superior to the *Homo erectus* populations that it eventually replaced them everywhere.

If the first *Homo sapiens* evolved in Africa, they were probably dark-skinned;

those who migrated northward into Eurasia lost their pigmentation. But it is just as possible that the first *Homo sapiens* appeared in northern climes, descendants of white-skinned *Homo erectus*. These could have migrated southward toward Africa, evolving darker skins. All modern races, incidentally, arose long after the brain had reached its present size in all parts of the world.

North-south variations in pigmentation are quite common among mammals and birds. The tropical races tend to be darker in fur and feather, the desert races tend to be brown, and those near the Arctic Circle are lighter colored.

There are exceptions among humans. The Indians of the Americas, from the Arctic to the southern regions of South America, do not conform to the north-south scheme of coloration. Though most think of Indians as being reddish-brown, most Indians tend to be relatively light skinned, much like their presumed Mongoloid ancestors in Asia. The ruddy complexion that lives in so many stereotypes of Indians is merely what years of heavy tanning can produce in almost any light-skinned person. Anthropologists explain the color consistency as a consequence of the relatively recent entry of people into the Americas—probably between 12,000 and 35,000 years ago. Perhaps they have not yet had time to change.

Only a few external physical differences other than color appear to have adaptive significance. The strongest cases can be made for nose shape and stature.

What's in a Nose

People native to colder or drier climates tend to have longer, more beak-shaped noses than those living in hot and humid regions. The nose's job is to warm and humidify air before it reaches sensitive lung tissues. The colder or drier the air is, the more surface area is needed inside the nose to get it to the right temperature or humidity. Whites tend to have longer and beakier noses than blacks or Orientals. Nevertheless, there is great variation within races. Africans in the highlands of East Africa have longer noses than Africans from the hot, humid lowlands, for example.

Stature differences are reflected in the tendency for most northern peoples to have shorter arms, legs and torsos and to be stockier than people from the tropics. Again, this is an adaptation to heat or cold. One way of reducing heat loss is to have less body surface, in relation to weight or volume, from which heat can escape. To avoid overheating, the most desirable body is long limbed and lean. As a result, most Africans tend to be lankier than northern Europeans. Arctic peoples are the shortest limbed of all.

Hair forms may also have a practical role to play, but the evidence is weak. It has been suggested that the more tightly curled hair of Africans insulates the top of the head better than does straight or wavy hair. Contrary to expectation, black hair serves better in this role than white hair. Sunlight is absorbed and converted to heat at the outer surface of the hair blanket; it radiates directly into the air. White fur, common on Arctic animals that need to absorb solar heat, is actually transparent and transmits light into the hair blanket, allowing the heat to form within the insulating layer, where it is retained for warmth.

Aside from these examples, there is little evidence that any of the other visible differences among the world's people provide any advantage. Nobody knows, for example, why Orientals have epicanthic eye folds or flatter facial profiles. The thin lips of Caucasoids and most Mongoloids have no known advantages over the Negroid's full lips. Why should middle-aged and older Caucasoid men go bald so much more frequently than the men of other races? Why does the skin of Bushmen wrinkle so heavily in the middle and later years? Or why does the skin of Negroids resist wrinkling so well? Why do the Indian men in one part of South America have blue penises? Why do Hottentot women have such unusually large buttocks?

There are possible evolutionary explanations for why such apparently useless differences arise.

One is a phenomenon known as sexual selection. Environmentally adaptive traits arise, Darwin thought, through natural selection—the environment itself chooses who will thrive or decline. In sexual selection, which Darwin also suggested, the choice belongs to the prospective mate.

In simple terms, ugly individuals will be less likely to find mates and reproduce their genes than beautiful specimens will. Take the blue penis as an example. Women might find it unusually attractive or perhaps believe it to be endowed with special powers. If so, a man born with a blue penis will find many more opportunities to reproduce his genes than his ordinary brothers.

Sexual selection can also operate when males compete for females. The moose with the larger antlers or the lion with the more imposing mane will stand a better chance of discouraging less well-endowed males and gaining access to females. It is possible that such a process operated among Caucasoid males, causing them to become markedly hairy, especially around the face.

Attractive Traits

Anthropologists consider it probable that traits such as the epicanthic fold or the many regional differences in facial features were selected this way.

Yet another method by which a trait can establish itself involves accidental selection. It results from what biologists call genetic drift.

Suppose that in a small nomadic band a person is born with perfectly parallel fingerprints instead of the usual loops, whorls or arches. That person's children would inherit parallel fingerprints, but they would confer no survival advantages. But if our family decides to strike out on its own, it will become the founder of a new band consisting of its own descendants, all with parallel fingerprints.

Events such as this, geneticists and anthropologists believe, must have occurred many times in the past to produce the great variety within the human species. Among the apparently neutral traits that differ among populations are:

Ear Wax

There are two types of ear wax. One is dry and crumbly and the other is wet and sticky. Both types can be found in every major population, but the frequencies differ. Among northern Chinese, for example, 98 percent have dry ear wax. Among American whites, only 16 percent have dry ear wax. Among American blacks the figure is 7 percent.

Scent Glands

As any bloodhound knows, every person has his or her own distinctive scent. People vary in the mixture of odoriferous compounds exuded through the skin—most of it coming from specialized glands called apocrine glands. Among whites, these are concentrated in the armpits and near the genitals and anus. Among blacks, they may also be found on the chest and abdomen. Orientals have hardly any apocrine glands at all. In the words of the Oxford biologist John R. Baker, "The Europids and Negrids are smelly, the Mongoloids scarcely or not at all." Smelliest of all are northern European, or so-called Nordic, whites. Body odor is rare in Japan. It was once thought to indicate a European in the ancestry and to be a disease requiring hospitalization.

Blood Groups

Some populations have a high percentage of members with a particular blood group. American Indians are overwhelmingly group O—100 percent in some regions. Group A is most common among Australian aborigines and the Indians in western Canada. Group B is frequent in northern India, other parts of Asia and western Africa.

Advocates of the pure-race theory once seized upon blood groups as possibly unique to the original pure races. The proportions of groups found today, they thought, would indicate the degree of mixing. It was subsequently found that chimpanzees, our closest living relatives, have the same blood groups as humans.

Taste

PTC (phenylthiocarbamide) is a synthetic compound that some people can taste and others cannot. The ability to taste it has no known survival value, but it is clearly an inherited trait. The proportion of persons who can taste PTC varies in different populations: 50 to 70 percent of Australian aborigines can taste it, as can 60 to 80 percent of all Europeans. Among East Asians, the percentage is 83 to 100 percent, and among Africans, 90 to 97 percent.

Urine

Another indicator of differences in body chemistry is the excretion of a compound known as BAIB (beta-amino-isobutyric acid) in urine. Europeans seldom excrete large quantities, but high levels of excretion are common among Asians and American Indians. It had been shown that the differences are not due to diet.

No major population has remained isolated long enough to prevent any unique genes from eventually mixing with those of neighboring groups. Indeed, a map showing the distribution of so-called traits would have no sharp boundaries, except for coastlines. The intensity of a trait such as skin color, which is controlled by six pairs of genes and can therefore exist in many shades, varies gradually from one population to another. With only a few exceptions, every known genetic possibility possessed by the species can be found to some degree in every sizable population.

Ever-Changing Species

One can establish a system of racial classification simply by listing the features of populations at any given moment. Such a concept of race is, however, inappropriate to a highly mobile and ever-changing species such as *Homo sapiens*. In the short view, races may seem distinguishable, but in biology's long haul, races come and go. New ones arise and blend into neighboring groups to create new and racially stable populations. In time, genes from these groups flow into other neighbors, continuing the production of new permutations.

Some anthropologists contend that at the moment American blacks should be considered a race distinct from African blacks. They argue that American blacks are a hybrid of African blacks and European whites. Indeed, the degree of mixture can be calculated on the basis of a blood component known as the Duffy factor.

In West Africa, where most of the New World's slaves came from, the Duffy factor is virtually absent. It is present in 43 percent of American whites. From the number of American blacks who are now "Duffy positive" it can be calculated that whites contributed 21 percent of the genes in the American black population. The figure is higher for blacks in northern and western states and lower in the South. By the same token, there are whites who have black ancestors. The number is smaller because of the tendency to identify a person as black even if only a minor fraction of his ancestors were originally from Africa.

The unwieldiness of race designations is also evident in places such as Mexico where most of the people are, in effect, hybrids of Indians (Mongoloid by some classifications) and Spaniards (Caucasoid).

Many South American populations are tri-hybrids—mixtures of Mongoloid, Caucasoid and Negroid. Brazil is a country where the mixture has been around long enough to constitute a racially stable population. Thus, in one sense, new races have been created in the United States, Mexico and Brazil. But in the long run, those races will again change.

Sherwood Washburn, a noted anthropologist, questions the usefulness of racial classification: "Since races are open systems which are intergrading, the number of races will depend on the purpose of the classification. I think we should require people who propose a classification of races to state in the first place why they wish to divide the human species."

The very notion of a pure race, then, makes no sense. But, as evolutionists know full well, a rich genetic diversity within the human species most assuredly *does*.

Are Blacks Natural Athletes?

James Peoples and Garrick Bailey

As you read:

1. What social reasons account for the cultural perception that African-Americans have greater innate athletic abilities than other ethnic groups?

An interesting exploration of the notion that racial differences are important influences on differences in behavior and performance of skills is the overrepresentation of black Americans in the nation's three most popular spectator sports: baseball, football, and basketball. Over one-fifth of professional baseball players are black, nearly half of National Football League players are black, and blacks comprise nearly three-fourths of all players in the National Basketball Association. A high percentage of boxers and track and field athletes also are black. Since only 12 percent of Americans are black, black men are doing exceptionally well in these sports—certainly better overall than whites. Why?

One possible reason is biological factors. There may be something about the bone structure, stamina, strength, coordination, or size of blacks that makes them better natural athletes than whites. If so, then blacks do so well in these sports because they have greater natural talents than whites. Less skilled athletes are eliminated as they pass through increasing levels of competition in high school and college, so that by the time one has made it as a pro, only the very best are left. The fact that so many of these are black must mean that the best blacks are better endowed biologically for sports than the best whites.

Sensible as this argument seems, it does not show that the overrepresentation of blacks in American sports is explained entirely or even to any significant degree by biological factors. First, notice that blacks are successful in only a few sports. Why are there so few black figure skaters, tennis players, gymnasts, skiers, swimmers, divers, and golfers? Whatever biological factors make blacks so successful at baseball, basketball, football, boxing, and track and field would be expected to carry over into other athletic competition. Yet blacks are underrepresented in these sports.

Second, notice that hardly anyone uses physical differences to explain why people of different nationalities perform well or poorly at particular sports. Physical factors do not explain why Germans do so well in swimming; Canadians in ice hockey; Swiss in skiing; Russians in gymnastics; Brazilians or Argentinians in soccer; British in cricket; Taiwanese, Koreans, and Japanese in the martial arts; or Cubans in boxing. Minnesota and Maine produce more hockey players than Florida and Texas—is this because of biological differences between residents of northern and southern states?

Third, notice that there was a period when various immigrants into the United States were overrepresented in sports. Contemporary Americans know that boxing today is dominated by blacks and Hispanics. How many of us know that other ethnic groups once dominated this sport? Large numbers of Irish came to the United States in the late nineteenth century following the potato famine in their homeland. In the first two decades of the twentieth century most of the great boxers were of Irish extraction. Later, Jews and Italians arrived in large numbers, and from the 1920s through 1930s, Jews and Italians did very well in boxing. An observer during the early decades of the twentieth century might have concluded that Irish, Jews, and Italians were naturally well-equipped for fighting, based on their dominance of professional boxing. But this statement sounds silly today, for now most descendants of these immigrants are so assimilated that we do not think of them as different from other whites.

For these and other reasons (see Edwards 1971 and 1973) there is no solid evidence that blacks dominate certain kinds of professional athletics because on average they are better natural athletes than whites. Then why do blacks perform so well? Part of the reason is the past and present racial discrimination experienced by blacks who pursue other lucrative careers. Sports offers young blacks the opportunity to become rich and famous in a country in which they have few other chances to make it really big. So they work harder at sports than at other things, since it offers them their best opportunity. In addition, young blacks have plenty of role models. Talented and highly visible men who have escaped the poverty of the inner cities by means of sports are bound to serve as examples for other blacks.

But the existence of opportunities in sports and athletic role models cannot alone explain why blacks do so well in certain sports. Before there can be viable role models, a fair number of blacks must already have done well in college and pro sports. Why should they have done so well in such large numbers if not because of biological factors? And before they could

have done well, they must have had the opportunity to participate. Why should they have had such opportunities, when they have been denied equal opportunity in so many other professions? Is there anything special about sports that would lure blacks into it over other potential careers? Specifically, is there anything about sports that would make it especially likely for blacks to be able to overcome the effects of poverty, poor education, and racial prejudice that hamper their achievement in other careers?

At root, racial prejudice means that an individual is evaluated negatively because of his or her perceived membership in racial category. It means that individual blacks are not judged on the basis of their merits and abilities, for whites' perceptions of blacks' merits and abilities are clouded by whites' prejudices. Members of an ethnic or racial minority can overcome prejudice by pursuing careers in which their performance can be evaluated easily and objectively, so that to some degree their performance overcomes the perceptual barrier of prejudice. In sports, statistics are kept that identify the better players in a relatively objective way. Batting average, rushing yardage, points per game, speed for the 100 meters, number of knockouts—such numbers allow fans, coaches, owners, and other players to judge individual performance accurately. Many fans in Brooklyn, and many fellow major league players, did not like it when Jackie Robinson broke the "color barrier" in major-league baseball in 1947. But his ability was obvious from his record.

There are other special features of sports that explain why blacks are better able to overcome prejudice in athletics than in most other occupations. Teams are small groups, so the presence or absence of even one star player can make the difference between success and failure. The skills necessary for success are so rare that owners compete for the best talent. Any owner or coach who refused to hire or play a skilled black player would be at a competitive disadvantage with those teams who did not discriminate. For the same reason, white players are less likely to reveal overtly any prejudice they may harbor, since the success of the whole team (and their prestige and next year's contract) may be affected. Blacks therefore experience less overt prejudice from their co-workers (teammates).

Further, teams are organized in such a way that cooperation generally takes precedence over competition. More than in most other occupations, the success of an athlete is not achieved at the expense of his co-workers, for success does not lead to promotion to a position of authority. White teammates therefore do not have to worry about taking orders from successful blacks, since all team members are subject equally to the authority of coaches or managers. And, significantly, there are few blacks in managerial roles in which they would be making important decisions and issuing commands, for this would threaten whites. The one exception, college and professional basketball, has such a high percentage of black players that black coaches are giving orders to mostly black teams.

In sum, blacks suffer from less overt prejudice and discrimination in athletics than in most other lucrative careers, so they are more attracted to and more likely to succeed in such careers. They experience less discrimination because their abilities can be objectively measured and compared, because their bosses and teammates recognize that they need their skills to succeed, and because getting ahead need not be at the expense of someone else on the team. So it is the special nature of sports and of athletic competition, and not biology, that explains blacks' overrepresentation in sports.

This analysis also explains why blacks are overrepresented only in certain sports, which the natural-athlete explanation does not do. The sports in which blacks do well are cheap sports, meaning that free public facilities are available and equipment is inexpensive and durable. This contrasts with sports like golf and skiing, which require high expenses. With the exception of boxing, the sports in which blacks do well do not require expensive private coaching to acquire professional status (unlike gymnastics and tennis).

Although the claim that blacks are naturally better athletes than whites seems to be antiracist and even pro-black, a subtle form of racism is involved. For example, whites who do well at basketball are sometimes said to have worked hard and to be "thinking players," whereas blacks are said to have great "instincts" and to be "natural athletes." Implicity, to claim that blacks are physically superior is to deny them equal intellectual abilities. Finally, and more importantly, to use black biology as the explanation for superior athletic performance results in channeling the energies of black youngsters into sports careers for which they are held to be naturally suited. But only a tiny fraction succeed in these careers; for most blacks, sports offers a false hope.

Beyond the Melting Pot

William A. Henry III

As you read:
1. *What does the "browning of America" mean?*
2. *What opportunities and risks may be associated with the "browning of America?"*
3. *What is the difference between a multiracial society and a multicultural society?*

Someday soon, surely much sooner than most people who filled out their Census forms last week realize, white Americans will become a minority group. Long before that day arrives, the presumption that the "typical" U.S. citizen is someone who traces his or her descent in a direct line to Europe will be part of the past. By the time these elementary students at Brentwood Science Magnet School in Brentwood, Calif., reach midlife, their diverse ethnic experience in the classroom will be echoed in neighborhoods and workplaces throughout the U.S.

Already 1 American in 4 defines himself or herself as Hispanic or nonwhite. If current trends in immigration and birth rates persist, the Hispanic population will have further increased an estimated 21%, the Asian presence about 22%, blacks almost 12% and whites a little more than 2% when the 20th century ends. By 2020, a date no further into the future than John F. Kennedy's election is in the past, the number of U.S. residents who are Hispanic or nonwhite will have more than doubled, to nearly 115 million, while the white population will not be increasing at all. By 2056, when someone born today will be 66 years old, the "average" U.S. resident, as defined by Census statistics, will trace his or her descent to Africa, Asia, the Hispanic world, the Pacific Islands, Arabia—almost anywhere but white Europe.

While there may remain towns or outposts where even a black family will be something of an oddity, where English and Irish and German surnames will predominate, where a traditional (some will wistfully say "real") America will still be seen on almost every street corner, they will be only the vestiges of an earlier nation. The former majority will learn, as a normal part of everyday life, the meaning of the Latin slogan engraved on U.S. coins— E PLURIBUS UNUM, one formed from many.

Among the younger populations that go to school and provide new entrants to the work force, the change will happen sooner. In some places an America beyond the melting pot has already arrived. In New York State some 40% of elementary- and secondary-school children belong to an ethnic minority. Within a decade, the proportion is expected to approach 50%. In California white pupils are already a minority. Hispanics (who, regardless of their complexion, generally distinguish themselves from both blacks and whites) account for 31.4% of public school enrollment, blacks add 8.9%, and Asians and others amount to 11%—for a nonwhite total of 51.3%. This finding is not only a reflection of white flight from desegregated public schools. Whites of all ages account for just 58% of California's population. In San Jose bearers of the Vietnamese surname Nguyen outnumber the Joneses in the telephone directory 14 columns to eight.

Nor is the change confined to the coasts. Some 12,000 Hmong refugees from Laos have settled in St. Paul. At some Atlanta low-rent apartment complexes that used to be virtually all black, social workers today need to speak Spanish. At the Sesame Hut restaurant in Houston, a Korean immigrant owner trains Hispanic immigrant workers to prepare Chinese-style food for a largely black clientele. The Detroit area has 200,000 people of Middle Eastern descent; some 1,500 small grocery and convenience stores in the vicinity are owned by a whole subculture of Chaldean Christians with roots in Iraq. "Once America was a microcosm of European nationalities," says Molefi Asante, chairman of the department of African-American studies at Temple University in Philadelphia. "Today America is a microcosm of the world."

History suggests that sustaining a truly multiracial society is difficult, or at least unusual. Only a handful of great powers of the distant past—Pharaonic Egypt and Imperial Rome, most notably—managed to maintain a distinct national identity while embracing, and being ruled by, an ethnic mélange. The most ethnically diverse contemporary power, the Soviet Union, is beset with secessionist demands and near tribal conflicts. But such comparisons are flawed, because those empires were launched by conquest and maintained through an aggressive military presence. The U.S. was created, and continues to be redefined, primarily by voluntary immigration. This process has been one of the country's great strengths, infusing it with talent and energy. The "browning of America" offers tremendous opportunity for capitalizing anew on the merits of many peoples from many lands. Yet this fundamental change in the ethnic makeup of the U.S. also poses risks. The American character is resilient and thrives on change. But past periods of rapid evolution have also, alas, brought out deeper, more fearful aspects of the national soul.

Politics—New and Shifting Alliances

A truly multiracial society will undoubtedly prove much harder to govern. Even seemingly race-free conflicts will be increasingly complicated by an overlay of ethnic tension. For example, the expected showdown in the early 21st century between the rising number of retirees and the dwindling number of workers who must be taxed to pay for the elders' Social Security benefits will probably be compounded by the fact that a large majority of recipients will be white, whereas a majority of workers paying for them will be nonwhite.

While prior generations of immigrants believed they had to learn English quickly to survive, many Hispanics now maintain that the Spanish language is inseparable from their ethnic and cultural identity, and seek to remain bilingual, if not primarily Spanish-speaking, for life. They see legislative drives to make English the sole official language, which have prevailed in some fashion in at least 16 states, as a political backlash. Says Arturo Vargas of the Mexican American Legal Defense and Educational Fund: "That's what English-only has been all about—a reaction to the growing population and influence of Hispanics. It's human nature to be uncomfortable with change. That's what the Census is all about, documenting changes and making sure the country keeps up."

Racial and ethnic conflict remains an ugly fact of American life everywhere, from working-class ghettos to college campuses, and those who do not raise their fists often raise their voices over affirmative action and other power sharing. When Florida Atlantic University, a state-funded institution under pressure to increase its low black enrollment, offered last month to give free tuition to every qualified black freshman who enrolled, the school was flooded with calls of complaint, some protesting that nothing was being done for "real" Americans. As the numbers of minorities increase, their demands for a share of the national bounty are bound to intensify, while whites are certain to feel ever more embattled. Businesses often feel whipsawed between immigration laws that punish them for hiring illegal aliens and antidiscrimination laws that penalize them for demanding excessive documentation from foreign-seeming job applicants. Even companies that consistently seek to do the right thing may be overwhelmed by the problems of diversifying a primarily white managerial corps fast enough to direct a work force that will be increasingly nonwhite and, potentially, resentful.

Nor will tensions be limited to the polar simplicity of white vs. nonwhite. For all Jesse Jackson's rallying cries about shared goals, minority groups often feel keenly competitive. Chicago's Hispanic leaders have leapfrogged between white and black factions, offering support wherever there seemed to be the most to gain for their own community. Says Dan Solis of the Hispanic-oriented United Neighborhood Organization: "If you're thinking power, you don't put your eggs in one basket."

Blacks, who feel they waited longest and endured most in the fight for equal opportunity, are uneasy about being supplanted by Hispanics or, in some areas, by Asians as the numerically largest and most influential minority—and even more, about being outstripped in wealth and status by these newer groups. Because Hispanics are so numerous and Asians such a fast-growing group, they have become the "hot" minorities, and blacks feel their needs are getting lower priority. As affirmative action has broadened to include other groups—and to benefit white women perhaps most of all—blacks perceive it as having waned in value for them.

The Classroom—Whose History Counts?

Political pressure has already brought about sweeping change in public school textbooks over the past couple of decades and has begun to affect the core humanities curriculum at such élite universities as Stanford. At stake at the college level is whether the traditional "canon" of Greek, Latin and West European humanities study should be expanded to reflect the cultures of Africa, Asia and other parts of the world. Many books treasured as classics by prior generations are now seen as tools of cultural imperialism. In the extreme form, this thinking rises to a value-deprived neutralism that views all cultures, regardless of the grandeur or paucity of their attainments, as essentially equal.

Even more troubling is a revisionist approach to history in which groups that have gained power in the present turn to remaking the past in the image of their desires. If 18th, 19th and earlier 20th century society should not have been so dominated by white Christian men of West European ancestry, they reason, then that past society should be reinvented as pluralist and democratic. Alternatively, the racism and sexism of the past are treated as inextricable from—and therefore irremediably tainting—traditional learning and values.

While debates over college curriculum get the most attention, professors generally can resist or subvert the most wrongheaded changes and students generally have mature enough judgment to sort out the arguments. Elementary- and secondary-school curriculums reach a far broader segment at a far more impressionable age, and political expediency more often wins over intellectual honesty. Exchanges have been vituperative in New York, where a state task force concluded that "African-Americans, Asian-Americans, Puerto Ricans and Native Americans have all been victims of an intellectual and educational oppression. . . . Negative characterizations, or the absence of positive references, have had a terribly damaging effect on the psyche of young people." In urging a revised syllabus, the task force argued, "Children from European culture will have a less arrogant perspective of being part of a group that has 'done it all'." Many intellectuals are outraged. Political scientist Andrew Hacker of Queens College lambastes a task-force suggestion that children be taught how "Native Americans were here to welcome new settlers from Holland, Senegal, England, Indonesia, France, the Congo, Italy, China, Iberia." Asks Hacker: "Did the Indians really welcome all those groups? Were they at Ellis Island when the Italians started to arrive? This is not history but a myth intended to bolster the self-esteem of certain children and, just possibly, a platform for advocates of various ethnic interests."

Values—Something in Common

Economic and political issues, however much emotion they arouse, are fundamentally open to practical solution. The deeper significance of America's becoming a majority nonwhite society is what it means to the national psyche, to individuals' sense of themselves and their nation—their idea of what it is to be American. People of color have often felt that whites treated equality as a benevolence granted to minorities rather than as an inherent natural right. Surely that condescension will wither.

Rather than accepting U.S. history and its meaning as settled, citizens will feel ever more free to debate where the nation's successes sprang from and what its unalterable beliefs are. They will clash over which myths and icons to invoke in education, in popular culture, in ceremonial speechmaking from political campaigns to the State of the Union address. Which is the more admirable heroism: the courageous holdout by a few conquest-minded whites over Hispanics at the Alamo, or the

anonymous expression of hope by millions who filed through Ellis Island? Was the subduing of the West a daring feat of bravery and ingenuity, or a wretched example of white imperialism? Symbols deeply meaningful to one group can be a matter of indifference to another. Says University of Wisconsin chancellor Donna Shalala: "My grandparents came from Lebanon. I don't identify with the Pilgrims on a personal level." Christopher Jencks, professor of sociology at Northwestern, asks, "Is anything more basic about turkeys and Pilgrims than about Martin Luther King and Selma? To me, it's six of one and half a dozen of the other, if children understand what it's like to be a dissident minority. Because the civil rights struggle is closer chronologically, it's likelier to be taught by someone who really cares."

Traditionalists increasingly distinguish between a "multiracial" society, which they say would be fine, and a "multicultural" society, which they deplore. They argue that every society needs a universally accepted set of values and that new arrivals should therefore be pressured to conform to the mentality on which U.S. prosperity and freedom were built. Says Allan Bloom, author of the best-selling *The Closing of the American Mind*: "Obviously, the future of America can't be sustained if people keep only to their own ways and remain perpetual outsiders. The society has got to turn them into Americans. There are natural fears that today's immigrants may be too much of a cultural stretch for a nation based on Western values."

The counterargument, made by such scholars as historian Thomas Bender of New York University, is that if the center cannot hold, then one must redefine the center. It should be, he says, "the ever-changing outcome of a continuing contest among social groups and ideas for the power to define public culture." Besides, he adds, many immigrants arrive committed to U.S. values; that is part of what attracted them. Says Julian Simon, professor of business administration at the University of Maryland: "The life and institutions here shape immigrants and not vice versa. This business about immigrants changing our institutions and our basic ways of life is hogwash. It's nativist scare talk."

Citizenship—Forging a New Identity

Historians note that Americans have felt before that their historical culture was being overwhelmed by immigrants, but conflicts between earlier-arriving English, Germans and Irish and later-arriving Italians and Jews did not have the obvious and enduring element of racial skin color. And there was never a time when the nonmainstream elements could claim, through sheer numbers, the potential to unite and exert political dominance. Says Bender: "The real question is whether or not our notion of diversity can successfully negotiate the color line."

For whites, especially those who trace their ancestry back to the early years of the Republic, the American heritage is a source of pride. For people of color, it is more likely to evoke anger and sometimes shame. The place where hope is shared is in the future. Demographer Ben Wattenberg, formerly perceived as a resister to social change, says, "There's a nice chance that the American myth in the 1990s and beyond is going to ratchet another step toward this idea that we are the universal nation. That rings the bell of manifest destiny. We're a people with a mission and a sense of purpose, and we believe we have something to offer the world."

Not every erstwhile alarmist can bring himself to such optimism. Says Norman Podhoretz, editor of *Commentary:* "A lot of people are trying to undermine the foundations of the American experience and are pushing toward a more Balkanized society. I think that would be a disaster, not only because it would destroy a precious social inheritance but also because it would lead to enormous unrest, even violence."

While know-nothingism is generally confined to the more dismal comers of the American psyche, it seems all too predictable that during the next decades many more mainstream white Americans will begin to speak openly about the nation they feel they are losing. There are not, after all, many nonwhite faces depicted in Norman Rockwell's paintings. White Americans are accustomed to thinking of themselves as the very picture of their nation. Inspiring as it may be to the rest of the world, significant as it may be to the U.S. role in global politics, world trade and the pursuit of peace, becoming a conspicuously multiracial society is bound to be a somewhat bumpy experience for many ordinary citizens. For older Americans, raised in a world where the numbers of whites were greater and the visibility of nonwhites was carefully restrained, the new world will seem ever stranger. But as the children at Brentwood Science Magnet School, and their counterparts in classrooms across the nation, are coming to realize, the new world is here. It is now. And it is irreversibly the America to come.

910
8 | 75
12

122
 47
 75

WOMEN AND MEN

A few years ago, anthropologist Michael Olien wrote an introductory anthropology text which he titled *The Human Myth.* A myth is a story which is believed to be true by those to whom it belongs; and by this book title, Olien meant that anthropologists are creators of myth, telling us stories about the human condition, stories which are true based upon the existing state of anthropological "knowledge."

Anthropology developed as a discipline in nineteenth-century Europe; and, since anthropologists cannot entirely divorce themselves from their native culture, early anthropology included as part of the myth of the human condition the Eurocentric view of male dominance. And it was easy to find examples beyond Europe to support this view—China, where women with bound feet paid proper homage first to father and then to husband; India, where widows followed their deceased husbands onto the funeral pyre; among Middle Eastern cultures, where male honor required women to be kept in seclusion behind the veil.

The excerpt from Susan Davis' book, *Patience and Power: Women's Lives in a Moroccan Village*, illustrates a society in which women traditionally have been expected to defer to the wishes of their male relatives. This article is followed, however, by two others which question male dominance as a universal human condition. In "The Status of Women" (excerpted from her book *Myths of Male Dominance*), Eleanor Leacock cites ethnographic data pertaining to the Montagnais-Naskapi Indians of Labrador and the Australian Aborigines to question the myth of male dominance among hunter-gatherers. As she indicates, the European Jesuit missionaries frowned upon the independent behavior of Montagnais-Naskapi women and were disappointed with Montagnais-Naskapi men's indifference to their wives' behavior.

Thus, women in a number of nonwestern societies displayed a degree of social autonomy; but, what about authority, the right to govern? Certainly nineteenth-century male anthropologists were aware of examples wherein females held positions of authority—Elizabeth I of England, Catherine the Great of Russia, for examples—however, these might conveniently be set aside as exceptions rather than the norm. Looking at non-European cultures, however, one could cite the Iroquois as another society which challenged the myth of male dominance. Men held public positions of authority but it was the decision of their female relatives which put them in those positions. Also, in this matrilineal, horticultural society, the longhouse and cultivated crops were the property of women.

The final article in this section, "Rape-free or Rape-prone," also suggests that male dominance, exhibited as violence toward women (rape), is not inherently a part of the human condition. Citing cross-cultural studies of rape, Beryl Benderly indicates that the incidence of rape may be correlated with such cultural factors as the status of women, values governing relations between males and females, and attitudes taught to boys.

It seems clear, to modern anthropologists at least, that the human myth does not include male dominance as the inevitable relationship between women and men.

Women's Lives in a Moroccan Village: Engagement and Marriage

Susan S. Davis

⫩⫩⫩⫩⫩

As you read:

1. *What is the rationale behond arranged marriages in Moroccan society?*
2. *Who arranges martriages in Moroccan culture? What is bride price?*
3. *What changes in marriage pattern does Davis note?*

⫩⫩Two ceremonies, involving both males and females, occur during adolescence. Engagement is the first, and marriage marks the end of this stage and the beginning of adulthood for both sexes. Although both sexes are honored (usually separately because men and women do not mix at parties), engagement and especially marriage are more centered around the female. Her main goal in life is to be married and have her own family, and her engagement is the first step toward it.

Marriages in Sidi Embarek are all arranged by the parents of the couple involved, although the parties on occasion may make suggestions, or veto those of their parents. The author heard an older woman describe, with obvious glee, how she had foiled her parents' plans for her. The prospective groom's family sent a donkey bearing baskets full of ripe grapes and a large sack of *henna* (a cosmetic made of powdered leaves, used to color hair red in the U.S.) as a gift. To show her disapproval, Fatna dumped all the grapes on the ground, sprinkled the *henna* over them, and set the chickens loose in the mess—and ran away to hide. When her parents found her, they chained her ankles

together so she could not run far, and went ahead with the wedding plans. But Fatna was not about to be subdued, and a girl friend helped her remove the chain from one ankle. She put this over her shoulder and ran off to a nearby French farm where she knew some Moroccan workers, and they interceded with the owner. He let her stay, and when her parents came for her persuaded them to delay the marriage. According to Fatna, she was fourteen at the time, and she did not marry (and then it was someone else) for another several years.

Legally, a girl now has the right to refuse the match and is asked if she agrees to it during the engagement ceremony, but the legal prerogative does not always match the reality of the situation. If a girl fears a beating, or lack of further support from her family, she will agree publicly to the marriage, whatever her personal preferences (which are just beginning to be important in village marriages). Traditionally, marriage is an alliance between two families. It was said to often be of the patrilateral parallel cousin type, in which a boy married his father's brother's daughter, which had the effect of keeping jointly owned property in the same patrilineal family. Since the families involved were related and may even have lived together as an extended family, it also meant that it was easier to assess

Susan S. Daivs, *Patience and Power; Women's Lives in a Moroccan Village* (Rochester, VT: Schenkman Books, Inc., © 1987), pp. 26-30. Reprinted with permission.

both the types of relationships being entered into and the characters of the actors. Data collected in Sidi Embarek, however, show that in only three of twenty-four cases did persons related by blood (not only parallel cousins) marry, while in the other twenty-one marriages the partners were unrelated. While this was not a random or representatively selected sample, it does indicate that marriage often occurs between unrelated couples.

Since marriage is mainly an alliance between two families, the partners do not have expectations of Western-style "love" (although movies and magazines are beginning to arouse such expectations), but rather work as a partnership with the object of raising a family. In this context arranged marriages are not resented, as many Western observers suspect, but rather accepted as the most sensible way to go about the matter. Even if a girl and boy in the village decide they want to marry, the decision is probably based on only a few meetings, since the sexes do not usually mix and in rural Morocco there is nothing like the custom of dating. Parents have more experience in life and more knowledge of the families which may be involved, so they are the logical agents.

The age at marriage of village girls is considerably higher than was that of their mothers. Many women recall that they had barely reached puberty when they were married ("I hardly had any breasts yet"), were afraid of their husbands, and ran away several times before finally settling down. There is now a Moroccan law setting the minimum age at marriage for girls as sixteen years and boys as eighteen, but this can easily be circumvented (an agreement with the proper official, or a change in the birth certificate) and is thus unlikely to be the cause of the higher age at marriage, now usually seventeen or eighteen for girls and the early or midtwenties for boys. Unmarried teenage girls are still seen as a threat to the family honor, and in other rural regions of Morocco (e.g., the

Southeast, near the Sahara) may still be married when they are eleven or twelve years old. The higher age at marriage in Sidi Embarek is probably due to the general lack of agriculturally based extended families living as a single household unit that could absorb and support the new couple. Marriages now usually do not occur until the male has a job with which he can support his new family, and when the job is not involved with family agriculture (and given the general shortage of jobs available), he is usually in his twenties before he can afford to be married. Thus age at marriage is higher, and most girls approve of this (although some of the boys get impatient). However, girls are still regarded as likely to be old maids if they are not married by the time they are twenty.

It is the male's family which selects the wife for its son and makes the first overtures to her family. The first sign the girl has of her impending marriage (it is improper for a father and daughter to discuss such things) is a visit paid to her home by a few female members of the groom's family, including his mother. While the males of the groom's family are important in selecting with which family they desire further ties, since they are men they can play little part in personally assessing the worthiness of the proposed bride. The women of the family are given this task, both because they can interact with her face-to-face, and because they will be more accurate judges of her housekeeping skills. In fact, household skills and honor are highly correlated; one would not expect to find an honorable girl a sloppy housekeeper, and a messy house suggests also a looseness in a woman's moral character. In this way, even if the women have been overruled initially by the men in the choice of the bride, they still have the opportunity to influence the decision in their favor.

If the groom's family is pleased with the reputation, demeanor (very shy and retiring), and household skills of the potential bride, males of the two families discuss the bride price (*sdaq* in Morocco, *mahr* in classical Arabic and in the Middle East). This sum is included in the marriage contract, and may either be given as a large lump sum to the family of the bride, or given only in part at the marriage with the other portion to be paid only in case of divorce or death of the husband. In either case, the bride price contributes to the stability of the marriage. A man considers seriously before divorcing a woman when it means he will have to pay her family additional money. Even if he has paid the total amount initially, he must still raise the bride price for another wife, for men seldom live as bachelors. Usually his family contributes to the bride price, and their hesitance to invest any further money leads them to put pressure on him to sustain his current marriage.

The inflation of bride prices in recent years is a problem for many bachelors and has also contributed to the rising age at marriage. The family of a country girl in 1972 demanded $100.00 or $200.00, while that of a city girl asked between $700.00 and $1,000.00 (village girls fell in between), in a country where the per capita income was then $80.00 a year. Divorcees and widows are much more easily attainable; their price fell within the $20.00 to $40.00 range (and did not require a large wedding celebration either), but usually only a man who has in some way lost his first wife will marry a woman who is not a virgin.

The Moroccan case also refutes (once again) those who suggest that a bride price involves the "selling" of a daughter. The money is paid to the bride's father, but it is used to buy jewelry for the bride or household furnishings for the new couple, and to finance the elaborate and costly wedding celebration. Guests do bring gifts, but these are usually something personal for the bride (such as a slip or nightgown) or cash, and are not large enough to furnish a house. The bride's father may manage to retain some of the money (for this reason some prospective grooms attempt to provide the furnishings themselves rather than giving cash to the bride's family to do so, confident that in this way they can be more economical), but not a great deal in any case. Rather, he is expected to contribute a similar sum as a dowry, to be used for the celebration, the bride's garments, and household furnishings.

If a bride price is agreed upon by the two families, there are exchanges of gifts and meals between them and a contract is prepared. The legal part of the ceremony of signing the marriage contract in rural Morocco (literally, "they do the paper") is considered as part of the engagement, but is actually also the only legal part of the marriage. If one decides afterwards to break the "engagement," one must obtain a divorce. The marriage is usually not consummated until months or even years later at a marriage ceremony (which is purely secular and consists of several days of celebration and feasting), but it is legally binding from the signing of the contract at the engagement.

The signature of the contract is done at home in the presence of a judge or his assistant and attended by members of each family. The bride is present but is spoken for by her father (or other male relative) except when asked if she agrees to the marriage. Otherwise she maintains a demure silence, her eyes cast down.

Myths of Male Dominance: The Status of Women in Egalitarian Societies

Eleanor Leacock

𝓍𝓍𝓍𝓍𝓍

As you read:

1. What is the relationship between social organization and male dominance?

2. What type of relationship exists between men and women in egalitarian societies?

3. How does this article affect our understanding of the relationship between men and women in contemporary American society?

𝓍𝓍With regard to the autonomy of women, nothing in the structure of egalitarian band societies necessitated special deference to men. There were no economic and social liabilities that bound women to be more sensitive to men's needs and feelings than vice versa. This was even true in hunting societies, where women did not furnish a major share of the food. The record of seventeenth-century Montagnais-Naskapi life in the *Jesuit Relations* makes this clear. Disputes and quarrels among spouses were virtually nonexistent, Le Jeune reported, since each sex carried out its own activities without "meddling" in those of the other. Le Jeune deplored the fact that the Montagnais "imagine that they ought by right of birth, to enjoy the liberty of wild ass colts, rendering no homage to any one whomsoever." Noting that women had "great power," he expressed his disapproval of the fact that men had no apparent inclination to make their wives "obey"

them or to enjoin sexual fidelity upon them. He lectured the Indians of this failing, reporting in one instance, "I told him then that he was the master, and that in France women do not rule their husbands." LeJeune was also distressed by the sharp and ribald joking and teasing into which women entered along with the men. "Their language has the foul odor of the sewers," he wrote. The *Relations* reflect the program of the Jesuits to "civilize" the Indians, and during the course of the seventeenth century they attempted to introduce principles of formal authority, lectured the people about obeying newly elected chiefs, and introduced disciplinary measures in the effort to enforce male authority upon women. No data are more illustrative of the distance between hierarchical and egalitarian forms of organization than the Jesuit account of these efforts (Leacock 1977; Leacock and Goodman 1977).

Nonetheless, runs the argument for universal female subservience to men, the hunt and war, male domains, are associated with power and prestige to the disadvantage of women. What about this assumption?

Answers are at several levels. First, it is necessary to modify the exaggerations of male as hunter and warrior. Women did some individual hunting, as will be discussed below for the Ojibwa, and they participated in hunting drives that were often of great importance. Men did a lot of non-hunting. Warfare was minimal or non-existent. The association of hunting, war, and masculine assertiveness is not found among hunter-gatherers except, in a limited way, in Australia. Instead, it characterizes horticultural societies in certain areas, notably Melanesia and the Amazon lowlands.

It is also necessary to reexamine the idea that these male activities were in the past more prestigious than the creation of new human beings. I am sympathetic to the skepticism with which women may view the argument that their gift of fertility was as highly valued as or more highly valued than anything men did. Women are too commonly told today to be content with the wondrous ability to give birth and with the presumed propensity for "motherhood" as defined in saccharine terms. They correctly read such exhortations as saying, "Do not fight for a change in status." However, the fact that childbearing is associated with women's present oppression does not mean this was the case in earlier social forms. To the extent that hunting and warring (or, more accurately, sporadic raiding, where it existed) were areas of male ritualization, they were just that: areas of male ritualization. To a greater or lesser extent women participated in the rituals, while to a greater or lesser extent they were also involved in ritual elaborations of generative power, either along with men or separately. To presume the greater importance of male than female participants, or to casually accept the statements to this effect of latter-day male informants, is to miss the basic function of dichotomized sex-symbolism in egalitarian society. Dichotomization made it possible to ritualize the reciprocal roles of females and males that sustained the group. As ranking began to develop, it became a means of

asserting male dominance, and with the full-scale development of classes sex ideologies reinforced inequalities that were basic to exploitative structures.

Much is made of Australian Aboriginal society in arguments for universal deference of women toward men. The data need ethnohistorical review, since the vast changes that have taken place in Australia over the last two centuries cannot be ignored in the consideration of ritual life and of male brutality toward women. Disease, outright genocidal practices, and expulsion from their lands reduced the population of native Australians to its lowest point in the 1930s, after which the cessation of direct genocide, the mission distribution of foods, and the control of infant mortality began to permit a population increase. The concomitant intensification of ceremonial life is described as follows by Godelier.*

> This . . . phenomenon, of a politico-religious order, of course expresses the desire of these groups to reaffirm their cultural identity and to resist the destructive pressures of the process of domination and acculturation they are undergoing, which has robbed them of their land and subjected their ancient religious and political practices to erosion and systematic extirpation. (1973: 13) (Translation mine. E.L.) .

Thus ceremonial elaboration was oriented toward renewed ethnic identification, in the context of oppression. Furthermore, on the reserves, the economic autonomy of women vis-à-vis men was undercut by handouts to men defined as heads of families and by the sporadic opportunities for wage labor open to men. To assume that recent ritual data reflect aboriginal Australian symbolic structures as if unchanged is

*"Ce . . . phenomène, d'ordre politico-réligieux, traduit bien entendu la volunté de ces groupes de réaffirmer leur identité culturelle et de résister aux pressions déstructrices du procès de domination et d'acculturation qu'elles subissent, que les a privés de leur terre et soumet leurs anciennes pratiques réligieuses et politiques a un travail d'erosion et d'extirpation systématique."

to be guilty of freezing these people in some timeless "traditional culture" that does not change or develop, but only becomes lost; it is to rob them of their history. Even in their day, Spencer and Gillen (1968: 443) noted the probable decline in women's ceremonial participation among the Arunta.

Allusions to male brutality toward women are common for Australia. Not all violence can be blamed on European colonialism, to be sure, yet it is crass ethnocentrism, if not outright racism, to assume that the grim brutality of Europeans toward the Australians they were literally seeking to exterminate was without profound effect. A common response to defeat is to turn hostility inward. The process is reversed when people acquire the political understanding and organizational strength to confront the source of their problems, as has recently been happening among Australian Aborigines.

References to women of recent times fighting back publicly in a spirited style, occasionally going after their husbands with both tongue and fighting club, and publicly haranguing both men and women bespeak a persisting tradition of autonomy (Kaberry 1939: 25-26, 181). In relation to "those reciprocal rights and duties that are recognized to be inherent in marriage," Kaberry writes:

> *I, personally, have seen too many women attack their husbands with a tomahawk or even their own boomerangs, to feel that they are invariably the victims of ill treatment. A man may perhaps try to beat his wife if she has not brought in sufficient food, but I never saw a wife stand by in submission to receive punishment for her culpable conduct. In the quarrel she might even strike the first blow, and if she were clearly in danger of being seriously hurt, then one of the bystanders might intervene, in fact always did within my experience. (142-143)*

Nor did the man's greater strength tell in such a struggle, for the wife "will pack up her goods and chattels and move to the camp of a relative . . . till the loss of an economic partner . . . brings the man to his senses and he attempts a reconciliation"(143). Kaberry concludes that the point to stress about this indispensability of a woman's economic contribution is "not only her great importance in economics, but also her power to utilize this to her own advantage in other spheres of marital life."

A further point also needs stressing: such quarrels are not, as they may first appear, structurally at the same level as similar quarrels in our own society. In our case, reciprocity in marital rights and duties is defined in the terms of a social order in which subsistence is gained through paid wage labor, while women supply socially essential but unpaid services within a household. A dichotomy between "public" labor and "private" household service masks the household "slavery" of women. In all societies, women use the resources available to them to manipulate their situation to their advantage as best they can, but they are in a qualitatively different position, structurally, in our society from that in societies where what has been called the "household economy" is the *entire* economy. References to the autonomy of women when it comes to making decisions about their own lives are common for such societies. Concomitant autonomy of attitude is pointed out by Kaberry, again, for the Kimberly peoples: "The women, as far as I could judge from their attitudes," she writes, "remained regrettably profane in their attitude towards the men." To be sure, they much admired the younger men as they paraded in their ceremonial finery, but "the praise uttered was in terms that suggested that the spectators regarded the men as potential lovers, and not as individuals near unto gods" (230). In summary, Kaberry argues that "there can be no question of identifying the sacred inheritance of the tribe only with the men's ceremonies. Those of the women belong to it also" (277). As for concepts of "pollution," she says, "the women with regard to the men's rituals are profane and uninitiated; the men with regard to the women's ritual are profane and uninitiated" (277).

The record on women's autonomy and lack of special deference among the seventeenth-century Montagnais-Naskapi is unambiguous. Yet this was a society in which the hunt was overwhelmingly important. Women manufactured clothing and other necessities, but furnished much less food than was the usual case with hunter-gatherers. In the seventeenth century, women as well as men were shamans, although this is apparently no longer remembered. As powerful shamans, they might exhort men to battle. Men held certain special feasts to do with hunting from which women were excluded. Similarly, men were excluded from women's feasts about which we know nothing but that they were held. When a man needed more than public teasing to ensure his good conduct, or in times of crisis, women held their own councils. In relation to warfare, anything but dominance-deference behavior is indicated. In historic times, raids were carried on against the Iroquois, who were expanding their territories in search of furs. The fury with which women would enjoin men to do battle and the hideous and protracted intricacies of the torture of captives in which they took the initiative boggle the mind. Getting back at the Iroquois for killing their menfolk was central, however, not "hailing the conquering hero."

Rape-Free or Rape-Prone

Beryl Benderly

As you read:
1. *Is rape a universal human behavior?*
2. *How does enculturation affect the manifestation of rape in a society?*
3. *What are the general behavior patterns of rape-prone societies? of rape-free societies?*

The typical American rapist is not, as many people assume, sexually deprived. Rather he is a hostile, aggressive man who likes to do violence to women. Not until the women's movement, when victims became more willing to report rapes, did social scientists discover that rape is not so much a sexual act as a violent crime with profoundly damaging effects. Furthermore, scientists say it is far more pervasive than they had thought.

One highly significant observation, however, went along unnoticed: Rape is not an unavoidable fact of human nature. There are cultures in the world where it is virtually unknown. American women are several hundred times as likely to be raped as are women in certain other cultures. But there also are extremely violent societies where women are three times more likely to be attacked than they are in the United States.

New research suggests that the incidence of rape depends in particular on cultural factors: the status of women, the values that govern the relations between the sexes, and the attitudes taught to boys. Although the findings are tentative, they contradict the widely publicized feminist hypothesis that rape is inherent to the relations between men and women, an idea that received considerable attention in Susan Brownmiller's book, *Against Our Will*, published in 1975.

Now comes Peggy Reeves Sanday, a University of Pennsylvania anthropologist who has compared data from scores of cultures to find that rape is anything but universal. It does not stem from a biological drive, she believes, but is rather a conditioned response to the way certain kinds of societies are organized. Sexual violence is no more inherent to masculinity than football. Many American men may express their masculinity by making bone-jarring tackles or watching others do so, but that is because this culture encourages them to perform these strange rituals, not because their inherent nature demands linebacker blitzes or quarterback sneaks. Likewise, Sanday believes, "Human sexual behavior, though based on a biological need, is expressed in cultural terms." Human violence takes many forms, and rape is but one of them.

But what predisposes a culture toward or against rape? To find out, Sanday consulted a cross-cultural sample of 156 societies published in 1969 by George Peter Murdock and Douglas R. White. This sample, while accepted by many anthropologists as a standard basis for cross-cultural comparison, has its drawbacks as a research tool. The societies she referred

From *Science 82*, Vol. 3, No. 8, pp. 40–43. Copyright © 1982 by Beryl Lieff Bendely. Reprinted by permission of the author.

Prob. w/ study

to were studied at different times by different anthropologists interested in different aspects of each culture. Sensitive information, such as that on rape, might not have been disclosed to a visiting stranger who was not deliberately trying to find out about it. Nevertheless, Sanday found information on rape that she believes to be reliable for 95 of these societies.

Almost half of the reports (47 percent) Sanday studied were rape-free societies with sexual assault "absent or . . . rare." Less than a quarter (17 percent) proved to be "unambiguously rape-prone," displaying "the social use of rape to threaten or punish women or the presence of a high incidence of rape of their own or other women." Reports of rape exist for the remaining 36 percent, but the incidence is not known. Although some of these societies may actually have little rape, Sanday added them to the rape-prone to form the category "rape-present." Thus the split between sample societies that have rape and those that do not is close to even.

A model rape-free society, according to Sanday, is the Ashanti of West Africa. Their principal ethnographer, R.S. Rattray, mentions only a single incidence of rape, although he does not ignore other sexual offenses such as incest and adultery. Ashanti women are respected and influential members of the community. The Ashanti religion emphasizes women's contribution to the general well-being. The main female deity, the Earth Goddess, is believed to be the creator of past and future generations as well as the source of food and water. Women participate fully in religious life, taking as important a ritual role as men.

The Mbuti Pygmies, extensively described by anthropologist Colin Turnbull, present another aspect of rape-free social life. They hunt with nets in the jungle of central Africa and live harmoniously with the forest, which provides all their needs— food, clothing, shelter. The Mbuti believe that the forest takes offense at anger and discord. The people live in cooperative small bands, men and women sharing both work and decisions. No Mbuti attempts to dominate another, nor does the group as a whole seek to dominate nature. Indeed, they refer to the forest in terms of endearment, as they would a parent or lover. Here again women play important symbolic and political roles. The feminine qualities of nurturance and fertility rank among the culture's most valued traits.

Very different traits stand out in rape-prone societies such as the Gusii of Kenya. Anthropologist Robert LeVine reports that judicial authorities counted 47.2 rapes per 100,000 population in a year when the U.S. rate, one of the highest in the industrial world, was 13.85 per 100,000. "Normal heterosexual intercourse between Gusii males and females is conceived as an act in which a man overcomes the resistance of a woman and causes her pain," writes Sanday. It's customary for respectable old ladies to taunt the young bridegroom about his inadequate sexual equipment on the way to his wedding. He retaliates and asserts his manhood by bragging to his friends that he reduced his bride to tears on their wedding night, that she remained in pain the next morning. No wife respects a husband who fails to take her by force.

The degree of tension pervading the Gusii battle of the sexes may be unusual, but the use of rape to conquer unwilling brides or to keep women under tight control is not. Men of certain Plains Indian tribes once invited groups of friends to gang-rape unfaithful wives. Mundurucu men of the Amazon threaten to rape any woman approaching the sacred trumpets, which embody supernatural tribal power and are safeguarded in a special men's house.

As Sanday suspected, she found patterns of behavior common to rape-prone societies, and they differed markedly from traits of rape-free peoples. Societies with a high incidence of rape, she discovered, tolerate violence and encourage men and boys to be tough, aggressive, and competitive. Men in such cultures generally have special, politically important gathering spots off limits to women, whether they be in the Mundurucu men's club or the corner tavern. Women take little or no part in public decision making or religious rituals; men mock or scorn women's practical judgment. They also demean what they consider women's work and remain aloof from childbearing and rearing. These groups usually trace their beginnings to a male supreme being.

Men in such societies, Sanday says, often "perceive themselves as civilized animals." Indeed, the word *macho*, now slang for that attitude, is the Spanish for "male of an animal species," a significant qualification in a language that distinguishes, more carefully than English, the properties of beasts from those of humans.

In short, Sanday concludes, "Rape is not inherent in men's nature but results from their image of that nature." It is a product of a certain set of beliefs, which in turn derive from particular social circumstances. Male dominance, Sanday believes, serves its purpose. Rape-prone societies often have histories of unstable food supplies, warfare, or migration. Such rigors force men to the forefront to repel attackers and compete with others for scarce resources and land. A belief system that glorifies masculine violence, that teaches men to regard strength and physical force as the finest expression of their nature, reconciles them to the necessity of fighting and dying in society's interest. Unstable or threatened societies—gin-ridden, trigger-happy American frontiersmen, Southern planters outnumbered by their restive slaves, children of Israel approaching Canaan, the Azande conquerors of neighboring African tribes—depended for their survival on the physical prowess of their men. Danger brings soldiers and fighters to the front line and encourages the development of male-dominated social structures. And these often include concepts of men as bestial crea-

tures and women as property. It is interesting that a number of rape-prone societies provide restitution to the rape victim's husband rather than to the victim herself.

On the other hand, stable cultures that face no danger from predatory enemies and that harmoniously occupy ancestral surroundings neither need nor condone such violence. Their food supplies usually fluctuate little from season to season or year to year, so they face neither the threat of starvation nor the need to compete with neighbors for resources. Women and men share power and authority because both contribute equally to society's welfare, and fighters are not necessary. Rape-free societies glorify the female traits of nurturance and fertility. Many such peoples believe that they are the offspring of a male and female deity or that they descended from a universal womb.

Although data on hundreds of societies have been available to anthropologists for generations, Sanday is one of the first to dig out broad patterns of behavior relating to rape. Just as the general society paid little attention to rape until Brownmiller's book made the front pages, rape has also been a "nonsubject" in anthropology. But not, anthropologists hope, for long.

The way society trains its boys and girls to think about themselves and each other determines to a large extent how rape-prone or rape-free that society will be. Sanday believes we can mitigate the damage our unconscious biases do by raising boys, for example, with more reverence for nurturance and less for violence. We can encourage women to resist assault. "One must be careful," Sanday says, "in blaming men alone or women alone for the high incidence of rape in our society. In a way we all conspire to perpetuate it. We expect men to attack, just as we expect women to submit."

But we can do something about such patterns of thought. Rape is not inevitable.

RAISING CHILDREN

The experiences of childhood vary greatly among human societies. Child-rearing practices are different in every human culture, as is the cultural knowledge that children learn as they are enculturated. It is during childhood that children are taught their gender roles—the beliefs, values, and behaviors expected of them as a male or female in their society. In many societies, children are also considered a part of the household labor force; and they are expected to contribute their time to the household's work. The articles in this section offer some insight into the differences in children's enculturation around the world and the different cultural attitudes towards childhood.

Laura Shapiro, in "Guns and Dolls," focuses on children as she discusses the efforts of anthropologists, psychologists, and sociologists to discover whether biol-

ogy or culture is the basis of behavioral differences between males and females. As this article illustrates, cultural anthropologists tend to stress the importance of socially-learned behavior; thus, parents and other adults are recognized as having significant roles in the enculturation process of a child.

The other two articles relate to the traditional middle class American view of adults as protectors of children. In this view, parents have an obligation to provide a safe environment where children can be children. The contrast between this ideal and the facts of modern life in America is reflected in the now common terms "latch-key kid" and "home alone." "Moonrose Watched Through a Sunny Day" and "Child Labour in Naples" remind us that the situation is not new and that it is not confined to America.

Guns and Dolls

Laura Shapiro

As you read:
1. *How do American parents enculturate gender roles in children?*
2. *Does this article seem to support one or the other—biology or culture—as the primary source of gender differences?*

Meet Rebecca. She's 3 years old, and both her parents have full-time jobs. Every evening Rebecca's father makes dinner for the family—Rebecca's mother rarely cooks. But when it's dinner time in Rebecca's dollhouse, she invariably chooses the Mommy doll and puts her to work in the kitchen.

Now meet George. He's 4, and his parents are still loyal to the values of the '60s. He was never taught the word "gun," much less given a war toy of any sort. On his own, however, he picked up the word "shoot." Thereafter he would grab a stick from the park, brandish it about and call it his "shooter."

Are boys and girls *born* different? Does every infant really come into the world programmed for caretaking or war making? Or does culture get to work on our children earlier and more inexorably than even parents are aware? Today these questions have new urgency for a generation that once made sexual equality its cause and now finds itself shopping for Barbie clothes and G.I. Joe paraphernalia. Parents may wonder if gender roles are immutable after all, give or take a Supreme Court justice. But burgeoning research indicates otherwise. No matter how stubborn the stereotype, individuals can challenge it; and

they will if they're encouraged to try. Fathers and mothers should be relieved to hear that they do make a difference.

Biologists, psychologists, anthropologists and sociologists have been seeking the origin of gender differences for more than a century, debating the possibilities with increasing rancor ever since researchers were forced to question their favorite theory back in 1902. At that time many scientists believed that intelligence was a function of brain size and that males uniformly had larger brains than women—a fact that would nicely explain men's preeminence in art, science and letters. This treasured hypothesis began to disintegrate when a woman graduate student compared the cranial capacities of a group of male scientists with those of female college students; several women came out ahead of the men, and one of the smallest skulls belonged to a famous male anthropologist.

Gender research has become a lot more sophisticated in the ensuing decades, and a lot more controversial. The touchiest question concerns sex hormones, especially testosterone, which circulates in both sexes but is more abundant in males and is a likely, though unproven, source of aggression. To postulate a biological determinant for behavior in an ostensibly egalitarian society like ours requires a thick skin. "For a while I didn't dare talk about hormones, because women would get up and leave the room," says Beatrice Whiting, professor emeritus of education and anthropology at Harvard. "Now they seem to have more self-confidence. But they're skeptical. The data's not in yet."

Some feminist social scientists are staying away from gender research entirely— "They're saying the results will be used against women," says Jean Berko Gleason, a professor of psychology at Boston University who works on gender differences in the acquisition of language. Others see no reason to shy away from the subject. "Let's say it were proven that there were biological foundations for the division of labor," says Cynthia Fuchs Epstein, professor of sociology at the City University of New York, who doesn't, in fact, believe in such a likelihood. "It doesn't mean we couldn't do anything about it. People can make from scientific findings whatever they want." But a glance at the way society treats those gender differences already on record is not very encouraging. Boys learn to read more slowly than girls, for instance, and suffer more reading disabilities such as dyslexia, while girls fall behind in math when they get to high school. "Society can amplify differences like these or cover them up," says Gleason. "We rush in reading teachers to do remedial reading, and their classes are almost all boys. We don't talk about it, we just scurry around getting them to catch up to the girls. But where are the remedial math teachers? Girls are *supposed* to be less good at math, so that difference is incorporated into the way we live."

No matter where they stand on the question of biology versus culture, social scientists agree that the sexes are much more alike than they are different, and that variations within each sex are far greater than variations between the sexes. Even differences long taken for granted have begun to disappear. Janet Shibley Hyde, a professor of psychology at the University of Wisconsin, analyzed hundreds of studies on verbal and math ability and found boys

and girls alike in verbal ability. In math, boys have a moderate edge; but only among highly precocious math students is the disparity large. Most important, Hyde found that verbal and math studies dating from the '60s and '70s showed greater differences than more recent research. "Parents may be making more efforts to tone down the stereotypes," she says. There's also what academics call "the file-drawer effect." "If you do a study that shows no differences, you assume it won't be published," says Claire Etaugh, professor of psychology at Bradley University in Peoria, Ill. "And until recently, you'd be right. So you just file it away."

The most famous gender differences in academics show up in the annual SAT results, which do continue to favor boys. Traditionally they have excelled on the math portion, and since 1972 they have slightly outperformed girls on the verbal side as well. Possible explanations range from bias to biology, but the socioeconomic profile of those taking the test may also play a role. "The SAT gets a lot of publicity every year, but nobody points out that there are more women taking it than men, and the women come from less advantaged backgrounds," says Hyde. "The men are a more highly selected sample: they're better off in terms of parental income, father's education and attendance at private school."

Another longstanding assumption does hold true: boys tend to be somewhat more active, according to a recent study, and the difference may even start prenatally. But the most vivid distinctions between the sexes don't surface until well into the pre-school years. "If I showed you a hundred kids aged 2, and you couldn't tell the sex by the haircuts, you couldn't tell if they were boys or girls," says Harvard professor of psychology Jerome Kagan. Staff members at the Children's Museum in Boston say that the boys and girls racing through the exhibits are similarly active, similarly rambunctious and similarly interested in model cars and model kitchens, until they reach first grade or so. And at New York's Bank Street preschool, most of the 3 year olds clustered around the cooking table to make banana bread one recent morning were boys. (It was a girl who gathered up three briefcases from the costume box and announced, "Let's go to work.")

By the age of 4 or 5, however, children start to embrace gender stereotypes with a determination that makes liberal-minded parents groan in despair. No matter how careful they may have been to correct the disparities in "Pat the Bunny" ("Paul isn't the *only* one who can play peekaboo, *Judy* can play peekaboo"), their children will delight in the traditional male/female distinctions preserved everywhere else: on television, in books, at day care and pre-school, in the park and with friends. "One of the things that is very helpful to children is to learn what their identity is," says Kyle Pruett, a psychiatrist at the Yale Child Study Center. "There are rules about being feminine and there are rules about being masculine. You can argue until the cows come home about whether those are good or bad societal influences, but when you look at the children, they love to know the differences. It solidifies who they are."

Water pistols

So girls play dolls, boys play Ghost-busters. Girls take turns at hopscotch, boys compete at football. Girls help Mommy, boys aim their water pistols at guests and shout, "You're dead!" For boys, notes Pruett, guns are an inevitable part of this developmental process, at least in a television-driven culture like our own. "It can be a cardboard paper towelholder, it doesn't have to be a miniature Uzi, but it serves as the focus for fantasies about the way he is going to make himself powerful in the world," he says. "Little girls have their aggressive side, too, but by the time they're

socialized it takes a different form. The kinds of things boys work out with guns, girls work out in terms of relationships—with put-downs and social cruelty." As if to underscore his point, a 4-year-old at a recent Manhattan party turned to her young hostess as a small stranger toddled up to them. "Tell her we don't want to play with her," she commanded. "Tell her we don't like her."

Once the girls know they're female and the boys know they're male, the powerful stereotypes that guided them don't just disappear. Whether they're bred into our chromosomes or ingested with our corn-flakes, images of the aggressive male and the nurturant female are with us for the rest of our lives. "When we see a man with a child, we say, 'They're playing'," says Epstein. "We never say, 'He's nurturant'."

The case for biologically based gender differences is building up slowly, amid a great deal of academic dispute. The theory is that male and female brains, as well as bodies, develop differently according to the amount of testosterone circulating around the time of birth. Much of the evidence rests on animal studies showing, for instance, that brain cells from newborn mice change their shape when treated with testosterone. The male sex hormone may also account for the different reactions of male and female rhesus monkeys, raised in isolation, when an infant monkey is placed in the cage. The males are more likely to strike at the infant, the females to nurture it. Scientists disagree—vehemently—on whether animal behavior has human par-allels. The most convincing human evi-dence comes from anthropology, where cross-cultural studies consistently find that while societies differ in their predilection toward violence, the males in any given society will act more aggressively than the females. "But it's very important to em-phasize that by aggression we mean only physical violence," says Melvin Konner, a physician and anthropologist at Emory

University in Atlanta. "With competitive, verbal or any other form of aggression, the evidence for gender differences doesn't hold." Empirical findings (i.e., look around you) indicate that women in positions of corporate, academic or political power can learn to wield it as aggressively as any man.

Apart from the fact that women everywhere give birth and care for children, there is surprisingly little evidence to support the notion that their biology makes women kinder, gentler people or even equips them specifically for motherhood. Philosophers—and mothers, too—have taken for granted the existence of a maternal "instinct" that research in female hormones has not conclusively proven. At most there may be a temporary hormonal response associated with childbirth that prompts females to nurture their young, but that doesn't explain women's near monopoly on changing diapers. Nor is it likely that a similar hormonal surge is responsible for women's tendency to organize the family's social life or take up the traditionally underpaid "helping" professions—nursing, teaching, social work.

Studies have shown that female newborns cry more readily than males in response to the cry of another infant, and that small girls try more often than boys to comfort or help their mothers when they appear distressed. But in general the results of most research into such traits as empathy and altruism do not consistently favor one sex or the other. There is one major exception: females of all ages seem better able to "read" people, to discern their emotions, without the help of verbal cues. (Typically researchers will display a picture of someone expressing a strong reaction and ask test-takers to identify the emotion.) Perhaps this skill—which in evolutionary terms would have helped females survive and protect their young—is the sole biological foundation for our unshakable faith in female selflessness.

Infant Ties

Those who explore the unconscious have had more success than other researchers in trying to account for male aggression and female nurturance, perhaps because their theories cannot be tested in a laboratory but are deemed "true" if they suit our intuitions. According to Nancy J. Chodorow, professor of sociology at Berkeley and the author of the influential book "The Reproduction of Mothering," the fact that both boys and girls are primarily raised by women has crucial effects on gender roles. Girls, who start out as infants identifying with their mothers and continue to do so, grow up defining themselves in relation to other people. Maintaining human connections remains vital to them. Boys eventually turn to their fathers for self-definition, but in order to do so must repress those powerful infant ties to mother and womanhood. Human connections thus become more problematic for them than for women. Chodorow's book, published in 1978, received national attention despite a dense, academic prose style; clearly, her perspective rang true to many.

Harvard's Kagan, who has been studying young children for 35 years, sees a different constellation of influences at work. He speculates that women's propensity for caretaking can be traced back to an early awareness of their role in nature. "Every girl knows, somewhere between the ages of 5 and 10, that she is different from boys and that she will have a child—something that everyone, including children, understands as quintessentially natural," he says. "If, in our society, nature stands for the giving of life, nurturance, help, affection, then the girl will conclude unconsciously that those are the qualities she should strive to attain. And the boy won't. And that's exactly what happens."

Kagan calls such gender differences "inevitable but not genetic," and he emphasizes—as does Chodorow—that they need have no implications for women's status, legally or occupationally. In the real world, of course, they have enormous implications. Even feminists who see gender differences as cultural artifacts agree that, if not inevitable, they're hard to shake. "The most emancipated families, who really feel they want to engage in gender-free behavior toward their kids, will still encourage boys to be boys and girls to be girls," says Epstein of CUNY. "Cultural constraints are acting on you all the time. If I go to buy a toy for a friend's little girl, I think to myself, why don't I buy her a truck? Well, I'm afraid the parents wouldn't like it. A makeup set would really go against my ideology, but maybe I'll buy some blocks. It's very hard. You have to be on the alert every second."

In fact, emancipated parents have to be on the alert from the moment their child is born. Beginning with the pink and blue name tags for newborns in the hospital nursery—I'M A GIRL/I'M A BOY—the gender-role juggernaut is overwhelming. Carol Z. Malatesta, associate professor of psychology at Long Island University in New York, notes that baby girls' eyebrows are higher above their eyes and that girls raise their eyebrows more than boys do, giving the girls "a more appealing, socially responsive look." Malatesta and her colleagues, who videotaped and coded the facial expressions on mothers and infants as they played, found that mothers displayed a wider range of emotional responses to girls than to boys. When the baby girls displayed anger, however, they met what seemed to be greater disapproval from their mothers than the boys did. These patterns, Malatesta suggests, may be among the reasons why baby girls grow up to smile more, to seem more sociable than males, and to possess the skill noted earlier in "reading" emotions.

The way parents discipline their toddlers also has an effect on social behavior later on. Judith G. Smetana, associate professor of education, psychology and pediatrics at the University of Rochester, found that mothers were more likely to deal differently with similar kinds of misbehavior depending on the sex of the child. If a little girl bit her friend and snatched a toy, for instance, the mother would explain why biting and snatching were unacceptable. If a boy did the same thing, his mother would be more likely to stop him, punish him and leave it at that. Misbehavior such as hitting in both sexes peaks around the age of 2; after that, little boys go on to misbehave more than girls.

Psychologists have known for years that boys are punished more than girls. Some have conjectured that boys simply drive their parents to distraction more quickly; but as Carolyn Zahn-Waxler, a psychologist at the National Institute of Mental Health, points out, the difference in parental treatment starts even before the difference in behavior shows up. "Girls receive very different messages than boys," she says. "Girls are encouraged to care about the problems of others, beginning very early. By elementary school, they're showing more caregiver behavior, and they have a wider social network."

Children also pick up gender cues in the process of learning to talk. "We compared fathers and mothers reading books to children," says Boston University's Gleason. "Both parents used more inner-state words, words about feelings and emotions, to girls than to boys. And by the age of 2, girls are using more emotion words than boys." According to Gleason, fathers tend to use more directives ("Bring that over here") and more threatening language with their sons than their daughters, while mothers' directives take more polite forms ("Could you bring that to me, please?"). The 4-year-old boys and girls in one study were duly imitating their fathers and mothers in that very conversational pattern. Studies of slightly older children found that boys talking among themselves use more threatening, commanding, dominating language than girls, while girls emphasize agreement and mutuality. Polite or not, however, girls get interrupted by their parents more often than boys, according to language studies—and women get interrupted more often than men.

Despite the ever-increasing complexity and detail of research on gender differences, the not-so-secret agenda governing the discussion hasn't changed in a century: how to understand women. Whether the question is brain size, activity levels or modes of punishing children, the traditional implication is that the standard of life is male, while the entity that needs explaining is female. (Or as an editor put it, suggesting possible titles for this article: "Why Girls Are Different.") Perhaps the time has finally come for a new agenda. Women, after all, are not a big problem. Our society does not suffer from burdensome amounts of empathy and altruism, or a plague of nurturance. The problem is men—or more accurately, maleness.

"There's one set of sex differences that's ineluctable, and that's the death statistics," says Gleason. "Men are killing themselves doing all the things that our society wants them to do. At every age they're dying in accidents, they're being shot, they drive cars badly, they ride the tops of elevators, they're two-fisted hard drinkers. And violence against women is incredibly pervasive. Maybe it's men's raging hormones, but I think it's because they're trying to be a *man*. If I were the mother of a boy, I would be very concerned about societal pressures that idolize behaviors like that."

Studies of other cultures show that male behavior, while characteristically aggressive, need not be characteristically deadly. Harvard's Whiting, who has been analyzing children cross-culturally for half a century, found that in societies where boys as well as girls take care of younger siblings, boys as well as girls show nurturant, sociable behavior. "I'm convinced that infants elicit positive behavior from people," says Whiting. "If you have to take care of somebody who can't talk, you have to learn empathy. Of course there can be all kinds of experi-

Where Little Boys Can Play with Nail Polish

For 60 years, America's children have been raised on the handiwork of Fisher-Price, makers of the bright plastic cottages, school buses, stacking rings and little, smiley people that can be found scattered across the nation's living rooms. Children are a familiar sight at corporate headquarters in East Aurora, N.Y., where a nursery known as the Playlab is the company's on-site testing center. From a waiting list of 4,000, local children are invited to spend a few hours a week for six weeks at a time playing with new and prototype toys. Staff members watch from behind a one-way mirror, getting an education in sales potential and gender tastes.

According to Kathleen Alfano, manager of the Child Research Department at Fisher-Price, kids will play with everything from train sets to miniature vacuum cleaners until the age of 3 or 4; after that they go straight for the stereotypes. And the toy business meets them more than halfway. "You see it in stores," says Alfano. "Toys for children 5 and up will be in either the girls' aisles or the boys' aisles. For girls it's jewelry, glitter, dolls, and arts and crafts. For boys it's model kits, construction toys and action figures like G.I. Joe. Sports toys, like basketballs, will be near the boys' end."

The company's own recent venture into gender stereotypes has not been successful. Fisher-Price has long specialized in what Alfano calls "open gender" toys, aimed at boys and girls alike, ages 2 to 7. The colors are vivid and the themes are often from daily life: music, banking, a post office. But three years ago the company set out to increase profits by tackling a risky category known in the industry as "promotional" toys. Developed along strict sex-role lines and heavily promoted on children's television programs, these toys for ages 5 and up are meant to capture kids' fads and fashions as well as their preconceptions about masculinity and feminin-

ity. At Fisher-Price they included an elaborate Victorian dollhouse village in shades of rose and lavender, a line of beauty products including real makeup and nail polish, a set of battery-operated racing cars and a game table outfitted for pool, Ping-Pong and glide hockey. "The performance of these products has been very mixed," says Ellen Duggan, a spokesperson for Fisher-Price. "We're now refocusing on toys with the traditional Fisher-Price image." (The company is also independent for the first time in 21 years. Last month longtime owner Quaker Oats divested itself of Fisher-Price.)

Even where no stereotypes are intended, the company has found that some parents will conjure them up. At a recent session for 3 year olds in the Playlab, the most sought-after toy of the morning was the fire pumper, a push toy that squirts real water. "It's for both boys and girls, but parents are buying it for boys," says Alfano. Similarly, "Fun with Food," a line of kitchen toys including child-size stove, sink, toaster oven and groceries, was a Playlab hit; boys lingered over the stove even longer than girls. "Mothers are buying it for their daughters," says Alfano.

Children tend to cross gender boundaries more freely at the Playlab than they do elsewhere, Alfano has noticed. "When 7-year-olds were testing the nail polish, we left it out after the girls were finished and the boys came and played with it," she says. "They spent the longest time painting their nails and drying them. This is a safe environment. It's not the same as the outside world."

ences that make you extinguish that eliciting power, so that you no longer respond positively. But on the basis of our data, boys make very good baby tenders."

In our own society, evidence is emerging that fathers who actively participate in raising their children will be steering both sons and daughters toward healthier gender roles. For the last eight years Yale's

Pruett has been conducting a groundbreaking longitudinal study of 16 families, representing a range of socioeconomic circumstances, in which the fathers take primary responsibility for child care while the mothers work full time. The children are now between 8 and 10 years old, and Pruett has watched subtle but important differences develop between them and their peers. "It's not that they have conflicts about their gender identity—the boys are masculine and the girls are feminine, they're all interested in the same things their friends are," he says. "But when they were 4 or 5, for instance, the stage at preschool when the boys leave the doll corner and the girls leave the block corner, these children didn't give up one or the other. The boys spent time playing with the girls in the doll corner, and the girls were building things with blocks, taking pride in their accomplishments."

Little Footballs

Traditionally, Pruett notes, fathers have enforced sex stereotypes more strongly than mothers, engaging the boys in active play and complimenting the girls on their pretty dresses. "Not these fathers," says Pruett. "That went by the boards. They weren't interested in bringing home little footballs for their sons or little tutus for the girls. They dealt with the kids according to the individual. I even saw a couple of the mothers begin to take over those issues— one of them brought home a Dallas Cowboys sleeper for her 18-month-old. Her husband said, 'Honey, I thought we weren't going to do this, remember?' She said, 'Do what?' So that may be more a function of being in the second tier of parenting rather than the first."

As a result of this loosening up of stereotypes, the children are more relaxed about gender roles. "I saw the boys really enjoy their nurturing skills," says Pruett. "They knew what to do with a baby, they didn't see that as a girl's job, they saw it as a

human job. I saw the girls have very active images of the outside world and what their mothers were doing in the workplace—things that become interesting to most girls when they're 8 or 10, but these girls were interested when they were 4 or 5."

Pruett doesn't argue that fathers are better at mothering than mothers, simply that two involved parents are better than "one and a lump." And it's hardly necessary for fathers to quit their jobs in order to become more involved. A 1965-66 study showed that working mothers spent 50 minutes a day engaged primarily with their children, while the fathers spent 12 minutes. Later studies have found fathers in two-career households spending only about a third as much time with their children as mothers. What's more, Pruett predicts that fathers would benefit as much as children from the increased responsibility. "The more involved father tends to feel differently about his own life," he says. "A lot of men, if they're on the fast track, know a lot about competitive relationships, but they don't know much about intimate relationships. Children are experts in intimacy. After a while the wives in my study would say, 'He's just a nicer guy'."

Pruett's study is too small in scope to support major claims for personality development; he emphasizes that his findings are chiefly theoretical until more research can be undertaken. But right now he's watching a motif that fascinates him. "Every single one of these kids is growing something," he says. "They don't just plant a watermelon seed and let it die. They're really propagating things, they're doing salad-bowl starts in the backyard, they're breeding guinea pigs. That says worlds about what they think matters. Generativity is valued a great deal, when both your mother and your father say it's OK." Scientists may never agree on what divides the sexes; but someday, perhaps, our children will learn to relish what unites them.

Moonrose Watched Through a Sunny Day

Erika Friedl

As you read:
1. *How do rural Iranians view childhood?*
2. *What contribution does Goli make to her family?*
3. *How does Goli's life compare to that of an American child?*

There isn't a rose in sight where Moonrose lives: not in the large, dung-strewn courtyard, not in the alleys along the water channel, and not on the sun-bleached, brown-mottled hills behind the village. In spring, the hedge roses around the orchards—small, nearly white blossoms on prickly stems—bloom for a short while, but they wilt quickly and don't smell like much. Yet Rose is a common name for women in the village. Moonrose is Mahgol; everybody except her mother calls her Goli.

Goli is a tiny flower, nine years old, small, scrawny, with narrow-set brown eyes and a long nose. Her pointy face is framed by a pinkish gray scarf that mats down her many dark, thin braids. She has just finished third grade. Goli's mother is up somewhere in the greenish haze behind the gray rocks of Snow Mountain, gone for the summer with the sheep and goats. Her father makes the four-hour trek several times a week along the steep trails radiating out of the village toward the cool valleys and high plains where the herds are in pasture camps. He is on his feet from well before dawn until after nightfall, day after day, all summer long.

Goli's grandmother went up with him a few days ago, to help Goli's mother at the birth of a sixth child. Goli, all skin and bones and sinew under her tattered gray sweater, long, heavy skirt, and dark, dusty pants frayed at the ankles, was left at home to take care of her father and her brothers all by herself.

The family's mud-brick living quarters have been built atop barns and sheds. Goli's father's two rooms are between his brother's rooms and her grandmother's room, which doubles as a storage space. A flat, extended dirt roof shades a narrow porch running along the front of the house. Beyond it, a wide, uncovered veranda (roof to barns and sheds below) stretches to its unprotected edge some ten steps away. In the shade of her porch, the wife of Goli's uncle, her eyes closed, weak and tired as usual, leans against the gritty wall and rocks a cradle. Two of Goli's little cousins throw rocks at chickens in the yard. The midsummer sun scorches the air, bakes the walls, the dirt floor.

Goli almost burns her hands on the aluminum tray propped against a roof post; she needs it to take a heap of dirty clothes down to the water faucet. With her foot, she pushes the tray into the shade to cool while she shuffles next door in her father's large, plastic flip-flops. "I need soap from Grandmother's room," she says to her half-dozing aunt. "Give me the key." Without opening her eyes, the woman finds it in the inside pocket of her red velvet jacket. "Wash the baby's rags too, dear, will you?" she asks. Goli pulls a face of disgust, but the woman does not see it. When Goli brings back the big pile of wash she carried to the water, the sun is high, her back aches, her arms are red, and the skin on her fingers is wrinkled.

Goli is sitting on the floor in the shade of the roofed porch outside her father's kitchen-living room, bent over a mound of rice on a shallow aluminum tray. With a flick of her fingers she scatters a handful of rice kernels toward her on the silvery surface, picks out little stones and seeds, chaff and dirt, and heaps the clean rice along the wall of the tray. One of her cousins, a square little boy a couple of years younger than she, with a runny nose, dirty hands, and dirtier feet, squats on the other side of the tray, helping her. When Goli turns her head to call his sister away from the dangerous edge of the veranda, his fast, grimy fingers grab a handful of clean rice from Goli's side and drop it on his small pile. Goli has seen it. She laughs, pinches his hand, kicks him with her foot. "Rascal," she says. "Work right or else I'll kill you." On his feet in a flash, the boy slaps his hands hard into the hill of rice. The dry kernels scatter all over, the boy runs out into the sun. "Get lost," Goli shouts, "I'll kill you for sure."

Holding her uncle's baby under his armpits, Goli swings him slightly. She sits with her back pressed against a big sack of fleece on her uncle's porch. "Oh, baby dear, oh, little boy," she hums. He smiles. Goli moves him faster, lifting and dropping him jerkily, chanting: "The moon is so bright, the moon is so bright, the wolf will get the shah's sheep tonight. The moon is so bright, the moon. . . ." The boy, red faced, dangling limply, head crammed between his squeezed shoulders, screws his eyes shut and whines. "Don't like it?" Goli asks, swinging him sideways and panting from the exertion. He whines louder. "Listen to this: 'Hosein dear, Hosein dear, beets are gone, turnips are here'. . . well?" The baby is crying now; his cotton pants have slid down and his ragged T-shirt is bunched

around his neck. Standing him on her lap, Goli slides him back into his pants and then props him against her knees. "Don't cry, don't cry dear, dear," she says, touching his chin, his lips, his chin again to make him smile, but he does not stop crying. She catches a hen and slaps the baby's hand on its brown back. "Hit it, hit it," she tells him. As the cackling and flapping hen pecks at his hand, he starts crying bitterly. Goli lets go of the hen and cradles the baby in her arms, rocking him gently. "Lalai, lalai," she sings, as if putting him to sleep. As he quiets down, she pulls his cap up, smooths his shirt, and jingles the amulets—beads, a tiny iron spit, a smooth, polished salt crystal—pinned to his shirt. She waves flies away from his watery eyes, wipes his snotty nose with her skirt. He stops crying, and she holds him still, studying his face intently.

At the water faucet in the alley, Goli washes the picked-over rice in a battered aluminum pot. A neighbor girl fetches water in a white plastic can, and one of Goli's aunts scrubs a big copper pot with sandy mud from around the cement-encased faucet. Goli swishes the rice around in the milky-gray water—back and forth, up and down, round and round. The smooth, pearly-hard grains trickle through her fingers. Straw floats to the surface, and Goli skims it off before she drains the dirty water, tilting the pot ever so carefully. The neighbor girl pours fresh water over the rice, and Goli again swishes and sloshes and drains. Straightening up, she yanks her scarf down over her face and then back over her forehead in a swift, practiced movement that packs her untidy hair under the washed-out pink buds on her scarf.

She picks up her pot for a last rinse, turning to the faucet jutting out of the chipped and crumbling concrete block. The faucet is tricky: turned a little too low or too high, the water will squirt every way but down. Impatient or just unmindful, Goli turns the wobbly brass lever a notch too far and is instantly doused from her face down to her knees. "Watch it, girl." her aunt cries, leaning away from the jet of water. Goli clonks the pot down on the muddy grille and wipes her face with her arms. "Death and ashes on my head!" she cries, jumping up and down. "You'll catch cold," warns her aunt. Goli is still jumping up and down. "I am cold, I am wet, a water sack is on my back," she chants, flapping the frayed sleeves of her soaked sweater. She picks up the pot and, legs bent to balance herself, shuffles up the steep, short stairway across the channel to her house. "I am cold, I am wet, a water sack is on my back," she chants loudly to the rhythm of her shlap-shlapping shoes.

Crouching in front of the fireplace, Goli coaxes a fire of brush and oak branches. The fireplace, a curbed niche at the foot of a mud-brick wall, is black with the soot of years. Heavy gray smoke billows up from the brush. Goli leans forward, blowing with all her might, cheeks full of air, like bellows. The smoke is choking her and burning her eyes although she has them shut tight. She coughs and wipes her eyes. The fire will not catch. She has carried the wood up from the shed below because there was no gas in the bottle under the gas stove in the kitchen. With a deep breath she blows a long, sustained stream of air, ending with some fierce huffs, which make the gray ash of a dead fire fly up and settle on her head and arms. She gets up and brings a bottle of kerosene from the kitchen. Standing back a step, she pours the kerosene over the smoking wood and puts the bottle into a niche in the wall. Then she lights a match and drops it onto the smoky pile, shielding her face with her arm. The evaporating kerosene explodes in a high yellow flame. The wood is on fire.

Goli's younger brother and her cousin are ambling across the veranda. "I want bread," her brother cries, "I am hungry."

"Get lost," Goli says crossly, without looking up. Leaning against the porch beams, the boys watch the fire and Goli as she pours the washed rice from the alu-minum pot into a copper cooking pot. The copper is black from the smoke of countless fires; inside, it is tinned, silver bright. Goli fetches a water kettle from the kitchen and swings it toward her brother's belly. "Go get water," she tells him.

"No," he says, "I want bread." Goli shrugs as if she never expected compliance anyway and leaves for the water faucet. The little boy runs after her, hammering his fists into her back. "Bread, bread," he yells. Goli ignores him.

Back with the dripping kettle, her brother in tow, Goli rinses the last grain of rice from the aluminum pot into the cooking pot. The fire is dying again in smoke; kneeling down, she blows life into it vigorously. "Black death on the damn thing," she mutters, but then turns and unleashes her fury on her brother, who is pulling down her scarf. "Beat it or I'll thrash you!" Her brother disappears into the kitchen and comes out with his hands full of bread. He has ripped it from the neatly folded, paper-thin flatbreads that are stored there. Goli watches the fire. Behind her back, her brother swipes the matches she had left on the floor—matches are scarce, a prized possession. She notices both thefts as she is about to take the kerosene bottle back to the kitchen. But a furious yell and a streak across the wide, sunny veranda in her bare feet are futile: the boys have vanished.

With a black smear along the side of her nose, a hot, flushed, and disheveled Goli drops an iron tripod over the low-burning wood and heaves the cooking pot onto it. She pours water from the kettle over the rice, and more water after yet another trip to the water faucet. She pours a handful of salt from a yellow tin can into the rice pot, stirring it slowly with a long-handled, flat aluminum ladle. While the rice is popping up and down in the bubbling water, Goli takes a stubbly broom from a corner and sweeps the breadcrumbs out toward the edge of the veranda, where a small hen is leading three chirping chicks. Her agitated clucking at the bread brings two more hens and a rooster running. The rooster and the hens are much faster than the chicks. Goli throws dirt at the hens, but it scares the little chicks more than the hens. They peep and run and flap their tiny yellow wings. Goli shrugs her shoulders. "Little ones are always hungry," she says.

Her uncle's wife helps Goli strain the half-cooked rice through a sieve. The chickens are waiting for the few spilled rice grains. Goli spoons a ladleful of yellow, coarse cooking fat from a big square tin can into the empty copper pot on the tripod again and pours the rice back in, adding a bowl of cooked lentils. Her little cousin is yanking at Goli's skirt, whining for rice. Goli ladles some back into the sieve for her. "It is not cooked yet, you'll get a tummy ache," she says. Despite her own warning, she scoops a ladleful out for herself, blowing at it and then swallowing fast, while the toddler sits at the kitchen sill, out of the range of heat from the fireplace, eating with both hands. "Sit down right, eat right," says Goli. The little girl licks her fingers.

Goli sprinkles water over the rice and lentils, spreads a singed rag over the pot, then presses the lid down tightly over the cloth. Carefully, she ties the corners over the lid so that the rag does not burn. Surveying the scene, she collects the sieve, the ladle, and the aluminum pot and wipes her face with her skirt. Then she climbs a few feet up the wall, using rough mud bricks as holds, and shouts over the top:, "Hoi, Fateme, hoi, hoi, I'm ready, hear me?" And from somewhere beyond, Fateme answers, "I'm coming."

Under an apricot tree in one of Goli's father's gardens, Goli and Fateme squat face to face. Propped against the tree are two woven backbags filled with grass. Two sickles lie in the withered weeds. The afternoon is dry, dusty, heavy with hot, shimmery heat. For Goli and Fateme, the visible world ends at the dark, high brambles around them. It is filled with sunlight, filtered and softened by dense leaves above them, with the twitter of sparrows in the tree, the irritating buzzing of countless flies, the gurgling of water from an irrigation ditch nearby. On the almost bare ground between them is a handful of smooth pebbles for playing *haftuk*. Fateme holds a pebble in her right fist. "Watch it," she says. She throws it straight up in the air, following it with her eyes, while her hand picks up a pebble so fast that it is ready to catch the first one as it is falling. Next, Fateme throws up two pebbles, grabs a third, catches both; at the third move, one of the three pebbles in the air spins sideways and falls to the ground uncaught. Now it is Goli's turn. Goli, mouth puckered in concentration, catches one, two, three, four pebbles. At the fifth turn she misses a catch. "The sun blinded me, it was the sun!" she cries.

"Lies, lies, you just missed," says Fateme, raking in the pebbles. Goli throws her pebbles to the ground and gets up. "Let's go," she says. Staggering a little under its weight, she heaves a sack onto her back by its straps. Fateme throws a few more pebbles into the air, misses, abandons the game. Goli has already climbed over the hedge.

Walking along the path between hedge roses and blackberry hedges and the irrigation channel, the girls cut some grass growing in clumps here and there along the water. When they reach the village, the minty smell of the cut grass on their backs and in their arms blocks the pungent odor of trampled dust hanging in the alley between the hot walls.

Next to the kitchen door, Goli's father and elder brother sit on the threadbare rug Goli has spread for them. On a small, shiny tray between them is a bowl holding lumps of sugar and two small glasses on gold-rimmed china saucers. Goli's father pours tea and water from a dented yellow enamel teapot and a water kettle, black with burned-in soot. The man and the boy had driven their donkeys back from the nearby wheat fields, loaded with straw stuffed in huge net bags. By the time they had unloaded and come upstairs, Goli had steeped the tea and put the tray on the rug. Now she sits on the floor a little away from her father, leaning against the house bricks, feet tucked under her skirt, looking at the sunburned faces of her father and her brother, the straw in their hair, the dusty jackets. She watches them slurp tea from the saucers. While her father refills the glasses from the pot and the kettle, her brother, without looking up, says: "Get me water." Goli fetches a small leather bag with an aluminum cup over its neck from the far side of the porch, filling the cup on her way back. The boy takes a sip and spits it out behind him. "Warm," he says with a grimace, pouring the rest on the floor. "Get cold water." Goli, walking across the wide veranda toward the stairs, empties the leather bag with sweeping splashes. Little dust clouds burst where the water hits the dirt floor. The men do not wait for her, however, but stop to drink the water from the faucet on their way out of the house. Goli watches them drive the two donkeys out through the open door on a trail of golden straw. Then she sits down by the teapot and pours herself a glass of dark tea, adding hardly any water at all. She pushes the saucer off the sugar bowl, where her father had put it to keep the flies out, and pops two lumps into her mouth before taking a big sip of tea. She pours more tea, drinks it over more sugar, pours another glass and yet another, until the pot is empty and the sugar all but gone.

From the kitchen door, Goli yells at her little girl-cousin squatting near the edge of the veranda. "Black death, girl-brat, nothing but troubles all day long, may an evil spirit get you. What are you doing there? Sarah! I'll kill you!" she shouts, "I'll tell your mother for sure. Woe to me, ashes on my head for having to watch such a brat." The little girl stirs mud into a pile of chicken shit with her fingers. "I am making bread dough," she says. "Leave me alone."

"Dirty, filthy," Goli yells, pushing her backward. "Ugly brat, look at your hands, look at your face!" She yanks her up by her shoulders, and half lifting and half pulling her by her left arm, and staggering under the weight, drags her down to the water, accompanying the child's screams with a stream of curses. At the faucet, she clamps Sarah tightly between her legs while she scrubs her face, hands, and arms until they are red with cold and both she and Sarah are drenched.

A little later, picking dry clothes from the line, the wall, and the ground, Goli finds Sarah huddled with two other little girls in the wide shade of a wall, mixing earth with water from a long-spouted, green plastic toilet can. Goli stops and looks down at them over the big pile of wash in her arms. One of the girls is forming small mud balls between her hands, On a flat rock Sarah is rolling out a ball of mud dough with a twig stripped of bark. "Dear, dear, my dough is ripping," she mumbles, patting it into shape with her hand. Goli shifts her feet as if to squat down but then thinks better of it. "It needs more kneading," she says from up high. "Don't you touch my dough," Sarah says. "Go away, your hands are dirty." And Goli slowly turns and leaves.

In the kitchen, dim light falls on Goli from the half-closed door and a small window set deep in the thick mud-brick wall. She kneels on the gray gypsum floor, bent over a heap of flour in a large round basin. Fateme slowly pours water from an aluminum pitcher on the flour. Goli, sweater sleeves rolled up above her bony elbows, mixes dough from the flour and water. She had measured twenty double-handfuls of wheat flour into the basin, and she had gotten Fateme to help her. Making dough and baking bread requires the strength and experience of a woman. But Goli, a helper to her mother at this chore for a long time, has baked alone before this summer, and anyway, what choice was there? Barely enough bread was left for the morning meal.

When the girls decide that the dough has enough water, Fateme kneels at the other side of the basin, turns up her sleeves, fastens her headscarf, says, "Bismillah o Raham o Rahim" (in the name of God, the merciful and compassionate), as her mother does when she starts this work, and pushes one knuckled fist into the dough, then the other, in and out, just as Goli does on her side. Their heads almost touch. When they have covered all the dough with their knuckles, they fold half of it over the other half and punch it down again. The dough sticks to their hands. Goli rubs her shoulder against an itchy spot on her cheek. Her scarf has slipped off her braids, and three red beads on a string in her left earlobe are bobbing up and down. The girls are breathing hard as they punch, fold, and punch in a perfect harmony of sound and movement, as if somebody is keeping time for them. Slowly, the dough is turning smooth, sticking to itself rather than to the hands and the basin. Goli decides it is done.

They wash their hands on the veranda with water from the kettle. Fateme leaves, flapping her arms to shake off the water. Back in the kitchen, Goli pats the dough a little before pushing the tray into a corner and covering it with heavy sacking. The dough will rest here overnight. Early tomorrow, Goli will roll the breads on her mother's heavy oak board and bake them on the griddle. It will take all morning, but perhaps her uncle's wife will help her.

Goli sits on the kitchen sill, elbows on her knees, chin in her hands, chewing gum. The sun is down. Goli has fed the chickens some bread dough and locked them up for the night. She has washed the tea things. The aluminum pot is at her side, ready to be used as a milk pail as soon as the cows are home. From the walnut tree in the yard, where a flock of sparrows gather every evening, comes loud twittering and chirping. Two boys at the other side of the courtyard shoot at the birds with rubber slings. There is a sharp, cracking sound, and the bird noise stops suddenly. Goli blows a pink bubble that sticks to her lips when it pops. Dusk is falling from the pale sky, is creeping out of corners. The coals in the fireplace on the porch glimmer faintly under the water kettle. Goli's aunt talks to her crying baby. From behind the wall a woman yells for Fateme. Goli blows another big bubble and looks down at it along her nose, cross-eyed. The bird noise has started again. A breeze touches Goli's cheek. She is waiting for the cow; for her father and her brothers; for the dinner she will serve on the rug; for the neighbors' lamps; for the stars above the roofs—for the short night under her heavy cotton quilt.

Child Labour in Naples

Victoria Goddard

As you read:
1. *What does Goddard mean when she says that "child" and "work" are culturally and historically specific categories?*
2. *What is outwork? Why do families choose to allow children to participate in outwork?*

In January 1981 the Anti-Slavery Society held a workshop on child labour at the Institute of Development Studies. The intention of this workshop was to bring together social scientists and policy-makers to discuss a problem which has proved to be elusive. In particular, it was hoped that the contribution of anthropologists and historians would help to rectify a weakness which runs through much of the political and social literature on the subject of child labour: a tendency to take a moralistic standpoint which universalizes the category "child" and uncritically transposes European urban middle-class expectations to this category wherever and whenever it may be found.

It was agreed at the workshop that both the category "child" and the category "work" were culturally and historically specific. In the attempt to develop more rigorous frameworks, it was important to rid oneself of mystifications and romanticizations, both those associated with extending "European" concepts and values and also those associated with the idealization of "traditional" or "primitive" society and its institutions—which is equally dangerous (Cf. IDS, 1981).

The social scientist studying child labour is faced bluntly with her or his preconceptions and sentiments. A satisfactory treatment of the subject has to go beyond the boundaries of sociological categories. Concepts which in other contexts have been powerful tools of analysis, such as "exploitation," fall short of dealing with the various ways in which the time and labour of children is used and appropriated. With these points in mind, I will briefly look at the question of child labour in the organization of outwork in Naples, Southern Italy.

Children and Work in Naples

Even the briefest visit to Naples will reveal to the often surprised tourist the existence of child workers. As you sit in any café you will see a nine or ten-year-old boy flit in and out of office buildings carrying his tray of cups of coffees, or hanging around during his workbreak, with a cigarette dangling from his mouth in expert fashion. A more adventurous visitor, exploring the narrow streets of the old quarters of the city, will see small boys covered in grease helping out at a car mechanic's workshop or bicycle-shop. And there are the small groups of boys practicing guerrilla warfare tactics on tourists, as well as those windscreen cleaners who make their services necessary by taking the precaution of wiping a dirty cloth over your windscreen as soon as the traffic lights turn red (Cf. Anti-Slavery Society, 1980 & 1981).

I was not in Naples to study child labour, but my search for outworkers in different trades led to one particular sector of the child labour-market. Outworkers are the last link in the chain of subcontracting, whereby industrial or commercial enterprises hand out all or part of the process of production to smaller units or individual workers who provide goods or services in their own homes.[1] This system operates worldwide and for good reason. It presents many advantages to the entrepreneur: it reduces costs, since often (and in the Neapolitan case almost always) the machines used belong to the workers and they shoulder the costs of repair, electricity and sometimes the secondary material, such as thread, as well. The outwork system allows the entrepreneur a greater degree of flexibility in the use of labour, because the worker is paid on a piece-rate basis, so that the oscillations of demand can be handled without a paid workforce standing idle at times when demand is low. Usually, labour-power on piecework systems is cheaper because the workers so employed are not unionized and, being scattered and usually isolated, are in a more vulnerable position than most factory workers. They can thus be paid lower rates of pay.

The entrepreneur escapes not only the limitations imposed on his business by trade unions but also taxes and various conditions of employment imposed by the state—one of these being the prohibition against employing minors.[2] Many enterprises do employ people under the legal age limit, but large-scale companies, sensitive to public opinion and state intervention, fight shy of doing this. Being defined as illegal, child workers are pushed out of those work-places where labour relations are better regulated and where safety and hygiene conditions may be more adequate. Instead, it is in the small workshop or sweatshop, unnoticed by either public or State, and cramped into unhygienic conditions by its lack of capital, that we find the bulk of minors employed in industrial work.

The Neapolitan outworker is usually a woman. The productive work she may carry out for a shoe, glove or toy factory will be interspersed with her household chores. It is the assumption that her responsibility as housewife and mother (either in the present or projected into the future) which is usually given as a justification for her working in the home rather than in a factory (Goddard, 1977).

Households in Naples differ in their composition, and their boundaries fluctuate; but in all cases there is a clear division between the sexes in respect of tasks and responsibilities. Domestic tasks are the women's concern. This means that little girls start work in the home, helping their mothers at a younger age than most boys start to work. In fact, if a mother has to work outside the home, her daughter(s) take over most of her household duties, and if the mother works at home, she or they may start housework when still very young.

There is also a division of labour by age in the household, which may take many forms, according to the needs and aspirations of parents. An elder son or daughter may start work at a very young age, to ease the burden on the parents while the brothers and sisters are still young. An elder child may even work to help put his/her siblings through the education system, even through university. A younger daughter on the other hand runs the risk of taking over more and more household responsibilities, thus freeing the labour of her mother and older sisters who can earn more—and older sisters are likely to marry and leave the household anyway. Of course older daughters can also meet this fate. Whatever the case, it is frequent to find a "specialization" within the household whereby the women allocate different tasks to each other. Thus some young women are specialist paid workers, having worked in production from a very early age. Their skills in the domestic sphere are hence very limited. Others are specialist housewives and can run a household but have no other skills. This specialization in the household from an early age has important consequences for their future lives. Where the girl starts paid work at an early age—especially factory work—she is likely to have problems in adapting to her role as wife at marriage. Where, however, a girl specializes as a domestic worker, she is likely to join the ranks of the most poorly paid unskilled category of outworkers when the economic situation of the household which she has formed at marriage forces her to make a monetary contribution.

Children's paid work is usually parallel to schooling. Where there is a family workshop or other business, the children will almost certainly be expected to spend many hours helping out after school. Where the mother only is involved in production in the home, there may be less pressure but it is usual for little girls to help their mothers. Not so little boys, who help only (and this very casually) when they are quite young. As they grow older the sexual division of labour establishes itself: the mother is doing a woman's job and the women and girls around her should help her and learn her skills. But both boys and girls may be apprenticed out to a neighbor or kin to learn a trade. The burden of carrying out two activities—or more in the case of little girls who may help in the home and work for money and go to school—is a heavy one. Absenteeism from school is high in certain areas of Naples and there is a tendency for numbers to drop progressively from the first grade onwards.[3]

Training Versus Education

In order to consider why parents may impose such a burden on their children it is important to take into account the eco-nomic structure of Naples and the Italian South as a whole. Naples is a city of contrasts in its production profile as well as in so many other aspects. The giant steelworks at Bagnoli was established when the Italian State experimented with the concept of "poles of development" to reverse the poverty of the South; there is also the large Alfa Sud car plant in Pomigliano d'Arco and a few medium-sized enterprises. A privileged few will find jobs in such places and will try to keep them; in fact many pass them on to their children. The majority of working-class Neapolitans, however, will be competing for jobs in small factories and tiny workshops, which characteristically emerge and disappear almost overnight. Unemployment is massive. In spite of certain actions which have been taken by Neapolitans, such as electing a Communist mayor and organizing combative leagues of unemployed workers, complex problems relating to insufficient work opportunities remain unsolved.

Given this backdrop, it is important to point out that neither the Neapolitan working-class nor the lumpen-proletariat are homogeneous. Not only are there important variations in terms of their occupational status; there are also differences in attitude and expectations, for example regarding their children. Thus, many Neapolitan couples opt for having two or no more than three, children so that they can provide for them adequately and give them a solid basis for their adult lives. They look down upon couples who have many children, considering them uncaring and selfish. Many such do not wish their own fate on their children: they find their own work tiring and dull, and want something better for their offspring. Most would consider a graduate, professional status for their children to be overambitious and seem happy to settle for a white-collar or secretarial job. Some however do hope to get at least one of their children through university, and with the joint efforts of both themselves and other offspring they may achieve this.

But there has been growing disaffection with education as a solution and as a way out of the hard life of the working class, now that more and more university graduates join the ranks of the unemployed, to the extent of forming their own league of "organized unemployed."

As a result of the economic conditions in Naples and disillusion with formal education, most parents prefer to play both alternatives: sending their children to school for as long as this is feasible, while at the same time inserting them in the economic structure of the city, preferably as an apprentice in a trade. In the case of a daughter, apprenticing her out to an outworker in the shoe trade is considered a wise move. Women, some of whom are very highly skilled, can always find work in this traditional Neapolitan export industry. In addition it is a skill which they can use either in a factory or at home, so that the factory can be left on marriage. Thus the sexual division of labour, and the values which dictate a preference for women to be at home, are protected. So training, that is, preparing a child for his or her adult responsibilities, is an important objective of parents who put their children in paid work.

The Economic Contribution of Children

The financial motive is important as well. Very few children after a certain age can get away with living in a household without making some contribution, however small and erratic. In the case of young girls working with outworkers, their earnings are negligible for the first years of their training. Daughters working with their mothers are unlikely to get any wages at all, and their contribution to the household is made directly through their labour.

In the shoe trade, the task of the young apprentice is to place glue on the rim of pieces of leather which will form the upper part of the shoe. Another, more difficult task, is to fold the edges of the leather onto the glue and hammer them down without distorting the shape. To do this really well requires a lot of practice, and there are many adult workers who specialize in the folding task rather than move on to the machine work which will render them a fully fledged *orlatrice*. This in turn means higher rates of pay and better opportunities both for factory workers and outworkers. It is to such women, usually a kinswoman or neighbor, that a young girl will be apprenticed out at about the age of 10 or 12 (if she is learning from a mother this could start much earlier, say at the age of 7).

From the point of view of the teacher, initially, such an apprentice may not help very much; but, as the child becomes more skilful she allows her to increase her output, since the more glued and folded pieces there are, the more a machinist can sew—which is of course very significant in piecerate work. It is difficult to say to what extent, if at all, these apprentices are exploited by their teachers. In any case the situation will be acceptable to the girl's parents and often to the girl herself, since after such a period of training she will be in a position to enter a factory or workshop at about the age of 14, when her wages will increase considerably.

A girl's earnings are usually handed over to her mother. She may take them as a contribution towards the costs of keeping the family fed and dressed, or she may use them to pay for the needs of this particular daughter. As the daughter gets older, the mother may subtract a certain amount each week from this income for the girl's *corredo:* the various items such as bed linen which a girl should have when she marries. The *corredo* can in some cases be the major reason for a girl's employment, once she is engaged to marry. So earnings are important economically but not necessarily for immediate purposes: that is to say, earnings must be seen in relation to longer-term and more general objectives.

The Question of Control

Girls in general, because of the forms their work takes, and those boys who are apprenticed out or work in a family business, are very much under adult control. But those children, mostly boys, who are involved in various "street activities" can obtain a greater degree of autonomy from their parents and other adults as well. It is unlikely that they can totally escape adult authority, or the "seniority system" as Diane Elson has called it (Elson, 1982) but they have a better chance than others to keep or spend a part of their takings without having to consult adults. Children who work in the context of a family or kinship-based unit of production are under much greater control, and there may well be a compounding of the authority of work relations with the authority of parent-child relations.

Machado Neto (1981, 1982), writing on her research in Bahia, Brazil, points out that the work children carry out in the household or neighbourhood is closely controlled by the family or the neighbourhood. As the child grows older, s/he is likely to venture further afield than the neighbourhood—girls usually being employed as domestic servants and boys more probably involved in various street activities. Street activities take place far from the neighbourhood, which allows these boys considerable freedom, although various adult figures will attempt to control their labour and their incomes. Interestingly those who are most successful in escaping adult control are those who are most likely to join up with gangs involved with petty crime, who are both feared and respected.

So it appears that boys have more opportunities of becoming relatively autonomous and wide-ranging in their movements than girls, who are in most cases restricted to the home and its immediate surround-ings, or are employed in conditions where strong control is exercised over them. In the City of Mexico, on the other hand, although boys dominate many street activities, both boys and girls engage in petty vending or begging away from the home. This difference between the Mexican and Neapolitan situations could be related in part to ideological differences related to the degree of control considered necessary for girls; but given the importance attributed to female virginity in Mexico, it is more likely that the explanation will be found in Mexico City's larger "floating population" and in the economic organization of Naples which may provide opportunities for women's economic pursuits to take place in the home or the neighbourhood.

It would appear that adult Mexican women are more likely than their Neapolitan counterparts to be involved in street activities in which they also involve their children, whether male or female. There is an important link to be considered here between the activities of children and those of women. The conditions which determine women's status also shape the lives of children (for an interesting example of this see Schildkrout, 1978 and 1979).

Conclusion

To sum up:
1. Child labour has to be located within the context of social and economic relations and to understand it we must take into account ideological factors.

2. Although economic necessity is a central motive for child labour, in the case of the child outworkers of Naples this must be understood in a broad context. Furthermore this economic necessity must be seen to be shaped and conditioned by ideological factors which emphasize control over women's sexuality, and therefore movement from an early age, the importance of marriage, the

institution of the *corredo* and the relative importance of formal education in comparison to other forms of preparation for adulthood.

3. The division of labour between adult men and women and the position allocated to women in a given society have important repercussions for children: especially, and more enduringly, for girl children. In other words, the activities of mothers (and of women generally) largely determine the activities of children, and the sexual division of labour which holds for both adult men and women can also be seen to operate at the level of childhood.

4. Although a child may be more "protected" when working within the context of a family or kinship-based enterprise, this does not necessarily mean that the child is better off from the point of view of health or finances. In fact, the child working in such a situation is liable to suffer much stricter control and exploitation than do many "street" children and may fall under the dual authority structures of kinship and work relations.

5. Legislation is a double-edged sword. By declaring child workers to be illegal the State enhances children's already existing social vulnerability. Because of their illegality, child workers are concentrated in small, unsafe work-places where their working conditions cannot be monitored. This has, in fact, resulted in more than one tragedy such as the episode when three girls died in a fire in a Casavatore workshop in 1976, because all exits were blocked with boxes and machinery. Furthermore, the glues used in the leather trades can be very toxic. This is especially true of the cheaper glues which because of the pressures on small workshops and factories are used widely. The toxic elements from these glues cause a neuromuscular disease which affect women workers and working and non-working children alike, since babies and toddlers play close to their outworkermothers' machines and materials (Cf. Berlinguer *et al,* 1977).

6. We should be cautious when appraising the significance of formal education. Education in this sense should not be considered only in institutional terms; but rather its forms and content must be related to its socioeconomic context. Thus the negative attitude of some Neapolitans towards schooling can be seen either as a failure to appreciate the value of formal education or as an accurate assessment of the local labour-market.

Notes

1. For a survey of the outwork system for Italy as a whole see Frey, *L. et al* (1975). For the informal sector, including outwork in Naples see De Marco & Talamo 1976.

2. According to the 1967 Act the minimum age for admission to employment (including apprentices) is 15 years.

3. According to a survey carried out in 1977 (quoted in ASS 1981) 74% of the children interviewed said they had left school because of work; 45% of children left school before the final year of primary education. 15% left during the final year and 19% left during the first year of middle school (at the ages of 10 and 12 respectively).

References

Allum, P. 1973. *Politics and Society in Post-War Naples,* Cambridge.

Anti-Slavery Society 1980. *Child Labour in Italy— Report for 1980 to the United Nations Working Group Experts on Slavery.*

Anti-Slavery Society 1980. *Child Labour: Published and Unpublished Material* compiled by A. Hill Black.

Anti-Slavery Society 1981. *Child Labour in Italy,* Report No. 5 by Marina Valcarenghi.

Belmonte, T. 1979. *The Broken Fountain,* Columbia University Press, N.Y.

Berlinguer, G., L. Cecchini, & F. Terranova 1977. *Gli Infortuni sul lavaro dei Minori.* Il Pensiero Scientifico Editore, Rome.

Challis, J.,& D. Elliman 1979. *Child Workers Today,* Quartermaine House

De Marco, C., & M. Talamo 1976. *Lavoro Nero,* Gabriele Mazzotta editore.

Elson, D. 1982. The Differentiation of Children's Labour in the Capitalist Labour Market, in *Development and Change,* Vol. 13, No. 4.

Frey, L., G. De Santis, & R. Livraghi 1975. *Lavoro a domicilio e decentramento dell'attivita produttiva nei settori tessili e dell'abbigliamento in Italia,* Franco Angelo Ed., Collana ISVET, No. 30, Milano.

Goddard, V. 1977. Research Note: Domestic Industry in Naples in *Critique of Anthropology,* Vol. 3, No. 9 & 10.

Goddard, V. 1981. *Child Labour—An Introduction to Some of the Issues,* mimeo Child Labour Workshop, I.D.S., Sussex.

Institute of Development Studies 1981. *Working Children—An International Perspective,* Report of a Child Labour Workshop at the I.D.S., Sussex.

Machado Neto, Z. 1981. See I.D.S. 1981.

Machado Neto, Z. 1982. Work, Poverty, Starvation, in *Development and Change,* Vol. 13, No. 4.

Mendelievich, E. 1979. Italy, in *Children at Work,* ed. by Mendelievich, I.L.O., Geneva.

Rouard, D. 1979. Enfants au Travail, in Le *Monde de L'Education,* No. 53, Sept. Paris.

Schildkrout, E. 1978. Age and Gender in Hausa Society: Socio-Economic Roles of Children in Urban Kano, in *Sex and Age as Principles of Social Differentiation,* ASA Monograph No. 7, ed. by J.S. LaFountaine, Academic Press.

Schildkrout, E. 1979. Women's Work and Children's Work: Variations Among Moslems in Kano, in *Social Society of Work,* ASA Monograph No. 19, ed. by S. Wallman, London, Academic Press.

HEALTH, POVERTY, AND POPULATION

In many areas of the world, traditional societies have had to alter their food-producing practices and their culture as they have been incorporated into the modern global economy. The change in food production usually leads to a lower level of nutrition and health. Traditional cultural practices that help to limit population growth are also disrupted, and there are changes in the social relations between people that lead to the breakdown of networks of social support. These same people usually also find themselves assimilated into modern nations as the lowest economic class, with little opportunity to improve their standard of living. The consequences of this process are population increase, poverty, malnutrition, and disease.

This process can also result in the development of cultural practices that allow people to survive and cope in the deprived and brutal conditions of chronic poverty. In "Lifeboat Ethics: Mother Love and Child Death in Brazil," Nancy Scheper-Hughes describes the dehumanizing conditions that have resulted from poverty in rural Brazil, including the cultural attitudes towards child-rearing that have developed as people attempt to cope with the high infant mortality rate. Stanley and Ruth Freed discuss the cultural practices that contribute to rapid population growth in India and demonstrate that there are no simple reasons for, or solutions to, the problem in their article, "One Son Is No Sons."

Ronald Frankenburg discusses the global epidemic of AIDS and the social conditions and cultural practices that have facilitated the disease's spread in "AIDS and Anthropologists." In "The Prejudice Against Men," Peter Marin discusses cultural prejudices against men that make them the primary victims of homelessness in this article on poverty and homelessness in the United States. Finally, Jack McIver Weatherford describes the effects of cocaine production on the economy and culture of people in rural Bolivia as a result of their incorporation into the global economy in "Cocaine and the Economic Deterioration of Bolivia." Together these articles provide us with an understanding of the overwhelming economic, health, and social problems confronting people around the world.

Lifeboat Ethics: Mother Love and Child Death in Brazil

Nancy Scheper-Hughes

As you read:
1. *What is lifeboat ethics?*
2. *What are the cultural attitudes towards children in Alto do Cruzeiro? Why have these attitudes developed and how do they help people cope with the high rate of infant mortality?*
3. *Based upon your reading of this article, what can you say about mother love as natural, instinctive behavior?*

I have seen death without weeping
The destiny of the Northeast is death
Cattle they kill
To the people they do something worse

— Geraldo Vendré (1965)

"Why do the church bells ring so often?" I asked Nailza de Arruda soon after I moved into a corner of her tiny mudwalled hut near the top of the shantytown called the Alto do Cruzeiro (Crucifix Hill). I was then a Peace Corps volunteer and a community development/health worker. It was the dry and blazing hot summer of 1965, the months following the military coup in Brazil, and save for the rusty, clanging bells of N.S. das Dores Church, an eerie quiet had settled over the market town that I call Bom Jesus da Mata. Beneath the quiet, however, there was chaos and panic. "It's nothing," replied Nailza, "just another little angel gone to heaven."

Nailza had sent more than her share of little angels to heaven, and sometimes at night I could hear her engaged in a muffled but passionate discourse with one of them, two-year-old Joana. Joana's photograph, taken as she lay propped up in her tiny cardboard coffin, her eyes open, hung on a wall next to one of Nailza and Ze Antonio taken on the day they eloped.

Nailza could barely remember the other infants and babies who came and went in close succession. Most had died unnamed and were hastily baptized in their coffins. Few lived more than a month or two. Only Joana, properly baptized in church at the close of her first year and placed under the protection of a powerful saint, Joan of Arc, had been expected to live. And Nailza had dangerously allowed herself to love the little girl.

In addressing the dead child, Nailza's voice would range from tearful imploring to angry recrimination: "Why did you leave me? Was your patron saint so greedy that she could not allow me one child on this earth?" Ze Antonio advised me to ignore Nailza's odd behavior, which he understood as a kind of madness that, like the birth and death of children, came and went. Indeed, the premature birth of a stillborn son some months later "cured" Nailza of her "inappropriate" grief, and the day came when she removed Joana's photo and carefully packed it away.

More than fifteen years elapsed before I returned to the Alto do Cruzeiro, and it was anthropology that provided the vehicle of my return. Since 1982 I have returned several times in order to pursue a problem that first attracted my attention in the 1960s. My involvement with the people of the Alto do Cruzeiro now spans a quarter of a century and three generations of parenting in a community where mothers and daughters are often simultaneously pregnant.

The Alto do Cruzeiro is one of three shantytowns surrounding the large market town of Bom Jesus in the sugar plantation zone of Pernambuco in Northeast Brazil, one of the many zones of neglect that have emerged in the shadow of the now tarnished economic miracle of Brazil. For the women and children of the Alto do Cruzeiro the only miracle is that some of them have managed to stay alive at all.

The Northeast is a region of vast proportions (approximately twice the size of Texas) and of equally vast social and developmental problems. The nine states that make up the region are the poorest in the country and are representative of the Third World within a dynamic and rapidly industrializing nation. Despite waves of migrations from the interior to the teeming shantytowns of coastal cities, the majority still live in rural areas on farms and ranches, sugar plantations and mills.

Life expectancy in the Northeast is only forty years, largely because of the appallingly high rate of infant and child mortality. Approximately one million children in Brazil under the age of five die each year. The children of the Northeast, especially those born in shantytowns on the periphery of urban life, are at a very high risk of death. In these areas, children are born without the traditional protection of breastfeeding, subsistence gardens, stable marriages, and multiple adult caretakers that exists in the interior. In the hillside shantytowns that spring up around cities or, in this case, interior market towns, marriages are brittle, single parenting is the norm, and women are frequently forced into the shadow economy of domestic work in the homes of the rich or into unprotected and oftentimes "scab" wage labor on the surrounding sugar plantations, where they clear land for planting and weed for a pittance, sometimes less than a dollar a day. The women of the Alto may not bring their babies with them into the homes of the wealthy, where the often-sick infants are considered sources of contamination, and they cannot carry the little ones to the riverbanks where they wash clothes because the river is heavily infested with schistosomes and other deadly parasites. Nor can they carry their young children to the plantations, which are often several miles away. At wages of a dollar a day, the women of the Alto cannot hire baby sitters. Older children who are not in school will sometimes serve as somewhat indifferent caretakers. But any child not in school is also expected to find wage work. In most cases, babies are simply left at home alone, the door securely fastened. And so many die alone and unattended.

Bom Jesus da Mata, centrally located in the plantation zone of Pernambuco, is within commuting distance of several sugar plantations and mills. Consequently, Bom Jesus has been a magnet for rural workers forced off their small subsistence plots by large landowners wanting to use every available piece of land for sugar cultivation. Initially, the rural migrants to Bom Jesus were squatters who were given tacit approval by the mayor to put up temporary straw huts on each of the three hills overlooking the town. The Alto do Cruzeiro is the oldest, the largest, and the poorest of the shantytowns. Over the past three decades many of the original migrants have become permanent residents, and the primitive and temporary straw huts have been replaced by small homes (usually of two rooms) made of wattle and daub, sometimes covered with plaster. The more affluent residents use bricks and tiles. In most Alto homes, dangerous kerosene lamps have been replaced by light bulbs. The once tattered rural garb, often fashioned from used sugar sacking, has likewise been replaced by store-bought clothes, often castoffs from a wealthy *patrão* (boss). The trappings are modern, but the hunger, sickness, and death that they conceal are traditional, deeply rooted in a history of feudalism, exploitation, and institutional dependency.

My research agenda never wavered. The questions I addressed first crystallized during a veritable "die-off" of Alto babies during a severe drought in 1965. The food and water shortages and the political and economic chaos occasioned by the military coup were reflected in the handwritten entries of births and deaths in the dusty, yellowed pages of the ledger books kept at the public registry office in Bom Jesus. More than 350 babies died in the Alto during 1965 alone—this from a shantytown population of little more than 5,000. But that wasn't what surprised me. There were reasons enough for the deaths in the miserable conditions of shantytown life. What puzzled me was the seeming indifference of Alto women to the death of their infants, and their willingness to attribute to their own tiny offspring an aversion to life that made their death seem wholly natural, indeed all but anticipated.

Although I found that it was possible, and hardly difficult, to rescue infants and toddlers from death by diarrhea and dehydration with a simple sugar, salt, and water solution (even bottled Coca-Cola worked fine), it was more difficult to enlist a mother herself in the rescue of a child she perceived as ill-fated for life or better off dead, or to convince her to take back into her threatened and besieged home a baby she had already come to think of as an angel rather than as a son or daughter.

I learned that the high expectancy of death, and the ability to face child death with stoicism and equanimity, produced patterns of nurturing that differentiated between those infants thought of as thrivers and survivors and those thought of as born already "wanting to die." The survivors were nurtured, while stigmatized, doomed infants were left to die, as mothers say, *a mingua,* "of neglect." Mothers stepped back and allowed nature to take its course. This pattern, which I call mortal selective neglect, is called passive infanticide by anthropologist Marvin Harris. The Alto situation, although culturally specific in the form that it takes, is not unique to Third World shantytown communities and may have its correlates in our own impoverished urban communities in some cases of "failure to thrive" infants.

I use as an example the story of Zezinho, the thirteen-month-old toddler of one of my neighbors, Lourdes. I became involved with Zezinho when I was called in to help Lourdes in the delivery of another child, this one a fair and robust little tyke with a lusty cry. I noted that while Lourdes showed great interest in the newborn, she totally ignored Zezinho who, wasted and severely malnourished, was curled up in a fetal position on a piece of urine- and feces-soaked cardboard placed under his mother's hammock. Eyes open and vacant, mouth slack, the little boy seemed doomed.

When I carried Zezinho up to the community daycare center at the top of the hill, the Alto women who took turns caring for one another's children (in order to free themselves for part-time work in the cane fields or washing clothes) laughed at my efforts to save Ze, agreeing with Lourdes that here was a baby without a ghost of a chance. Leave him alone, they cautioned. It makes no sense to fight with death. But I did do battle with Ze, and after several months of force-feeding (malnourished babies lose their interest in food), Ze began to succumb to my ministrations. He acquired some flesh across his taut chest bones, learned to sit up, and even tried to smile. When he seemed well enough, I returned him to Lourdes in her miserable scrap-material lean-to, but not without guilt about what I had done. I wondered whether returning Ze was at all fair to Lourdes and to his little brother. But I was busy and washed my hands of the matter. And

Lourdes did seem more interested in Ze now that he was looking more human.

When I returned in 1982, there was Lourdes among the women who formed my sample of Alto mothers—still struggling to put together some semblance of life for a now grown Ze and her five other surviving children. Much was made of my reunion with Ze in 1982, and everyone enjoyed retelling the story of Ze's rescue and of how his mother had given him up for dead. Ze would laugh the loudest when told how I had had to force-feed him like a fiesta turkey. There was no hint of guilt on the part of Lourdes and no resentment on the part of Ze. In fact, when questioned in private as to who was the best friend he ever had in life, Ze took a long drag on his cigarette and answered without a trace of irony, "Why my mother of course!" "But of course," I replied.

Part of learning how to mother in Alto do Cruzeiro is learning when to let go of a child who shows that it "wants" to die or that it has no "knack" or no "taste" for life. Another part is learning when it is safe to let oneself love a child. Frequent child death remains a powerful shaper of maternal thinking and practice. In the absence of firm expectation that a child will survive, mother love as we conceptualize it (whether in popular terms or in the psychobiological notion of maternal bonding) is attenuated and delayed with consequences for infant survival. In an environment already precarious to young life, the emotional detachment of mothers toward some of their babies contributes even further to the spiral of high mortality—high fertility in a kind of macabre lock-step dance of death.

The average woman of the Alto experiences 9.5 pregnancies, 3.5 child deaths, and 1.5 stillbirths. Seventy percent of all child deaths in the Alto occur in the first six months of life, and 82 percent by the end of the first year. Of all deaths in the community each year, about 45 percent are of children under the age of five.

Women of the Alto distinguish between child deaths understood as natural (caused by diarrhea and communicable diseases) and those resulting from sorcery, the evil eye, or other magical or supernatural afflictions. They also recognize a large category of infant deaths seen as fated and inevitable. These hopeless cases are classified by mothers under the folk terminology "child sickness" or "child attack." Women say that there are at least fourteen different types of hopeless child sickness, but most can be subsumed under two categories—chronic and acute. The chronic cases refer to infants who are born small and wasted. They are deathly pale, mothers say, as well as weak and passive. They demonstrate no vital force, no liveliness. They do not suck vigorously; they hardly cry. Such babies can be this way at birth or they can be born sound but soon show no resistance, no "fight" against the common crises of infancy: diarrhea, respiratory infections, tropical fevers.

The acute cases are those doomed infants who die suddenly and violently. They are taken by stealth overnight, often following convulsions that bring on head banging, shaking, grimacing, and shrieking. Women say it is horrible to look at such a baby. If the infant begins to foam at the mouth or gnash its teeth or go rigid with its eyes turned back inside its head, there is absolutely no hope. The infant is "put aside"—left alone—often on the floor in the back room, and allowed to die. These symptoms (which accompany high fevers, dehydration, third-stage malnutrition, and encephalitis) are equated by Alto women with madness, epilepsy and worst of all, rabies, which is greatly feared and highly stigmatized.

Most of the infants presented to me as suffering from chronic child sickness were tiny, wasted famine victims, while those labeled as victims of acute child attack seemed to be infants suffering from the deliriums of high fever or the convulsions that can accompany electrolyte imbalance in dehydrated babies.

Local midwives and traditional healers, praying women, as they are called, advise Alto women on when to allow a baby to die. One midwife explained: "If I can see that a baby was born unfortuitously, I tell the mother that she need not wash the infant or give it a cleansing tea. I tell her just to dust the infant with baby powder and wait for it to die." Allowing nature to take its course is not seen as sinful by these often very devout Catholic women. Rather, it is understood as cooperating with God's plan.

Often I have been asked how consciously women of the Alto behave in this regard. I would have to say that consciousness is always shifting between allowed and disallowed levels of awareness. For example, I was awakened early one morning in 1987 by two neighborhood children who had been sent to fetch me to a hastily organized wake for a two-month-old infant whose mother I had unsuccessfully urged to breast-feed. The infant was being sustained on sugar water, which the mother referred to as *soro* (serum), using a medical term for the infant's starvation regime in light of his chronic diarrhea. I had cautioned the mother that an infant could not live on *soro* forever.

The two girls urged me to console the young mother by telling her that it was "too bad" that her infant was so weak that Jesus had to take him. They were coaching me in proper Alto etiquette. I agreed, of course, but asked, "And what do *you* think?" Xoxa, the eleven-year-old, looked down at her dusty flip-flops and blurted out, "Oh, Dona Nanci, that baby never got enough to eat, but you must never say that!" And so the death of hungry babies remains one of the best kept secrets of life in Bom Jesus da Mata.

Most victims are waked quickly and with a minimum of ceremony. No tears are shed, and the neighborhood children form a tiny procession, carrying the baby to the town graveyard where it will join a multitude of others. Although a few fresh flowers may be scattered over the tiny grave, no stone or wooden cross will mark the place, and the same spot will be reused within a few months' time. The mother will never visit the grave, which soon becomes an anonymous one.

What, then, can be said of these women? What emotions, what sentiments motivate them? How are they able to do what, in fact, must be done? What does mother love mean in this inhospitable context? Are grief, mourning, and melancholia present, although deeply repressed? If so, where shall we look for them? And if not, how are we to understand the moral visions and moral sensibilities that guide their actions?

I have been criticized more than once for presenting an unflattering portrait of poor Brazilian women, women who are, after all, themselves the victims of severe social and institutional neglect. I have described these women as allowing some of their children to die, as if this were an unnatural and inhuman act rather than, as I would assert, the way any one of us might act reasonably and rationally, under similarly desperate conditions. Perhaps I have not emphasized enough the real pathogens in this environment of high risk: poverty, deprivation, sexism, chronic hunger, and economic exploitation. If mother love is, as many psychologists and some feminists believe, a seemingly natural universal maternal script, what does it mean to women for whom scarcity, loss, sickness, and deprivation have made that love frantic and robbed them of their grief, seeming to turn their hearts to stone?

Throughout much of human history—as in a great deal of the impoverished Third World today—women have had to give birth and to nurture children under ecological conditions and social arrangements hostile to child survival, as well as to their own well-being. Under circumstances of high childhood mortality, patterns of selective neglect and passive infanticide may be seen as active survival strategies.

They also seem to be fairly common practices historically and across cultures. In societies characterized by high childhood mortality and by a correspondingly high (replacement) fertility, cultural practices of infant and child care tend to be organized primarily around survival goals. But what this means is a pragmatic recognition that not all of one's children can be expected to live. The nervousness about child survival in areas of northeast Brazil, northern India, or Bangladesh, where a 30 percent or 40 percent mortality rate in the first years of life is common, can lead to forms of delayed attachment and a casual or benign neglect that serves to weed out the worst bets so as to enhance the life chances of healthier siblings, including those yet to be born. Practices similar to those that I am describing have been recorded for parts of Africa, India, and Central America.

Life in the Alto do Cruzeiro resembles nothing so much as a battlefield or an emergency room in an overcrowded inner-city public hospital. Consequently, morality is guided by a kind of "lifeboat ethics," the morality of triage. The seemingly studied indifference toward the suffering of some of their infants, conveyed in such sayings as "little critters have no feelings," is understandable in light of these women's obligation to carry on with their reproductive and nurturing lives.

In their slowness to anthropomorphize and personalize their infants, everything is mobilized so as to prevent maternal overattachment and, therefore, grief at death. The bereaved mother is told not to cry, that her tears will dampen the wings of her little angel so that she cannot fly up to her heavenly home. Grief at the death of an angel is not only inappropriate, it is a symptom of madness and of a profound lack of faith.

Infant death becomes routine in an environment in which death is anticipated and bets are hedged. While the routinization of death in the context of shantytown life is not hard to understand, and quite possible to empathize with, its routinization in the formal institutions of public life in Bom Jesus is not as easy to accept uncritically. Here the social production of indifference takes on a different, even a malevolent, cast.

In a society where triplicates of every form are required for the most banal events (registering a car, for example), the registration of infant and child death is informal, incomplete, and rapid. It requires no documentation, takes less than five minutes, and demands no witnesses other than office clerks. No questions are asked concerning the circumstances of the death, and the cause of death is left blank, unquestioned and unexamined. A neighbor, grandmother, older sibling, or common-law husband may register the death. Since most infants die at home, there is no question of a medical record.

From the registry office, the parent proceeds to the town hall, where the mayor will give him or her a voucher for a free baby coffin. The full-time municipal coffinmaker cannot tell you exactly how many baby coffins are dispatched each week. It varies, he says, with the seasons. There are more needed during the drought months and during the big festivals of Carnaval and Christmas and São Joao's Day because people are too busy, he supposes, to take their babies to the clinic. Record keeping is sloppy.

Similarly, there is a failure on the part of city-employed doctors working at two free clinics to recognize the malnutrition of babies who are weighed, measured, and immunized without comment and as if they were not, in fact, anemic, stunted, fussy, and irritated starvation babies. At best the mothers are told to pick up free vitamins or a health "tonic" at the municipal chambers. At worst, clinic personnel will give tranquilizers and sleeping pills to quiet the hungry cries of "sick-to-death" Alto babies.

The church, too, contributes to the routinization of, and indifference toward, child death. Traditionally, the local Catholic church taught patience and resignation to domestic tragedies that were said to reveal the imponderable workings of God's will. If an infant died suddenly, it was because a particular saint had claimed the child. The infant would be an angel in the service of his or her heavenly patron. It would be wrong, a sign of a lack of faith, to weep for a child with such fortune. The infant funeral was, in the past, an event celebrated with joy. Today, however, under the new regime of "liberation theology," the bells of N.S. das Dores parish church no longer peal for the death of Alto babies, and no priest accompanies the procession of angels to the cemetery where their bodies are disposed of casually and without ceremony. Children bury children in Bom Jesus da Mata. In this most Catholic of communities, the coffin is handed to the disabled and irritable municipal gravedigger, who often chides the children for one reason or another. It may be that the coffin is larger than expected and the gravedigger can find no appropriate space. The children do not wait for the gravedigger to complete his task. No prayers are recited and no sign of the cross made as the tiny coffin goes into its shallow grave.

When I asked the local priest, Padre Marcos, about the lack of church ceremony surrounding infant and childhood death today in Bom Jesus, he replied: "In the old days, child death was richly celebrated. But those were the baroque customs of a conservative church that wallowed in death and misery. The new church is a church of hope and joy. We no longer celebrate the death of child angels. We try to tell mothers that Jesus doesn't want all the dead babies they send him." Similarly, the new church has changed its baptismal customs, now often refusing to baptize dying babies brought to the back door of a church or rectory. The mothers are scolded by the church attendants and told to go home and take care of their sick babies. Baptism, they are told, is for the living; it is not to be confused with the sacrament of extreme unction, which is the anointing of the dying. And so it appears to the women of the Alto that even the church has turned away from them, denying the traditional comfort of folk Catholicism.

The contemporary Catholic church is caught in the clutches of a double bind. The new theology of liberation imagines a kingdom of God on earth based on justice and equality, a world without hunger, sickness, or childhood mortality. At the same time, the church has not changed its official position on sexuality and reproduction, including its sanctions against birth control, abortion, and sterilization. The padre of Bom Jesus da Mata recognizes this contradiction intuitively, although he shies away from discussions on the topic, saying that he prefers to leave questions of family planning to the discretion and the "good consciences" of his impoverished parishioners. But this, of course, sidesteps the extent to which those good consciences have been shaped by traditional church teachings in Bom Jesus, especially by his recent predecessors. Hence, we can begin to see the seeming indifference of Alto mothers toward the death of some of their infants is but a pale reflection of the official indifference of church and state to the plight of poor women and children.

Nonetheless, the women of Bom Jesus are survivors. One woman, Biu, told me her life history, returning again and again to the themes of child death, her first husband's suicide, abandonment by her father and later by her second husband, and all the other losses and disappointments she had suffered in her long forty-five years. She concluded with great force, reflecting on the days of Carnaval '88 that were fast approaching:

No, Dona Nanci, I won't cry, and I won't waste my life thinking about it from morning to night. . . . Can I argue with

God for the state I am in? No! And so I'll dance and I'll jump and I'll play Carnaval! And yes, I'll laugh and people will wonder at a pobre like me who can have such a good time.

And no one did blame Biu for dancing in the streets during the four days of Carnaval—not even on Ash Wednesday, the day following Carnaval '88 when we all assembled hurriedly to assist in the burial of Mercea, Biu's beloved *casula,* her last-born daughter who had died at home of pneumonia during the festivities. The rest of the family barely had time to change out of their costumes. Severino, the child's uncle and godfather, sprinkled holy water over the little angel while he prayed: "Mercea, I don't know whether you were called, taken, or thrown out of this world. But look down at us from your heavenly home with tenderness, with pity, and with mercy." So be it.

Postscript

The essay you have just read is controversial and provocative. It disturbs. In some ways it is misleading, for in the space allowed, I could not possibly do justice to the painful subject that it treats. Much of the necessary context and explanation are missing. These are provided in my forthcoming book, *Death Without Weeping: the Madness of Hunger in Northeast Brazil* (University of California Press, 1991).

What we learn about others and about ourselves through anthropology is not always pleasing or exalting. I neither defend, celebrate, nor condemn the mortal selective neglect of frail infants in the shantytown, a practice born of great misery and

of reduced life chances. The mothers of the Alto are not "bad' people suffering from a cancer of the soul, any more than are the bishops and priests of Bom Jesus who are deeply troubled and confused about which way to turn in order to help mothers and children in their communities. There are no simple solutions. Sometimes I have tried to intervene directly in saving a child and often I have repented later.

Birth control and abortion cannot solve the problems of hunger and child death in Brazil. People in the shantytown are not poor and hungry because they have so many children. They have so many children because they are poor. Women get pregnant to replace children who have died as sick infants. They pray for strong, big, and healthy newborns, infants with a thirst and a knack for life. The rescue of doomed infants through medical techniques such as immunization and oral rehydration therapies often prolongs the deaths from hunger and neglect. International rescue and adoption programs often promote pernicious forms of "baby trade."

The chaos produced by Brazil's huge international debt has made Brazil economic "hostage" to the United States and reproduces more hunger and child death in the shantytown than is produced by high fertility. We in the United States have our own moral dilemmas and ambiguities to reflect upon. How do we value human life at its beginnings and toward its often medically prolonged end? How do our political and economic institutions produce "indifference" toward the suffering of women and children at home and abroad? —NS-H

One Son Is No Sons

Stanley A. Freed and Ruth S. Freed

As you read:
1. *Why is one son no sons?*
2. *What are the social and cultural practices that contribute to Indian population growth?*

Devi and her five children were sitting in their village home in north India watching "Star Trek" on television. Caught up in the adventure, the children struggled to understand the English words. Their mother, meanwhile, was explaining why she was not interested in the government's program of birth control. Noting that her first four children had been girls, Devi said, "1 would have gotten sterilized if I had had sons instead of daughters in the beginning. My six-year-old son is very weak physically, which is why I want to have one more son. Girls get married and leave the village to live with their husbands; they are no longer your own. A son in the family is necessary."

Already endowed with five children and intending to have at least one more, Devi and her husband contribute to making India a demographic giant second only to China. In 1981, India had 684 million inhabitants, about 15 percent of the globe's population. This figure includes 136 million persons added since the census of 1971, an increment larger than the total population of Brazil, which ranks sixth in the world. The current annual increase of about 15 million is more than double the population of New York City. India's population, now estimated at 735 million, will approach one billion by 2001 and may surpass China's soon after 2025.

Devi and her husband are not illiterate, poverty-stricken villagers, often thought to be at the heart of India's problem of massive population growth. Devi finished five years of school, and her husband is a high school graduate with a well-paying clerical job in Delhi and a sizable farm in a nearby village. The family is quite prosperous. What impels people like Devi and her husband to continue to have large families in an era of largely free, easily available contraception is that sons are the only dependable insurance against misfortune, poverty, and the disabilities of old age. The vast majority of Indians have no social security, private pension plans, or annuities; they rely instead on their sons. Few couples are satisfied with just one son, for the rate of infant mortality, while steadily declining, is still high enough to make parents with only one son very anxious. "One eye is no eyes, and one son is no sons," runs a popular saying. People try to have two or three sons, hoping that one of them will survive to care for them in their old age.

While a great deal of modernization has taken place in India since independence in 1947, the basic economic arrangements, values, and family roles, which tend to support the desire for a large family, have been generally stable. Even though India's birthrate has dropped and the use of contraception has mounted, India's average annual rate of population growth increased slightly from the 1960s to the 1970s—from 2.20 percent to 2.23 percent—because of lowered mortality. It is this stubbornly high rate of population growth—three times the estimated rate for the United States in 1981—that the government of India is fighting to control. As the late Prime Minister Indira Gandhi was fond of saying, India adds an Australia a year to her population.

In 1951, the year of the first Indian census after independence, the size of the population was of sufficient concern to lead to a national program of family planning, but it was presented in terms of maternal and child health care rather than fertility control. Serious efforts to reduce fertility did not begin until the mid-1960s. The endeavor to check population growth was most intense during the political Emergency legally proclaimed by Prime Minister Gandhi on June 25, 1975, after a period of political unrest and demands that she resign. During the 21-month period of the Emergency, which lasted until March 21, 1977, couples were strongly urged—by publicity, plus a combination of cash payments and various disincentive measures—to undergo sterilization. The governmental slogan "Two or three children, enough!" was widely disseminated. Because the program was often perceived as coercive, the ruling Congress Party suffered a temporary electoral defeat. Despite the popular reaction against the excesses of the Emergency, however, the government of India did succeed, much faster than might otherwise have happened, in establishing sterilization as a routine and acceptable option for couples wishing to terminate childbearing.

Today sterilization is the principal contraceptive technique used in India. Because it permanently ends childbearing, parents do not use it until they have all the children they want or think they will need. The present government, concerned with fertility control, extols and publicizes the small

family of two or three children. Indian parents think in terms of two sons and one daughter as the ideal "small" family; but in trying for at least two sons they end up with an average of about 4.2 children. In general, the minority of Indian parents who choose to be sterilized do so about two children too late from the government's point of view, and the large majority shun sterilization altogether, wanting to be very sure that they will never be left without at least one son. "To be sterilized is to tempt fate" summarizes a common attitude.

The government would like to achieve a family norm of two children by the turn of the century, at which point India's population would begin to stabilize, reaching a plateau of 1.2 billion by the middle of the twenty-first century. Is this goal realistic? The answer must be sought chiefly in India's villages, where 76 percent of the population lives. At various times during the 25-year period from 1958 to 1983, we have had the opportunity to investigate population growth in a north Indian village we call Shanti Nagar (the name is fictitious). The study is of particular interest because it encompasses the demographic watershed between the time that family planning barely existed and the period when fertility control became a serious governmental concern and sterilization was established as the major contraceptive technique. Although one should be cautious about drawing conclusions from a single village, the study of a small community such as Shanti Nagar provides an appreciation of the motives and attitudes that underlie people's everyday decisions about childbearing, family size, and sterilization.

Shanti Nagar is typical of the region that includes the northern states of Punjab, Haryana, western Uttar Pradesh, and the Union Territory of Delhi. From the 1950s to the 1980s, Shanti Nagar has undergone an economic revolution. The village has acquired electricity, brick houses have replaced mud houses, and streets have been paved. In agriculture, bullock power and hand labor have largely given way to machinery. Paved roads and increased bus service make it easier to commute to urban areas, where many men have jobs. Radios are now commonplace, there are some TV sets, and newspapers are delivered daily. The educational level has risen dramatically for both men and women. The village has become more prosperous and better informed about government programs.

Although one would expect that the modernization of education, communications, and the economy would significantly alter family life, the village family has generally maintained its traditional form and functions. A single Indian family may include more people than just a couple and their children: often a family is composed of a couple, their married son (or sons), and his wife and children. Sometimes two or more married brothers live as members of the same family, the eldest brother acting as family head. Families are relatively large by American standards, consisting on average of more than seven members. Men are young when they marry, and women are very young, often beginning their married lives shortly after first menstruation. Men continue to live at their parental home after marriage and bring their brides to live with them. Women are expected to begin childbearing as soon as possible, for both the economic and political strength of a family and a woman's own status depend on the number of sons. "Marriage is not for pleasure," say the villagers. "It is the duty of a wife to have children."

Because attitudes in the 1950s were so strongly in favor of having a goodly number of children, we would have given family planning and, particularly, sterilization little chance of making significant headway. Therefore, when we returned to Shanti Nagar in 1978 after an absence of twenty years, we were startled to hear so many people discussing their own sterilizations or those of their neighbors. We eventually found that there were 68 sterilizations involving both males and females, tantamount to 26 percent of the women of childbearing age (15 to 45 years) at the time. By late 1983, there were 93 sterilized individuals.

Sterilization has run an uneven course in Shanti Nagar. It was accepted slowly at first. From 1968 to 1974, 3.4 individuals on the average were sterilized annually. Then came the twenty-one months of the Emergency, which began in 1975, and the average number of persons who underwent sterilization jumped to about 20 per year. After the Emergency, the figure returned almost to the pre-Emergency norm; from 1977 to late 1983, 4.7 persons were sterilized per year. The big jump in sterilizations during the Emergency was due to the strong campaign mounted by the government. Governmental pressure was especially effective with men holding government jobs. Most of the men sterilized during the Emergency were in government service.

When the Emergency ended, there was a noteworthy change in the proportion of men to women undergoing sterilization. Prior to 1977, 53 percent of the operations were performed on men; for the period from 1977 to late 1983, this figure had fallen to 15 percent. The shift is probably related to the introduction of the surgical technique of laparoscopy, which has made female sterilization easier. The government also suggested a somewhat higher payment to women undergoing sterilization, compared with the incentive to men. Moreover, villagers may not have been entirely convinced that vasectomy was foolproof. If a vasectomy is done improperly, a pregnancy can follow, exposing the unfortunate woman to suspicion of adultery and to village gossip and scorn. Why take that chance when a tubectomy will avoid the problem?

Most of those in Shanti Nagar who discussed reasons for not being sterilized or for postponing the operation cited an insufficient number of sons. On the other hand, the expense of raising children was overwhelmingly the main reason that villagers gave for undergoing sterilization. Couples also frequently cited the governmental sterilization campaign, principally its coercive aspects, as a motive for being sterilized, and a few people mentioned that sterilization was seen as the solution to specific health problems of women.

The emphasis on economic reasons focuses attention on the changing value of child labor. In rural India, where children participate on the family farm from an early age, the value of their labor remains considerable. However, the modernization of agriculture has reduced the need for child labor. At the same time, there has been an increase in employment opportunities that require an educational qualification. Many parents aspire to better jobs for their children and prefer fewer, more educated children to more numerous, uneducated offspring. Few can afford to educate all the children that they can possibly have.

The findings from Shanti Nagar suggest that a significant drop in the growth rate of the population cannot be expected in the near term. The parents in Shanti Nagar who chose sterilization did so generally after having four or five living children, and it must be borne in mind that most couples have not been sterilized. Overall, completed families in the 1970s were larger than those of the 1950s (averaging 5.2 versus 5.0 living children). Even the women who were sterilized (or whose husbands were sterilized) in 1978 had almost as many living children (an average of 4.9) as had the women with completed families in 1958, almost all of whom used no contraception.

On the other hand, persons who anticipate at least a slight downturn in the rate of population growth can find some grounds for optimism in the statistics from Shanti Nagar. In 1978, sterilized mothers had fewer living children than nonsterilized mothers who had completed their childbearing (4.9 versus 5.5 on the average).

Moreover, the effect of sterilization is becoming more pronounced: from the end of the Emergency in 1977 until late in 1983, couples underwent sterilization at a younger age and had fewer children than before 1977. But they still averaged 4.3 living children, enough to produce a rather high rate of population growth.

Sterilized couples had, on the average, about three sons and two daughters, an imbalance that appears to be increasing. From 1977 to 1983, sterilized couples averaged twice as many sons as daughters. This sexual disparity is no accident: couples aim for between two and three sons before undergoing sterilization, but almost no one desperately wants more than one daughter. It is important to note that sterilization by itself cannot influence the sex of children. However, if either by random chance or active intervention a couple has more sons than daughters, a sterilization operation makes the situation permanent, provided that there are no untimely deaths of sons. As is common in northern India, Shanti Nagar has slightly more males than females, a difference usually explained by the preference for sons and the suspected mistreatment of female children. It is also possible that female infants are undernumerated in censuses. One explanation does not preclude the other, and both may be involved.

From an American and Western European perspective, one might assume that population control could be achieved in India by instituting a system of social security, such as is found in the United States, to reduce the need for so many sons and make the two-child family possible for many couples. In developed countries, much of the economic support and care of the aged comes from outside the family; children may assume minor financial and custodial roles or none at all. This feature of Western society is not of recent origin: it appeared in England, for example, several centuries before the Industrial Revolution, the source of sustenance shifting through the centuries from the manor and the guild to the parish and to the state. But India is a different world, where the care and support of the aged have always been a family affair. Indians do not believe that the government or anyone but their sons will take care of them when they are old. Their experience is that governments and policies change too frequently to be trustworthy in the long term. A family with fewer than two sons makes no sense to most Indians. This attitude would persist even if the resources to institute a system of social security could be found.

Many Western analysts also assume that economic development to improve the standard of living will solve the problem of population growth in India. However, there is no evidence from Shanti Nagar or elsewhere in India that motivation to limit family size to two or three children develops after a certain economic status has been attained. Even the effect of the education of women—perhaps the most promising of the socioeconomic factors thought to lower fertility—is somewhat ambiguous in India and, in any case, has little impact until women achieve the college level and begin to work outside the home. In all probability, it will be a long time before a significant proportion of rural Indian females are sent to college.

Although sterilization is increasing in India and the birthrate has been declining for some time, these developments do not presage an imminent solution to the problem of India's population growth. For our part, we would be inclined to keep a sharp eye on the average size of completed families, for this statistic will provide greater insight into India's demographic future than the drop of a few points in the birthrate. If parity at completed childbearing shows signs of stabilizing at between four and five children, India will continue to live up to its reputation as a demographic juggernaut. In that case, India's currently voluntary program of family planning might have to be replaced by more Draconian measures, like those instituted in China. The Indian government fell from power when it previously tried to introduce a stringent program of fertility control. The challenge is to try to control population growth in a democracy where families of four or more children are, for very good reasons, considered necessary.

Stanley A. Freed is a curator and Ruth S. Freed is a research associate in the American Museum's Department of Anthropology. This article is based on the authors' study, "Fertility, Sterilization, and Population Growth in Shanti Nagar, India: A Longitudinal Ethnographic Approach," published in The Anthropological Papers of the American Museum of Natural History, *vol. 60, part 3, pp. 229-286, 1985.*

AIDS and Anthropologists

Ronald Frankenburg

As you read:
1. *What cultural patterns of behavior contributed to the global spread of AIDS?*

Some years ago, a commission was formed for urgent anthropology, and Claude Lévi-Strauss and others sought to save Amazonian groups who were not merely threatened here and now but whose whole future was in jeopardy. AIDS requires urgent anthropology on an even greater scale, for if the pandemic is not checked it is as capable of virtually destroying human life on earth as nuclear radiation or other ecological disasters. However, there is every hope of checking its progress, and for once there is no argument but that, as has slowly come to be realized, anthropology (social, ecological and through the study of the culture of risk) could and must be of major importance in stopping all three separate but related epidemics which WHO has recognized as making up a global pandemic.

AIDS itself is not a disease but a complex of symptoms and diseases which some (up to now about 80,000 known to WHO) if not all of the persons (between five and ten million worldwide—Mann 1988) infected with a virus called HIV are no longer able to resist because of damage to their immune system. ("HIV may cause neurological disease in infected patients in whom immune defense remains intact. This observation raises the possibility that neurological features may eventually come to dominate the clinical perception of HIV

related disease." OHE 1988.) There is as yet no cure nor vaccine against HIV in sight and even the most optimistic predictions of either—ten years' time—would be too late to avert catastrophe. Prevention is not merely better than cure, it is the cure: prevention of transmission of the virus (epidemic one), prevention of the development of the AIDS syndromes which HIV makes possible (epidemic two) and prevention of unnecessary suffering for the general population including the HIV seropositive and people with AIDS caused, not by biological, but by socially determined factors (epidemic three).

HIV is spread worldwide in the same ways through sexual intercourse (homosexual or heterosexual), through transfer of blood (transfusions, sharing or reuse of injection needles), and from mother to child (Acheson 1988).

The First Pattern—Industrial West, Australia, Latin America

As is now well known AIDS was first identified as a problem amongst Gay men in certain cities in the United States who began to present to medical institutions with rare cancers and a form of pneumonia. The presence and often co-presence of these conditions, it gradually became apparent (despite institutional resistance from those, especially in the National Institutes of Health, opposed to transmission theories of malignant disease—Shilts 1987), must arise from damage to the immune system and from a transmissible virus disease. Gay men paid and continue to pay a terrible price for this knowledge; but everyone, Gay or not, is given the possibility of salvation by the chance of the virus's identification among those people at that place and at that time. For the United States, despite all the faults of its health care system, has a medical infrastructure which makes it possible quickly to identify new medical disorders and to discover the categories of people affected and thus to identify causative mechanisms and modes of transmission and what needs to be done to prevent or cure them. Given the political will, it also has the financial means to cope with new epidemics. Second, there is in San Francisco a self-conscious, more or less solidary, articulate and politically active Gay community, which, after an unsurprisingly faltering beginning (Shilts 1987), took stock of the situation and demonstrated to other Gays and to the rest of the world what could be done humanely to care for those already infected, and to slow down or stop further transmission. Unfortunately, through no fault of theirs, it was already too late for many of their friends and lovers. Professor M. W. Adler, one of Britain's leading experts, has pointed out that the symptomless nature of HIV infection, and the long latent period (5-8 years) before its effects, including those on the immune system, become apparent, meant that the first cases of AIDS emerged in 1980 when nearly a quarter of a cohort of Gay men were HIV seropositive (*The Independent* 17 February 1988). Also unfortunately Gays elsewhere in the world were less well-placed to respond, although self-help organizations like the Terrence Higgins Trust and Body Positive did a major task in Britain; and non-Gays were not disposed to listen or to learn from people whom at best they saw as other than themselves and at worst feared and hated for the challenge they seemed to represent to accepted social and family order and their own hardly (in both senses) suppressed temptations

and desires. Even anthropologists failed to react constructively; as I reported in my A. T. article (February 1987) on the 1986 AAA meetings, AIDS was left to the Gay Caucus and put at the most unpopular time. When, at last, it became a prominent topic at the 1987 meetings, many still saw it as a purely Gay issue. Despite the negative reactions, we now know—as Hafdan Mahler, Director of WHO has forcibly pointed out—that it is possible to check the spread of even an intractable and insidious disease by health promotion at a societal or communal level even when biological methods seem to offer little help. This knowledge, where before was merely hope, holds out new and exciting potentials for what is coming to be called social epidemiology, epidemiology reciprocally enriched by the social and cultural understandings of anthropology and sociology.[1]

The tendency to associate modes of transmission by means of body fluids with "risk groups" instead of the more epidemiologically useful "risk behaviours," led to "drug addicts"—as, in popular parlance, non-legitimated intravenous drug users are unhelpfully called—being added to Gays as scapegoats. The wish to see AIDS as a problem for the other, non-respectable, the out-of-control, was intensified. It was further reinforced by the notion of the "innocent victim," the haemophiliac infected with Factor 8 and the HIV-positive baby. Thus the Pope showed his rational lack of fear of biological contagion by embracing a person with AIDS; to the approval of some Catholics and the dismay of others, his message was made ambiguous in relation to the fear of moral contagion by the fact that he chose a child with haemophilia. I felt that he might have reassured my Orthodox Jewish aunt who, when I was a child, warned me against Christianity whose Founder's best friend Mary Magdalene, she said, was a prostitute. Especially since, as in earlier epidemics of sexually transmitted disease (Brandt 1987), prostitutes and the promiscuous (people with more sexual experience than us) were singled out for blame together with people from outside the metropolitan Industrial West.[2]

The Second Pattern—Africa and the Caribbean

The reaction to the discovery of AIDS and HIV infection among Gay men and intravenous drug users was, as I have already suggested, at best distanced but reproving pity. They had scored an "own goal" as Princess Anne put it, more in sorrow than in anger, and at worst a theologically perverse, at least by New Testament standards, theory of divine anger and retribution was favored in Britain by some Chief Constables and Rabbis. The reaction to the discovery in one part of Africa of developed AIDS, and of widespread HIV positivity spread for the most part heterosexually and therefore equally prevalent among men and women, only just escaped from being catastrophic. Western ignorance of geography, and stereotypes of African promiscuity, together with hasty suggestions of still greater immigration and travel control over black (and sometimes poor) Africans in sharp contrast to the absence of such suggestions in relation to white (and often rich) Americans led, at first, understandably to outright denial of the problem. Careful diplomacy by WHO and others and the good sense and experience of African politicians and statesmen with President Kaunda characteristically giving a courageous lead, very quickly overcame this denial.[3]

Particularly in urban areas of South Central Africa, up to 25% of the population between 20 and 40 years old may be HIV positive, and in some areas also 5-15% or even more of pregnant women are. The implications of these figures are staggering. The urban elite, on whom further development and national economic recovery depend, may be more than decimated. The productive and skilled workers and educators may be rendered ineffective and a whole generation made virtually unable to reproduce itself. Orphans and the elderly may be left without support, and achievements in the field of health may be made impossible to maintain. This is also a danger in poor areas of Southern Europe and in parts of Latin America, and even ultimately Asia.

The Third Pattern

In Asia, most of the Pacific, the Middle East and much of Eastern Europe, there are very few cases of AIDS, and even HIV seems to have appeared more recently than in other parts of the world. In most of these countries it is believed that HIV came from outside either from sexual intercourse with foreigners or by the import of infected blood products. However there is now evidence of internal transmission in the usual ways, and even if these nations succeed, in fact, in carrying out the policies of isolation and control to which some of them, including India, China and the Soviet Union are, in part, committed, they will not entirely halt the spread of HIV. Fortunately despite their reservations they attended the recent WHO summit and are signatories of the London Declaration and thus pledged to world co-operation.

The Role of Anthropology

The first objective of WHO's Global AIDS strategy is to prevent HIV infection, but this cannot be done in isolation from, or with indifference towards, either the development of AIDS among those already infected or the social experience of people, rightly or wrongly, believed to be at special risk, as well as the HIV seropositive and persons with AIDS.

Surprisingly little is known about specific individual sexual behaviours or about culturally approved practices of groups and subgroups. Straightforward questionnaire techniques are difficult to apply and produce data of arguable validity. Among British sociologists, Coxon (1988) has developed an ingenious self-reporting diary technique to study sexual behaviour of Gay men. Social or cultural anthropologists have already specialist knowledge of, as well as the necessary skills to discover, patterns of sexual behaviour in different societies and sub-groups. They are unlikely even to be tempted to the view that "*we* have our regulated sexual patterns, *you* are a bit odd but understandable, *they* are just promiscuous." They can understand the social circumstances in which desires become practices and in turn symbolic markers of either individual or cultural and social identity. Their knowledge and study of other kinds of behaviour change can help them to see how changes of practice can be instituted from within a society in such a way as to leave cultural and personal identity unthreatened.

How valuable such a skill may be and how urgent its application is, can be demonstrated by the difference between say Danish and British television advertising aimed at young people, which deserves comparative analysis. The British seems based on an assumption that the culture of young people can be at once ignored and condemned as bad or at least amoral, and that decisions (about risk-taking for example) are purely personal or at most dyadic. Even if the disco culture portrayed has been researched and is accurate, the wider social context of sought-for approval and avoidance of disapproval by important others, especially among peers and coevals, is just not there. The Danish advertising, on the other hand, begins by accepting that there are adolescent hedonistic values, and while leaving the choice of fundamental change open to young people themselves, shows how existing patterns can be modified to make them safer. An even sharper contrast may be seen between the Australian Government's "fear of death based" TV campaign, which was aimed at the whole population, and that (presented as an example of "how to do it" at the London Summit) which Aborigi-

nal health promoters devised in co-operation with local people and which aimed not at instilling terror but at the enhancement of life with reduced danger. Clearly, involving groups in self-help health promotion is one of the more effective strategies for preventing the transmission of HIV, and one in which anthropologists have much to offer as facilitators.

Anthropologists have sometimes been criticized in the development field for being better at analyzing failure than helping to create success. As regards AIDS, this may be a useful fault. Health educators are aware that while smoking in Britain, for example, has in general decreased, smoking amongst working-class young people and women has risen. Anthropologists again have the skills, both theoretical and practical, to examine the meanings and practices which make such crucial differences occur.

There is a world of difference between talking of a disease that has hitherto mainly affected Gays, and talking of a "Gay disease," or still more if "queer" or even "homosexual" is substituted for Gay. Anthropologists have learned, what they may not themselves even recognize as being a rare, sensitivity to partly concealed linguistic elisions like using Lapp for Sami, or Eskimo for Inuit, which may be perceived by those named as adding a latent symbolic communication of lack of esteem to the use of surface signs.

Anthropologists study *disease* as manifested in its particular social context of *sickness* as well as carrying an individual meaning of *illness*. They are thereby both less surprised and better prepared to analyze situations where danger and sickness are attributed prematurely or even falsely to those identified as being at risk. The knowledge that healing, whether by shaman, surgeon or sacerdote, is a social process, laden with specifiable cultural meanings, gives anthropologists an important possible role in understanding and investigating how, for example, traditional healers may be encouraged within their own society and culture to do the sick no harm and to continue to protect the well. The anthropological literature on natural and especially body symbolism (Douglas 1973) has prepared its students to understand such cultural taboos and non-taboos as the ability of British television audiences to tolerate (even before nine in the evening) the pictorial representation of the unnatural breach of body boundaries by (illegitimate) needles in contrast to the impossibility of the explicit depiction (unlike elsewhere in Northern Europe) of, not necessarily per se disapproved, sexual penetration.

Furthermore, anthropological study of the myriad different cultural meanings of death (Frankenberg 1987, Bloch et al. 1982) puts its practioners in a strong position to help in the social adjustment already faced by many Gays and their relatives to a changing demographic pattern in which people are dying in their reproductively, productively and socially most active years, an actual and potential shift in the modal age of death upwards in the developing world, downwards in industrial society.

The advent of HIV and its mode of transmission have taken not only medicine and epidemiology by surprise, but have also found both the social and cultural anthropology of risk perception and behavior, and cultural ecology theories in anthropology, as yet insufficiently developed. Health promotion is central in countering the pandemic arising from HIV infection as well as future global pandemics. There is also a renewed realization of the social implications of measured mortality in terms of both changing age distributions of individual dying and the possibility that the future of human society is once again in question through potential ecological disaster. These developments have given a new potential importance not just to virology and immunology within core medical specialties, but also to the study of anthropology in general and medical anthropology within it. When WHO gathered together more Health Ministers than ever before at the London Summit in January last, the handful of invited independent observers included at least three anthropologists, and anthropologists also played a prominent part at the First International Conference on the global impact of AIDS in March. We are presented with a challenge which we are despite our deficiencies uniquely qualified to meet, and which for our own sakes and for the sake of the general good we cannot afford to shirk.

Notes

1. For examples in other fields see the work on developing societies of Patrick Vaughan, Carol MacCormack, Kris Heggenhougen and others at the London School of Hygiene and Jean La Fontaine's recent report on Child Abuse in Britain for ESRC (see *Anthropology Today*, October 1987, p. 1).

2. The London fieldwork and comparative analysis of LSE anthropologist Sophie Day has shown how simplistic and unjust this is in relation to prostitute women.

3. As is so often the case there remain contrary views; see Chirimuta and Chirimuta 1987 and *The Guardian* 5 February 1988 for a favorable review of this book which in my personal view is wrong. It has also been argued, without evidence strong enough to convince most epidemiologists or WHO, that both African and Gay prevalence of AIDS are synergistically affected by other sexually transmitted diseases. Poverty is, of course, even more prevalent in Africa.

References

Acheson, Sir D. 1988. Modes of Transmission: The Basis of Prevention Strategies. Paper to World Summit of Ministers of Health for AIDS Prevention. London WHO/UKG, January.

Bloch, M. and J. Parry. 1982. *Death and the Regeneration of Life*. Cambridge University Press.

Brandt, A. 1987. *No Magic Bullet* with additional chapter on AIDS. Oxford University Press.

Chirimuta, R. C. and R. J. 1987. AIDS, *Africa and Racism*. Chirimuta, Bretby, Derbyshire.

Coxon, A. P. M. 1988. The sexual diary as a research method in the study of sexual behaviour of gay males. *Sociological Review*. 36, 2, May (forthcoming).

Douglas, M. 1970 (1966). *Purity and Danger*. Penguin.

Douglas, M. 1973 (1970). *Natural Symbols*. Penguin.

Frankenberg, R. 1987. Life: Cycle, Trajectory or Pilgrimage? A Social Production Approach to Marxism, Metaphor and Mortality. Chapter XII, pp. 122-140 in Alan Bryman et al. *Rethinking the Life Cycle*. Macmillan.

LaFontaine, J. 1988. *Child Sexual Abuse*. An ESRC Research Briefing.

Mann, J. 1988. Global AIDS: Epidemiology, Impact, Projections and the Global Strategy. Paper to World Summit . . . (as under Acheson above).

Office of Health Economics. 1980. HIV and AIDS in the United Kingdom. Briefing no. 23, January, London.

Shilts, R. 1987. *And the Band Played On*. Penguin.

The Prejudice Against Men

Peter Marin

As you read:
1. *What cultural attitudes have contributed to the victimization of homeless men?*
2. *What are the attitudes of homeless men toward their problems?*

For the past several years advocates for the homeless have sought public support and sympathy by drawing attention to the large number of homeless families on our streets. That is an understandable tactic. Americans usually respond to social issues on the basis of sympathy for "innocent" victims—those whose blamelessness touches our hearts and whom we deem unable to care for themselves. Families, and especially children, obviously fill the bill.

But the fact remains, despite the claims of advocates, that the problem of chronic homelessness is essentially a problem of *single adult men.* Far more single adults than families, and far more men than women, end up homeless on our streets. Until we understand how and why that happens, nothing we do about homelessness will have much of an impact.

Most figures pertaining to the homeless come from limited studies or educated guesses that tend, when examined, to dissolve in one's hand. The most convincing figures I know can be found in James Wright's book *Address Unknown: The Homeless in America.* According to Wright's data, out of every 1,000 homeless people in America, 120 or so will be adults with children, another hundred will be children and the rest will be single adults. Out of that total, 156 will be single women and 580 will be single men. Now break that down into percentages. Out of all single homeless adults, 78 percent are men; out of all homeless adults, more than 64 percent are single men; and out of all homeless people—adults or children—58 percent are single men.

But even those figures do not give the full story. Our federal welfare system has been designed, primarily, to aid women with children or whole families. That means that most of the families and children on the streets have either fallen through the cracks of the welfare system or have not yet entered it. They will, in the end, have access to enough aid to get them off the streets and into some form of shelter, while most men will be left permanently on their own.

I do not mean to diminish here the suffering of families or children, nor to suggest that welfare provides much more than the meanest alternative to homelessness. It is a form of indentured pauperism so grim it shames the nation. But it does in fact eventually get most families off the streets, and that leaves behind, as the chronically homeless, single adults, of whom four-fifths are men. Seen that way, homelessness emerges as a problem involving what happens to men without money, or men in trouble.

By Peter Marin. From *The Nation,* July 8, 1991. Copyright © 1991 by Peter Marin. Reprinted by permission of the author.

Why do so many more men than women end up on the streets? Let me begin with the simplest answers.

First, life on the streets, as dangerous as it is for men, is even more dangerous for women, who are far more vulnerable. While many men in trouble drift almost naturally onto the streets, women do almost anything to avoid it.

Second, there are far better private and public shelters and services available to women.

Third, women are accustomed to asking for help while men are not; women therefore make better use of available resources.

Fourth, poor families *in extremis* seem to practice a form of informal triage. Young men are released into the streets more readily, while young women are kept at home even in the worst circumstances.

Fifth, there are cultural and perhaps even genetic factors at work. There is some evidence that men—especially in adolescence—are more aggressive and openly rebellious than women and therefore harder to socialize. Or it may simply be that men are allowed to live out the impulses women are taught to suppress, and that they therefore end up more often in marginal roles.

More important, still, may be the question of work. Historically, the kinds of work associated with transient or marginal life have been reserved for men. They brought in crops, worked on ships and docks, built roads and railroads, logged and mined. Such labor granted them a place in the economy while allowing them to remain on society's edges—an option rarely available to women save through prostitution.

And society has always seemed, by design, to produce the men who did such work. Obviously, poverty and joblessness forced men into marginality. But there was more to it than that. Schools produced failures, dropouts and rebels; family life and its cruelties produced runaways and throwaways; wars rendered men incapable of settled or domestic life; small-town boredom and provinciality led them to look elsewhere for larger worlds.

Now, of course, the work such men did is gone. But like a mad engine that cannot be shut down, society goes right on producing them. Its institutions function as they always did: The schools hum, the families implode or collapse, the wars churn out their victims. But what is there for them to do? The low-paying service-sector jobs that have replaced manual labor in the economy go mainly to women or high school kids, not the men who once did the nation's roughest work.

Remember, too, in terms of work, that women, especially when young, have one final option denied to men. They can take on the "labor" of being wives and companions to men or of bearing children, and in return they will often be supported or "taken care of" by someone else. Yes, I know: Such roles can often constitute a form of oppression, especially when assumed out of necessity. But nonetheless, the possibility is there. It is permissible (as well as often necessary) for women to become financially, if precariously, dependent on others, while such dependence is more or less forbidden to men.

Finally, there is the federal welfare system. I do not think most Americans understand how the system works, or how for decades it has actually sent men into the streets, creating at least some male homelessness while aiding women and children. Let me explain. There are two main programs that provide care for Americans in trouble. One is Social Security Disability Insurance. It goes to men or women who are unable, because of physical or mental problems, to work or take care of themselves. The other is Aid to Families with Dependent Children (A.F.D.C.). It is what we ordinarily call "welfare." With its roots early in this century, it was established more or less in its present form during the Depression. Refined and expanded again in the 1960s, A.F.D.C. had always been a program meant mainly for women and children and limited to households headed by women. As long as an adult man remained in the household as mate, companion or father, *no aid was forthcoming.* Changes have recently been made in the system, and men may remain in the household if they have a work history satisfying certain federal guidelines. But in poor areas and for certain ethnic groups, where unemployment runs high and few men have a qualifying work history, these changes have not yet had much of an impact and men remain functionally outside the welfare system.

When it comes to single and "able-bodied" or employable, adults, there is no federal aid whatsoever. Individual states and localities sometimes provide their own aid through "general assistance" and "relief." But this is usually granted only on a temporary basis or in emergencies. And in those few places where it is available for longer periods to large numbers of single adults—California, for instance, or New York—it is often so grudging, so ringed round with capricious requirements and red tape, that it is of little use to those in need.

This combination of approaches not only systematically denies men aid as family members or single adults. It means that the aid given to women has sometimes actually deprived men of homes, even as it has provided for women and children. Given the choice between receiving aid for themselves and their children and living with men, what do you think most women do? The regulations as they stand actually force men to compete with the state for women; as a woman in New Orleans once told me: "Welfare changes even love. If a man can't make more at a job than I get from welfare, I ain't even gonna look at him. I can't afford it."

Everywhere in America poor men have been forced to become ghost-lovers and ghost-fathers, one step ahead of welfare workers ready to disqualify families for having a man around. In many ghettos throughout the country you find women and children in their deteriorating welfare apartments, and their male companions and fathers in even worse conditions: homeless in gutted apartments and abandoned cars, denied even the minimal help granted the opposite sex.

Is it surprising, in this context, that many African-Americans see welfare as an extension of slavery that destroys families, isolates women and humiliates men according to white bureaucratic whim? Or is it accidental that in poor communities family structure has collapsed and more and more children are born outside marriage at precisely the same time that disfranchised men are flooding the streets? Welfare is not the only influence at work in all of this, of course. But before judging men and their failures and difficulties, one must understand that their social roles are in no way supported or made easier by the social policies that in small ways make female roles sustainable.

Is this merely an accidental glitch in the system, something that has happened unnoticed? Or does it merely have something to do with a sort of lifeboat ethic, where our scarce resources for helping people are applied according to the ethics of a sinking ship—women and children first, men into the sea?

I do not think so. Something else is at work: deep-seated prejudices and attitudes toward men that are so pervasive, so pandemic, that we have ceased to notice or examine them.

To put it simply: Men are neither supposed nor allowed to be dependent. They are expected to take care of both others *and* themselves. And when they cannot do it, or "will not" do it, the built-in assumption at the heart of the culture is that they are *less than men* and therefore unworthy of help. An irony asserts itself: Simply by being in need of help, men forfeit the right to it.

Think here of how we say "helpless as a woman." This demeans women. But it also does violence to men. It implies that a man cannot be helpless and still be a man, or that helplessness is not a male attribute, or that a woman can be helpless through no fault of her own, but that if a man is helpless it is or must be his own fault.

Try something here. Imagine walking down a street and passing a group of homeless women. Do we not spontaneously see them as victims and wonder what has befallen them, how destiny has injured them? Do we not see them as unfortunate and deserving of help and *want* to help them?

Now imagine a group of homeless men. Is our reaction the same? Is it as sympathetic? Or is it subtly different? Do we have the very same impulse to help and protect? Or do we not wonder, instead of what befell them, how they have got themselves where they are?

And remember, too, our fear. When most of us see homeless or idle men we sense or imagine danger; they make us afraid, as if, being beyond the pale, they are also beyond all social control—and therefore people to be avoided and suppressed rather than helped.

Here too work plays a crucial role. In his memoirs Hamlin Garland describes the transient farm workers who passed through the countryside each year at harvest time. In good years, when there were crops to bring in, they were tolerated: fed, housed and hired. But when the crops were bad and men weren't needed, then they were forced to stay outside of town or pass on unaided, having become merely threats to peace and order, barbarians at the gates.

The same attitude is with us still. When men work (or when they go to war—work's most brutal form), we grant them a right to exist. But when work is scarce, or when men are of little economic use, then they become in our eyes not only superfluous but a danger. We feel compelled to exile them from our midst, banish them from view, drive them away to shift for themselves in more or less the same way that our Puritan forebears, in their shining city on its hill, treated sinners and rebels.

One wonders just how far back such attitudes go. One thinks of the Bible and the myth of the Garden and the first disobedience, when women were cursed with childbirth and men with the sorrows of labor—destinies still, as if by intention, maintained by our welfare system and private attitudes.

And one thinks too of the Victorian era, when the idealized vision of women and children had its modern beginnings. They were set outside the industrial nexus and freed from heavy labor while being rendered more than ever dependent on and subservient to men. It was a process that obviously diminished women, but it had a parallel effect on men. It defined them as laborers and little else, especially if they came from the lower classes. The yoke of labor lifted from the shoulders of women settled even more heavily on the backs of certain men, confining them in roles as narrow and as oppressive as those to which women were assigned.

We are so used to thinking of ours as a male-dominated society that we tend to lose track of the ways in which some men are as oppressed, or perhaps even more oppressed, than most women. But race and class, as well as gender, play roles in oppression. And while it is true, in general, that men dominate society and women, in practice it is only *certain* men who are dominant; others, usually those from the working class and often darker skinned (at least 50 percent of homeless men are black or Latino), suffer endlessly from forms of isolation and contempt that often exceed what many women experience.

The irony at work in all of this is that what you often find among homeless men, and what seems at the heart of their troubles, is precisely what our cultural myths deny them: a helplessness they cannot overcome on their own. You find vulnerability, a sense of injury and betrayal and, in their isolation, a despair equal to what we accept without question in women.

Often this goes unadmitted. Even when in deep trouble men understand, sometimes unconsciously, that they are not to complain or ask for help. I remember several men I knew in the local hobo jungle. Most of them were vets. They had constructed a tiny village of half-caves and shelters among the trees and brush, and when stove smoke filled the clearing and they stood bare to the waist, knives at their hips, you would swear you were in an army jungle camp. They drank throughout the day, and at dusk there always came a moment when they wandered off individually to sit staring out at the mountains or sea. And you could see on their faces at such moments, if you caught them unawares, a particular and unforgettable look: pensive, troubled, somehow innocent—the look of lost children or abandoned men.

I have seen the same look multiplied hundreds of times on winter nights in huge shelters in great cities, where a thousand men at a time will sometimes gather, each encapsulated in solitude on a bare cot, coughing and turning or sometimes crying all night, lost in nightmares as terrible as a child's or as life on the street. In the mornings they returned to their masked public personas, to the styles of behavior and appearance that often frightened passers-by. But while they slept you could see past all that, and you found yourself thinking: These are still, even grown, *somebody's* children, and many fare no better on their own, as adults, than they would have as children.

I remember, too, a young man in my town who was always in trouble for beating up older drunken men. No one understood his brutality until he explained it one day to a woman he trusted: "When I was a kid my daddy ran off and my mother's drunken brothers disciplined me. Whenever I made a mistake they punished me by slicing my legs with a straight razor."

And he pulled up his pant-legs to reveal on each shin a ladder of scars marking each childhood error or flaw.

This can stand for countless stories I've heard. The feeling you get, over and over, is that most men on the street have been "orphaned" in some way, deprived somewhere along the line of the kinds of connection, support and sustenance that enable people to find and keep places in the social order. Of course economics plays a part in this—I do not mean to suggest it does not. But more often than not, something else is also at work, something that cuts close to the bone of social and psychological as well as economic issues: the dissolution of family structures and the vitiation of community; subtle and overt forms of discrimination and racism; and institutions—schools, for instance—that harm or marginalize almost as many people as they help.

For decades now, sociologists have called our attention to rents in our private social fabric as well as our public "safety nets," and to the victims they produce: abused kids, battered women, isolated adults, alcoholics, addicts. Why, I wonder, is it so hard to see homeless men in this context? Why is it so hard to understand that the machinery of our institutions can injure men as permanently as it does women? We know, for instance, that both male and female children are permanently injured by familial abuse and violence and "normal" cruelties of family life. Why, then, do we find it hard to see that grown men, as well as women, can be crippled by childhood, or that they often end up on the edges of society, unable to play expected roles in a world that has betrayed them?

And do not forget here the greatest violence done to men, the tyrannous demand made upon them when young by older and more powerful males: that they kill and die in war. We take that demand for granted in our society and for some reason fail to see it as a form of oppression. But why? Long before the war in

Vietnam had crowded our streets with vets—as far back as the Civil War—the male victims of organized state violence wandered across America unable to find or make places in the social world. The fact is that many men never fully recover from the damage done by war, having seen too much of death to ever again do much with life.

Nor is war the only form in which death and disaster have altered the lives of troubled men. They appear repeatedly in the stories men tell. Listening to these tales one thinks of Oedipus and Lear, of tragedy in its classical sense, of the furies and fates that the Greeks believed stalk all human lives and that are still at work among us, no matter how much we deny them.

Gene, a homeless man I know, was conceived when his mother slept with his father's best friend. Neither of his parents wanted him, so he was raised reluctantly by his mother's parents, who saw him only as the living evidence of her disgrace. As an adult he married and divorced twice, had two children he rarely saw later in life, and spent two years in jail for beating nearly to death a friend he found in bed with his second wife. When I first met him he was living in a cave he had dug by hand out of a hillside, and he spent the money he earned on dope or his friends. But then he met a woman on the streets and they moved together to a cheap hotel. He got her pregnant; they planned to marry; but then they argued and she ran off and either had an abortion or spontaneously miscarried—it was never clear which. When Gene heard about it he took to his bed for days and would not sleep, eat or speak. When I later asked him why, he said: "I couldn't stand it. I wanted to die. I was the baby she killed. It was happening to me all over again, that bad stuff back when I was a kid."

Not everything you hear on the street is so dramatic. There are a thousand quiet and gradual ways American lives can fall apart or come to nothing. Often it is simply "normal" life that proves too much for some men. Some have merely failed at or fled their assigned roles: worker, husband, father. Others lacked whatever it takes to please a boss or a woman or else decided it wasn't worth the trouble to learn how to do it. Not all of them are "good" men. Some have brutalized women or left families in the lurch or fled lives in which the responsibility and stress were more than they could handle. "Couldn't hack it," they'll say with a shrug, or "I had to get out." And others have been so cruel to women or proved so unreliable or sometimes so unsuccessful that women fled them, leaving notes on the table or refrigerator such as the one a man in Seattle once repeated to me: "Gone. Took the kids. So long."

Are such men irresponsible? Perhaps. But in working with homeless men over the years, I've seen how many of them are genuinely unable to handle the stress others can tolerate. Many manage, for instance, to steer clear of alcohol or drugs for a certain period of time and then return to them automatically as soon as they are subject again to the kinds of stress they once fled. It is as if their defenses and even their skins are so much thinner than those of the rest of us that they give way as soon as trouble or too much responsibility appears.

The fact is that most such men seem to have tried to make a go of things, and many are willing to try again. But if others have given up and said inside, *the hell with it* or . . . *it,* is that really astonishing? The curious world we've compounded in America of equal parts of freedom and isolation and individualism and demands for obedience and submission is a strange and wearing mix, and no one can be startled at the number of victims or recalcitrants it produces or at those who can't succeed at it.

Finally, I must add one more thing. Whatever particular griefs men may have experienced on their way to homelessness, there is one final and crippling sorrow all of them share: a sense of betrayal at society's refusal to recognize their needs. Most of us—men and women—grow up expecting that when things go terribly wrong someone, from somewhere, will step forward to help us. That this does not happen, and that all watch from the shore as each of us, in isolation, struggles to swim and then begins to sink, is perhaps the most terrible discovery that anyone in any society can make. When troubled men make that discovery, as all homeless men do sooner or later, then hope vanishes completely; despair rings them round; they have become what they need not have become: the homeless men we see everywhere around us.

What can be done about this? What will set it right? One can talk, of course, about confronting the root causes of marginalization: the failure of families, schools and communities; the stupidities of war, racism and discrimination; social and economic injustice; the disappearance of generosity and reciprocity among us. But what good will that do? America is what it is; culture has a tenacity of its own; and though it is easy to call for major kinds of renewal, nothing of the sort is likely to occur.

That leaves us with ameliorative and practical measures, and it will do no harm to mention them, though they too are not likely to be tried: a further reformation of the welfare system; the federalization of assistance to single adults; increases in the amount and duration of unemployment insurance; further raises in the minimum wage; expanded benefits for vets; detox centers and vocational education for those who want them; the construction of the kinds of low-cost hotels and boarding houses where men in trouble once stayed.

And remember that back in the Depression when the welfare system was established, it was paralleled by programs providing work for men: the Civilian Conservation Corps and the Works Progress Administration. The idea seems to have been welfare for women, work for men. We still have the welfare for women, but where is the work for those men, or women, who want it? Why no one is currently lobbying for contemporary forms of those old programs remains a mystery. Given the deterioration of the American infrastructure— roads, bridges, public buildings—such programs would make sense from any point of view.

But beyond all this, and behind and beneath it, there remains the problem with which we began: the prejudices at work in society that prevent even the attempt to provide solutions. Suggestions such as those I have made will remain merely utopian notions without an examination and renovation of our attitudes toward men. During the past several decades we have slowly, laboriously, begun to confront our prejudices and oppressive practices in relation to women. Unless we now undertake the same kind of project in relation to men in general and homeless men in particular, nothing whatever is going to change. That's as sure as death and taxes and the endless, hidden sorrows of men.

MENTAL ILLNESS

Cocaine and the Economic Deterioration of Bolivia

Jack McIver Weatherford

As you read:
1. *What have been the consequences of cocaine production on rural Bolivians?*
2. *How have efforts to stop coca production affected Bolivians?*

"They say you Americans can do anything. So, why can't you make your own cocaine and let our children come home from the coca plantations in the Chapare?" The Indian woman asked the question with confused resignation. In the silence that followed, I could hear only the rats scurrying around in the thatched roof. We continued shelling corn in the dark. The large house around us had once been home to an extended clan but was now nearly empty.

There was no answer to give her. Yet it was becoming increasingly obvious that the traditional Andean system of production and distribution built over thousands of years was now crumbling. Accompanying the destruction of the economic system was a marked distortion of the social and cultural patterns of the Quechua Indians. Since early in Inca history, the village of Pocona where I was working had been a trading village connecting the highlands which produced potatoes, with the lowlands, which produced coca, a mildly narcotic plant used by the Incas. Over the past decade, however, new market demands from Europe and the United States have warped this system. Now the commodity is cocaine rather than the coca leaves, and the trade route bypasses the village of Pocona.

Bolivian subsistence patterns range from hunting and gathering in the jungle to intensive farming in the highlands, and since Inca times many parts of the country have depended heavily on mining. In the 1980s all of these patterns have been disrupted by the Western fad for one particular drug. Adoption of cocaine as the "drug of choice" by the urban elite of Europe and America has opened up new jungle lands and brought new Indian groups into Western economic systems. At the same time the cocaine trade has cut off many communities such as Pocona from their traditional role in the national economy. Denied participation in the legal economy, they have been driven back into a world of barter and renewed isolation.

The vagaries of Western consumerism produce extensive and profound effects on Third World countries. It makes little difference whether the demand is for legitimate products such as coffee, tungsten, rubber, and furs marketed through legal corporations or for illegal commodities such as opium, marijuana, cocaine, and heroin handled through criminal corporations. The same economic principles that govern the open, legal market also govern the clandestine, illegal markets, and the effects of both are frequently brutal.

Before coming to this Bolivian village, I assumed that if Americans and Europeans wanted to waste their money on cocaine, it was probably good that some of the poor countries such as Bolivia profit from it. In Cochabamba, the city in the heart of the cocaine-producing area, I had seen the benefits of this trade among the *narco chic,* who lived in a new suburb of houses styled to look like Swiss chalets, Spanish *haciendas,* and English country homes. All these homes were surrounded by large wrought-iron fences, walls with broken glass set in the tops, and with large dogs that barked loudly and frequently. Such homes cost up to a hundred thousand dollars, an astronomical sum for Bolivia. I had also seen the narco elite of Cochabamba wearing gold chains and the latest Miami fashions and driving Nissans, Audis, Ford Broncos, an occasional BMW, or even a Mercedes through the muddy streets of the city. Some of their children attended the expensive English-speaking school; much of Cochabamba's meager nightlife catered to the elite. But as affluent as they may be in Bolivia, this elite would probably not earn as much as working-class families in such cities as Detroit, Frankfurt, or Tokyo.

Traveling outside of Cochabamba for six hours on the back of a truck, fording the same river three times, and following a rugged path for the last 25 kilometers, I reached Pocona and saw a different face of the cocaine trade. Located in a valley a mile and a half above sea level, Pocona is much too high to grow the coca bush. Coca grows best below 6 thousand feet, in the lush area called the Chapare where the eastern Andes meet the western edge of the Amazon basin and rain forest.

Like the woman with whom I was shelling corn, most of the people of Pocona are older, and community life is dominated by women together with their children who are still too young to leave. This particular woman had already lost both of her sons to the Chapare. She did not know it at the time, but within a few months, she was to lose her husband to the same work as well. With so few men, the women are left alone to plant, work, and harvest the fields of potatoes, corn, and fava beans, but with most of the work force missing, the productivity of Pocona has declined substantially.

In what was once a moderately fertile valley, hunger is now a part of life. The daily diet consists almost exclusively of bread, potato soup, boiled potatoes, corn, and tea. The majority of their daily calories comes from the potatoes and from the sugar that they put in their tea. They have virtually no meat or dairy products and very few fresh vegetables. These products are now sent to the Chapare to feed the workers in the coca fields, and the people of Pocona cannot compete against them. The crops that the people of Pocona produce are now difficult to sell because truck drivers find it much more profitable to take goods in and out of the Chapare rather than face the long and unprofitable trip to reach such remote villages as Pocona.

Despite all the hardships caused by so many people being away from the village, one might assume that more cash should be flowing into Pocona from the Chapare, where young men easily earn three dollars a day—three times the average daily wage of porters or laborers in Cochabamba. But this assumption was contradicted by the evidence of Pocona. As one widowed Indian mother of four explained, the first time her sixteen-year-old son came home, he brought bags of food, presents, and money for her and the younger children. She was very glad that he was working in the Chapare. On the second visit home he brought only a plastic bag of white powder for himself, and instead of bringing food, he took away as much as he could carry on the two-day trip back into the Chapare.

The third time, he told his mother that he could not find enough work in the Chapare. As a way to earn more money he made his mother bake as much bread as she could, and he took Mariana, his ten-year-old sister, with him to sell the bread to the workers in the Chapare. According to the mother, he beat the little girl and abused her repeatedly. Moreover, the money she made disappeared. On one of Mariana's trips home to get more bread, the mother had no more wheat or corn flour to supply her son. So, she sent Mariana away to Cochabamba to work as a maid. The enraged son found where Mariana was working and went to the home to demand that she be returned to him. When the family refused, he tried but failed to have her wages paid to him rather than to his mother. Mariana was separated from her family and community, but at least she was not going to be one more of the prostitutes in the Chapare, and for her mother that was more important.

The standard of living in Pocona was never very high, but with the advent of the cocaine boom in Bolivia, the standard has declined. Ten years ago, Pocona's gasoline-powered generator furnished the homes with a few hours of electric light each night. The electricity also allowed a few families to purchase radios, and occasionally someone brought in a movie projector to show a film in a large adobe building on the main square. For the past two years, the people of Pocona have not been able to buy gasoline for their generator. This left the village not only without electricity but without entertainment and radio or film contact with the outside world. A few boys have bought portable radios with their earnings from the Chapare, but their families were unable to replace the batteries. Nights in Pocona are now both dark and silent.

In recent years the national economy of Bolivia has been virtually destroyed, and peasants in communities such as Pocona are reverting to barter as the only means of exchange. The value of the peso may rise or fail by as much as 30 percent in a day; the peasants cannot take a chance on trading their crops for money that may be worth nothing in a week. Cocaine alone has not been responsible for the destruction of the Bolivian economy, but it has been a major contributor. It is not mere coincidence that the world's largest producer of coca is also the country with the world's worst inflation.

During part of 1986, inflation in Bolivia varied at a rate between 2,000 and 13,000 percent, if calculated on a yearly basis. Prices in the cities changed by the hour, and on some days the dollar would rise at the rate of more than 1 percent per hour. A piece of bread cost 150,000 pesos, and an American dollar bought between two and three million pesos on the black market. Large items such as airplane tickets were calculated in the billions of pesos, and on one occasion I helped a man carry a large box of money to pay for such a ticket. It took two professional counters half an hour to count the bills. Workers were paid in stacks of bills that were often half a meter high. Because Bolivia is too undeveloped to print its money, the importation of its own bills printed in West Germany and Brazil was one of the leading imports in the mid-1980s.

Ironically, by no longer being able to participate fully in the money economy, the villagers of Pocona who have chewed coca leaves for centuries now find it difficult to afford the leaves. The narcotics industry pays such a high price that the people of Pocona can afford only the rejected trash from the cocaine industry. Whether chewed or made into a tea, the coca produces a mild lift somewhat like a cup of coffee but without the jagged come down that follows a coffee high. Coca also reduces hunger, thirst, headaches, stomach pains, and the type of altitude sickness known as *sorroche.*

Were this all, coca use might be viewed as merely a bad habit somewhat like drinking coffee, smoking cigarettes, or overindulging in chocolates, but unlike these practices coca actually has a number of marked health benefits. The coca leaf is very high in calcium. In a population with widespread lactose intolerance and in a country without a national system of milk distribution, this calcium source is very important. The calcium also severely reduces cavities in a population with virtually no dental services outside the city. Coca also contains large amounts of vitamins A, C, and D, which are often lacking in the starchy diet of the mountain peasants.

Without coca, and with an excess of corn that they cannot get to market, the people of Pocona now make more *chicha*, a form of homefermented corn beer that tastes somewhat like the silage that American dairymen feed their cows. It is ironic that as an affluent generation of Americans are decreasing their consumption of alcohol in favor of drugs such as cocaine, the people of Pocona are drinking more alcohol to replace their traditional coca. *Chicha*, like most beers, is more nutritious than other kinds of distilled spirits but lacks the health benefits of the coca leaves. It also produces intoxication, something that no amount of coca leaves can do. Coca chewing is such a slow process and produces such a mild effect that a user would have to chew a bushel of leaves to equal the impact of one mixed drink or one snort of cocaine.

In many ways, the problems and complaints of Pocona echo those of any Third World country with a cash crop, particularly those caught in the boom-and-bust cycle characteristic of capitalist systems. Whether it is the sisal boom of the Yucatan, the banana boom of Central America, the rubber boom of Brazil, or the cocaine boom in Bolivia, the same pattern develops. Rural villages are depleted of their work forces. Family and traditional cultural patterns disintegrate. And the people are no longer able to afford certain local products that suddenly become valued in the West. This is what happened to Pocona.

Frequently, the part of a country that produces the boom crop benefits greatly, while other areas suffer greatly. If this were true in Bolivia, benefits accruing in the coca-producing area of the Chapare would outweigh the adjustment problems of such villages as Pocona. As it turns out, however, the Chapare has been even more adversely affected.

Most of the young men who go to the Chapare do not actually work in the coca fields. The coca bush originated in this area and does not require extensive care. One hectare can easily produce 800 kilograms of coca leaves in a year, but not much labor is needed to pick them. After harvesting, the leaves are dried in the sun for three to four days. Most of these tasks can easily be done by the farmer and his family. Wherever one goes in the Chapare one sees coca leaves spread out on large drying cloths. Old people or young children walk up and down these cloths, turning the drying leaves with their whisk brooms.

The need for labor, especially the labor of strong young men, comes in the first stage of cocaine production, in the reduction of large piles of leaves into a small quantity of *pasta*, or coca paste from which the active ingredient, cocaine, can then be refined. Three to five hundred kilograms of leaves must be used to make one kilogram of pure cocaine. The leaves are made into *pasta* by soaking them in vats of kerosene and by applying salt, acetone, and sulfuric acid. To make the chemical reaction occur, someone must trample on the leaves for several days—a process very much like tromping on grapes to make wine, only longer. Because the corrosive mixture dissolves shoes or boots, the young men walk barefooted. These men are called *pistacocas* and usually work in the cool of the night, pounding the green slime with their feet. Each night the chemicals eat away more skin and very quickly open ulcers erupt. Some young men in the Chapare now have feet that are so diseased that they are incapable of standing, much less walking. So, instead, they use their hands to mix the *pasta*, but their hands are eaten away even faster than their feet. Thousands and possibly tens of thousands of young Bolivian men now look like lepers with permanently disfigured hands and feet. It is unlikely that any could return to Pocona and make a decent farmer.

Because this work is painful, the *pistacocas* smoke addictive cigarettes coated with *pasta*. This alleviates their pain and allows them to continue walking the coca throughout the night. The *pasta* is contaminated with chemical residues, and smoking it warps their minds as quickly as the acids eat their hands and feet. Like Mariana's brother, the users become irrational, easily angered, and frequently violent.

Once the boys are no longer able to mix coca because of their mental or their physical condition, they usually become unemployed. If their wounds heal, they may be able to work as loaders or haulers, carrying the cocaine or transporting the controlled chemicals used to process it. By and large, however, women and very small children, called *hormigas* (ants), are better at this work. Some of the young men then return home to their villages; others wander to Cochabamba, where they might live on the streets or try to earn money buying and selling dollars on the black market.

The cocaine manufacturers not only supply their workers with food and drugs, they keep them sexually supplied with young girls who serve as prostitutes as well. Bolivian health officials estimate that nearly half of the people living in the Chapare today have venereal disease. As the boys and girls working there return to their villages, they take these diseases with them. Increasing numbers of children born to infected mothers now have bodies covered in syphilitic sores. In 1985, a worse disease hit with the first case of AIDS. Soon after the victim died, a second victim was diagnosed.

In an effort to control its own drug problem, the United States is putting pressure on Bolivia to eradicate coca production in the Andean countries. The army invaded the Chapare during January of 1986, but after nearly three weeks of being surrounded by the workers in the industry and cut off from their bases, the army surrendered. In a nation the size of Texas and California combined but with a population approximately of the city of Chicago, it is difficult for the government to control its own territory. Neither the Incas nor the Spanish conquistadores were ever able to conquer and administer the jungles of Bolivia, where there are still nomadic bands of Indians who have retreated deep into the jungle to escape Western encroachment. The army of the poorest government in South America is no better able to control this country than its predecessors. The government runs the cities, but the countryside and the jungles operate under their own laws.

One of the most significant effects of the coca trade and of the campaigns to eradicate it has come on the most remote Indians of the jungle area. As the campaign against drugs has pushed production into more inaccessible places and as the world demand has promoted greater cultivation of coca, the coca growers are moving into previously unexplored areas. A coca plantation has been opened along the Chimore river less than an hour's walk from one of the few surviving bands of Yuqui Indians. The Yuquis, famous for their 8-foot-long bows and their 6-foot arrows, are now hovering on the brink of extinction. In the past year, the three bands of a few hundred Yuquis have lost eleven members in skirmishes with outsiders. In turn, they killed several outsiders this year and even shot the missionary who is their main champion against outside invaders.

According to the reports of missionaries, other Indian bands have been enlisted as workers in the cocaine production and trafficking, making virtual slaves out of them. A Bolivian medical doctor explained to me that the Indians are fed the cocaine in their food as a way of keeping them working and preventing their escape. Through cocaine, the drug traffickers may be able to conquer and control these last remnants of the great Indian nations of the Americas. If so, they will accomplish what many have failed to do in the five-hundred-year campaign of Europeans to conquer the free Indians.

The fate of the Indians driven out of their homelands is shown in the case of Juan, a thirteen-year-old Indian boy from the Chimore river where the Yuquis live. I found him one night in a soup kitchen for street children operated in the corner of a potato warehouse by the Maryknoll priests. Juan wore a bright orange undershirt that proclaimed in bold letters Fairfax District Public Schools. I sat with him at the table coated in potato dust while he ate his soup with his fellow street children, some of whom were as young as four years old. He told me what he could remember of his life on the Chimore; he did not know to which tribe he was born or what language he had spoken with his mother. It was difficult for Juan to talk about his Indian past in a country where it is a grave insult to be called an Indian. Rather than talk about the Chimore or the Chapare, he wanted to ask me questions because I was the first American he had ever met. Was I stronger than everyone else because he had heard that Americans were the strongest people in the world? Did we really have wolves and bears in North America, and was I afraid of them? Had I been to the Chapare? Did I use cocaine?

In between his questions, I found out that Juan had come to Cochabamba several years ago with his mother. The two had fled the Chapare, but he did not know why. Once in the city they lived on the streets for a few years until his mother died, and he had been living alone ever since. He had become a *polilla* (moth), as they call such street boys. To earn money he washed cars and he sold cigarettes laced with *pasta*. When he tired of talking about himself and asking about the animals of North America, he and his two friends made plans to go out to one of the nearby *pasta* villages the next day.

Both the Chapare (which supplied the land for growing coca) and highland villages such as Pocona (which supplied the labor) were suffering from the cocaine boom. Where then is the profit? The only other sites in Bolivia are the newly developing manufacturing towns where cocaine is refined. Whereas in the past most of this refining took place in Colombia, both the manufacturers and the traffickers find it easier and cheaper to have the work done in Bolivia, closer to the source of coca leaves and closer to much cheaper sources of labor. The strength of the Colombian government and its closeness to the United States also make the drug trafficking more difficult there than in Bolivia, with its weak, unstable government in La Paz.

Toco is one of the villages that has turned into a processing point for cocaine town. Located at about the same altitude as Pocona but only a half-day by truck from the Chapare, Toco cannot grow coca, but the village is close enough to the source to become a major producer of the pasta. Traffickers bring in large shipments of coca leaves and work them in backyard "kitchens." Not only does Toco still have its young men at home and still have food and electricity, but it has work for a few hundred young men from other villages.

Unlike Pocona, for which there are only a few trucks each week, trucks flow in and out of Toco every day. Emblazoned with names such as Rambo, El Padrino (The Godfather), and Charles Bronson rather than the traditional truck names of San José, Virgen de Copacabana, or Flor de Urkupina, these are the newest and finest trucks found in Bolivia. Going in with a Bolivian physician and another anthropologist from the United States, I easily got a ride, along with a dozen Indians on a truck, which was hauling old car batteries splattered with what appeared to be vomit.

A few kilometers outside of Toco we were stopped by a large crowd of Indian peasants. Several dozen women sat around on the ground and in the road spinning yarn and knitting. Most of the women had babies tied to their shoulders in the brightly colored *awayu* cloth, which the women use to carry everything from potatoes to lambs. Men stood around with farm tools, which they now used to block the roads. The men brandished their machetes and rakes at us, accusing us all of being smugglers and *pistacocas*. Like the Indians on the truck with us, the three of us stood silently and expressionless in the melee.

The hostile peasants were staging an ad hoc strike against the coca trade. They had just had their own fields of potatoes washed away in a flash flood. Now without food and without money to replant, they were demanding that someone help them or they would disrupt all traffic to and from Toco. Shouting at us, several of them climbed on board the truck. Moving among the nervous passengers, they checked for a shipment of coca leaves, kerosene, acid, or anything else that might be a part of the coca trade. Having found nothing, they reluctantly let us pass with stern warnings not to return with cocaine or *pasta*. A few weeks after our encounter with the strikers, their strike ended and most of the men went off to look for work in the Chapare and in Toco; without a crop, the cocaine traffic was their only hope of food for the year.

On our arrival in Toco we found out that the batteries loaded with us in the back of the truck had been hollowed out and filled with acid to be used in making *pasta*. *Chicha* vomit had been smeared around to discourage anyone from checking them. After removal of the acid, the same batteries were then filled with plastic bags of cocaine to be smuggled out of Toco and into the town of Cliza and on to Cochabamba and the outside world.

Toco is an expanding village with new cement-block buildings going up on the edge of town and a variety of large plumbing pipes, tanks, and drains being installed. It also has a large number of motorcycles and cars. By Bolivian standards it is a rich village, but it is still poorer than the average village in Mexico or Brazil. Soon after our arrival in Toco, we were followed by a handful of men wanting to sell us *pasta*, and within a few minutes the few had grown to nearly fifty young men anxious to assist us. Most of them were on foot, but some of them circled us in motorcycles, and many of them were armed with guns and machetes. They became suspicious and then openly hostile when we convinced them that we did not want to buy *pasta*. To escape them we took refuge in the home of an Indian family and waited for the mob to disperse.

When we tried to leave the village a few hours later, we were trapped by a truckload of young men who did not release us until they had checked with everyone we had met with in the village. They wondered why we were there if not to buy *pasta*. We were rescued by the doctor who accompanied us; she happened to be the niece of a popular Quechua writer. Evoking the memory of her uncle who had done so much for the Quechua people, she convinced the villagers of Toco that we were Bolivian doctors who worked with her in Cochabamba, and that we were not foreigners coming to buy *pasta* or to spy on them. An old veteran who claimed that he had served in the Chaco War with her uncle vouched for us, but in return for having saved us he then wanted us to buy *pasta* from him.

The wealth generated by the coca trade from Bolivia is easy to see. It is in the European cars cruising the streets of Cochabamba and Santa Cruz, and in the nice houses in the suburbs. It is in the motorcycles and jeeps in Toco, Cliza, and Trinidad. The poverty is difficult to see because it is in the remote villages like Pocona, among the impoverished miners in the village Porco, and intertwined in the lives of peasants throughout the highland districts of Potosi and Oruro. But it is in these communities such as Pocona that 70 percent of the population of Bolivia lives.

For every modern home built with cocaine money in Cochabamba, a tin mine lies abandoned in Potosi that lost many of its miners when the world price for tin fell and they had to go to the Chapare for food. For every new car in Santa Cruz or every new motorcycle in Toco, a whole village is going hungry in the mountains.

The money for coca does not go to the Bolivians. It goes to the criminal organizations that smuggle the drugs out of the country and into the United States and Europe. A gram of pure cocaine on the streets of Cochabamba costs five dollars; the same gram on the streets of New York, Paris, or Berlin costs over a hundred dollars. The price increase occurs outside Bolivia.

The financial differential is evident in the case of the American housewife and mother sentenced to the Cochabamba prison after being caught with six and a half kilograms of cocaine at the airport. Like all the other women in the prison, she now earns money washing laundry by hand at a cold-water tap in the middle of the prison yard. She receives the equivalent of twenty cents for each pair of pants she washes, dries, and irons. In Bolivian prisons, the prisoner has to furnish his or her own food, clothes, medical attention, and even her own furniture.

She was paid five thousand dollars to smuggle the cocaine out of Bolivia to the Caribbean. Presumably someone else was then to be paid even more to smuggle it into the United States or Europe. The money that the American housewife received to smuggle the cocaine out of the country would pay the salary of eighty *pistacocas* for a month. It would also pay the monthly wages of 250 Bolivian schoolteachers, who earn the equivalent of twenty U.S. dollars per month in pay. Even though her price seemed high by Bolivian standards, it is a small part of the final money generated by the drugs. When cut and sold on the streets of the United States, her shipment of cocaine would probably bring in five to seven million dollars. Of that amount, however, only about five hundred dollars goes to the Bolivian farmer.

The peasant in the Chapare growing the coca earns three times as much for a field of coca as he would for a field of papayas. But he is only the first in a long line of people and transactions that brings the final product of cocaine to the streets of the West. At the end of the line, cocaine sells for four to five times its weight in gold.

The United States government made all aid programs and loans to Bolivia dependent on the country's efforts to destroy coca. This produces programs in which Bolivian troops go into the most accessible areas and uproot a few fields of aging or diseased coca plants. Visiting drug-enforcement agents from the United States together with American congressmen applaud, make their reports on the escalating war against drugs, and then retire to a city hotel where they drink hot cups of coca tea and cocktails.

These programs hurt primarily the poor farmer who tries to make a slightly better living by growing coca rather than papayas. The raids on the fields and cocaine factories usually lead to the imprisonment of ulcerated *pistacocas* and women and children *hormigas* from villages throughout Bolivia. Local authorities present the burned fields and full prisons to Washington visitors as proof that the Bolivian government has taken a hard stance against drug trafficking.

International crime figures with bank accounts in New York and Zurich get the money. Bolivia ends up with hunger in its villages, young men with their hands and feet permanently maimed, higher rates of venereal disease, chronic food shortages, less kerosene, higher school dropout rates, increased drug addiction, and a worthless peso.

MAKING A LIVING

One of the most significant problems facing humans today is the task of feeding all the people of the world. The amount of arable land in the world is decreasing at an alarming rate, mostly due to overuse of the land and poor agricultural practices. Much human suffering occurs in areas where poverty and increasing population allow the land little or no relief from these abuses. Attempts to increase agricultural production in many areas of the world through the use of new hybrid crops and increased inputs of fertilizer and pesticides have met limited success or outright failure. The expense of these technological approaches make them impractical in many areas of the world, and traditional food producing practices often make better sense since they are suited to the environmental limitations and social organization of respective societies. Increasingly, anthropologists attempt to help people improve their food production by working with their traditional cultural practices instead of attempting to replace them with expensive technological approaches.

Humans have devised five basic subsistence patterns, or ways of making a living from their environment. Hunting and gathering is the oldest form of human subsistence, and humans have been hunter-gatherers for about 99% of their existence. Hunting and gathering was the only form of subsistence until about ten thousand years ago, when agriculture was developed; and hunting and gathering is still pursued by people in a few societies today. Hunter-gatherers subsist by hunting animals and collecting wild plant foods.

Horticulture is food production based on gardening. Horticultural societies normally exist in forested areas of the world, where trees are cleared and burned and the resulting ash is used to fertilize the gardens. Horticulturists plant a wide variety of plants in their gardens. This diversity mimics naturally diverse ecosystems and helps the plants to resist blights and insect pests. It also provides the people with a varied diet. Gardens are normally used for several years, until production begins to decrease, before the clearing and planting process begins in a new location. The old garden then is allowed to regenerate into new forest growth.

Pastoralism is food production based on the herding of animals. Pastoral societies exist in areas of the world where grasslands are found; and they are usually nomadic, moving seasonally with their herds in search of pasturage and water.

Agriculture is the most widespread subsistence pattern in the world today. Traditional agriculture involves the use of human labor and draft animals to produce food. While traditional agriculture involves intensive labor, it normally provides a high ratio of food energy in return for the labor invested. Modern industrial agriculture involves the use of machinery, fertilizer, and pesticides and herbicides to produce large quantities of food. Industrial agriculture requires a high amount of energy input through fuel and provides a low ratio of food energy in return for the labor invested. One problem with industrial agri-

culture is that as fuel prices increase, the price of food also rises.

The readings in this section provide insight into the interaction between culture, the environment, and the problems of food production. In "A New Lay of the Land," Holly B. Brough outlines some of the causes of the problems that people in many areas of the world face as they attempt to make a living in environments that are overused and barely suitable for food production. In "When Brothers Share a Wife," Melvyn C. Goldstein describes the relationship between marriage patterns, subsistence, and the environment that has allowed a traditional society adapt to its environment. Susan H. Lees, in "Oaxaca's Spiraling Race for Water," describes the problems that resulted when new technology was introduced in the arid environment. Finally, Gerald F. Murray discusses, in "The Domestication of Wood in Haiti," a development project that combined anthropological research into the subsistence practices of Haitian farmers with involvement by those farmers in the creation of a successful reforestation project.

A New Lay of the Land

Holly B. Brough

As you read:
1. *What impact does the uneven distribution of arable land have on poor peasants? on the land?*

Fifty years after the tribes of Israel entered the Promised Land, their God declared a Jubilee celebration, when all land fortunes accumulated during those years were redivided among the original owners. Every half-century thereafter, the land was equitably distributed among the people. Today in most developing countries, the Promised Land looks more like a wasteland and a Jubilee is long overdue.

Land ownership in much of the developing world is highly skewed. While a few wealthy plantation owners and cattle ranchers monopolize fruitful land, thousands more peasants are pressed to the diminishing margins of soil and society. In Guatemala, for instance, a mere 2 percent of landowners claim 63 percent of agricultural land.

Worse, the world's growing contingent of landless peasants must rake fragile hillsides, torch rain forests, and plow near-deserts for their next meal, driving the environmental threats of global deforestation and desertification. Norman Myers, a British forestry analyst, estimates that landless peasants clear three-fifths of the 42 million acres of rain forest lost annually. Small farmers and their livestock also pose a major danger to the third of the earth's land surface that is threatened with desertification.

Land reform strikes at the heart of these problems by creating small farms for many, rather than large farms for a few. More equitably distributing agricultural land can stimulate rural economies and relieve poverty. Bolstered by efforts to curb population growth and promote soil conservation, land reform could help stem environmental destruction in many countries.

Yet land reform has been relegated to the darkest recesses of the international development effort. Promising a dramatic transformation of the rural power structure, as it does, reform is an ambitious undertaking more easily ignored than initiated.

Indeed, the odds against land reform are hard to overstate. The power of landed elites and tenacious practical obstacles make redistribution an unpopular policy among government leaders despite its appeal on election platforms. Resistance to reform is fierce, and often violent. Still, if the earth is to survive and its people prosper, land reform is indispensable.

The Lay of the Land

Across centuries and cultures, from the Incan empire to the feudal estates of pre-revolutionary France, land has been inequitably divided between haves and have-nots. As feudalism crumbled in Europe, however, its pattern re-emerged overseas. Many of the rural environmental problems facing developing countries today trace their roots to colonialism.

Colonialism spread European immigrants sparsely over fertile land in Africa, South America, and Asia, and pushed out the native majority. In Algeria, 20,000 Europeans seized 6 million acres of alluvial, water-blessed land, leaving 630,000 Algerians with 12 million acres of parched, thin-soiled earth. Spanish and Portuguese colonizers of Latin America recreated the sprawling estates of their mother countries, relegating native Indians to surrounding uplands.

Export crops have taken over where colonialism left off. Large farms devoted to bananas, cotton, sugar, and beef cattle have virtually monopolized the rich soils of Central America, according to Jeffrey Leonard, vice president for environmental quality at the World Wildlife Fund—Conservation Foundation in Washington, D.C. In the African Sahel, peanut and cotton plantations line the irrigated valleys of the southern Senegal and Niger rivers, pressing small farmers north into areas of sparse rainfall and poor soils.

Population growth further cuts into peasant holdings. Generations of dividing land among heirs has left mere patches of soil to family members. In Tamil Nadu, India, marginal holdings (less than 2.5 acres) shot up from 73 percent of farms in 1972, to 82 percent 10 years later. The remaining 18 percent control 76 percent of the land, but much of this is in plots not much larger than five acres. Complicating matters, properties are fragmented over time. Tilling scattered bits of land drains a farmer's time and investment, often ruling out conservation.

Land concentration figures highlight the legacy of colonialism and the impact of export-based agriculture. In El Salvador, where 2 percent of landowners hold 60 percent of the land, almost two-thirds of rural families have little or none. White farmers, who comprise less than 1 percent of Zimbabwe's people, command 39 percent of all land. Although statistics in Asia are less dramatic, 3 percent of Filipino landowners control a quarter of the country; 60 percent of rural families either can't survive on the little land they own or own no land at all.

Forced off good land by plantations and wealthier farms, many peasants return to work as wage-laborers. During critical planting and harvest times they must neglect their own scraps of earth, again precluding proper soil husbandry.

Those left behind try to wrench the greatest yield from already deficient soil. As one labor leader from the National Association of Farm Workers in El Salvador laments: "What does a poor *campesino* [peasant farmer] do? He starts working what little land he does have year after year without leaving it fallow to recuperate. Soon the land doesn't produce and becomes barren. The soil is gone." Within the memories of *campesinos* in the Honduran highlands, fallow periods have plummeted from an average of 15 to 20 years, to 0 to 7 years.

Without rest, soil loses the shallow seam of organic matter that contains crop-feeding nutrients. Soil structure gradually collapses, reducing the earth's ability to hold rainwater and resist erosion. The process only accelerates on hillsides.

Ambiguous rights to land place the environment in double jeopardy. For tenants unsure whether they will till the same earth next season, good soil husbandry makes little economic sense. Moreover, since some laws give tenants ownership of land they improve, landlords may protect their holdings by evicting tenants ambitious enough to try conservation.

Squatters likewise have no incentive to preserve the soil. According to a World Bank study of four provinces in Thailand, untitled farmers build "bunds"—raised earth walls that catch soil and water—at half the rate of farmers with clear land titles. Getting a bank loan to finance soil conservation is nearly impossible for those without a land title to put up as collateral.

As a last resort, cornered by poverty and tiny plots of infertile land, peasants flee to the frontier—forest or desert—often with their government's blessings, and try to scrape a living from smoldering tree ashes or shifting sands.

Life on the Edge

"We ate the forest like a fire. There was no forest left. We pulled the stumps and cut the limbs. We thought that after a year of this, it would get better, but it sent us downwards."

These words, spoken by an Ethiopian farmer uprooted from his ancestral home, epitomize the plight of the world's swelling ranks of landless peasants. Today in Honduras, 200,000 families, or about 35 percent of the rural population, subsist on forest lands; in Thailand, a million squatter families have cleared nearly one-fifth of forest reserves for farming.

Both migrant peasants and the indigenous tribes they displace suffer from the move to the forests. First, the indigenous practice of shifting slash-and-burn agriculture—a sustainable cycle of clearing, cropping, fallowing, then reclearing forest land—is interrupted as more landless flood the forest. Encroachment on tribal lands has forced the Palaw'ans of the Philippines to reduce fallow time from eight to two years.

Migrants adopt a far more destructive form of shifting agriculture. They farm cleared land until crop yields deteriorate with the soil, then move into the woods. Seventy percent of Peruvian farmers who migrate to the Amazon do not settle even for a few years, but continuously open up new land.

During the mid-1980s, shifting agriculture in Indonesia cleared away about a million acres of forests each year, believes Soedjarwo, Indonesia's former minister of forests. Logging felled less than one-fifth as much area during the same period. But forestry practices encourage peasant migration by building roads that the land-hungry follow.

In Latin America, cattle ranches trail in the wake of peasants, subsuming the abandoned land. Ranchers in Central America give settlers short-term leases on uncleared frontier, then move in their cattle once the leases are up. Expanding ranches constantly push the peasant frontline further into the forest.

Government laws also lock squatters into destructive ways. Ecuador's Institute for Agrarian Reform and Colonization, which has encouraged settlement of remote areas, grants title to forest plots only if at least half the land has been cleared. Similar laws exist in countries from Malaysia to Nicaragua. To secure this promised land, migrants clear as much as they can. A study of setters in Peru found that squatters cut forests at twice the rate of legal tenants—2.7 acres a year versus 1.3.

States have colonized fragile ecosystems in lieu of real land reforms to relieve pressure on overcrowded land and pacify angry peasants. Brazil's Amazon colonization scheme is perhaps the most notorious, but it is not alone. Bolivia, Ecuador, and Peru have similar programs, while Ethiopia has been relocating farmers from the war-torn north for years. An Indonesian program has resettled 722,000 Javanese peasant families on forest-blanketed outer islands since 1970, while at least 574,000 families have migrated on their own.

The environment has paid in full for these programs. From 1964 to 1985, the Amazon lost 7.4 million acres to Ecuador's colonization efforts, and Indonesian settlers leveled 500,000 to 700,000 acres of forests a year during the 1980s alone.

Burning forests causes soil to irretrievably lose its fertile organic matter, already at low levels in rain forests, where 90 percent is stored in vegetation. Repeated burning eradicates sensitive native flora, allowing weeds to invade. And, with the absorptive topsoil gone, water runs off, taking more earth with it. The western highlands of Guatemala annually lose as much as 16 tons of soil per acre. In India, tree and plant destruction allow 7 billion tons of soil to wash into the sea each year, including 6 million tons of plant nutrients.

Downstream, flooding increases and water supplies are depleted. The flood-prone area of Honduras has doubled in the last 10 years from 50 to 100 million acres, damaging crops, roads, bridges, and dams. Silt fills reservoirs, like the one supplying Honduras's capital of Tegucigalpa, while eroded hillsides, now impervious to water, cannot replenish groundwater supplies.

In the fragile arid and semi-arid regions of Africa, many of the same factors are at work. The Jebel al-Awilya Dam in Sudan's Western Nile province irrigates tenant farms of 5 to 18 acres along the river's basins. Farmers excluded from the project have been pushed to sandy uplands and a belt consisting of dunes and clay soil, where the combination of population and poor soils has forced them to forsake fallow periods and cultivate more land simply to feed themselves. According to Sudanese geographer Anwar Abdu, formerly stable dunes in this area have begun to spread.

The problem is aggravated by drought. Threatened by dry spells, peasants pull as much marginal land into production as possible in the hope that at least some will yield crops. In western Sudan, the cultivation of millet (a staple crop for the poor) has expanded northwards 120 miles beyond the accepted growing region into delicate Saharan soils. Since these soils are most fragile during drought, erosion problems are compounded.

Herculean Challenge

The benefits of effective land reform are indisputable. Farmers who own their land are better stewards of it. Small family farms absorb more labor than mechanized plantations—employing family members who might otherwise head for forests or job-scarce cities. While sheer numbers preclude settling all peasants who need land,

A Common Tragedy

For all the ecological ravages attributable to inequitable land distribution, the collapse of common property ownership can be equally destructive. From African pastoralists controlling access to watering holes, to Indian villagers monitoring tree cutting in local forests, traditional forms of common resource management have minimized human impacts on fragile resources and ecosystems.

Forests, grasslands, fisheries, and water all constitute common properties, subject to use but not ownership. But contrary to the familiar "tragedy of the commons" scenario, where each user exploits a resource for private profit, common property systems are not "free-for-alls." Recognized authorities control access and preserve the resource.

Among the Berber herders of Morocco, land susceptible to degradation was carefully monitored by each subtribal group's amghar n'tougga (chief of grass). Vested with authority to decide when and where to move livestock, the chief of grass would close grazing areas seasonally to allow the trampled range to regenerate.

Forest resources are protected similarly. In the Indian hill village of Silpar in Uttar Pradesh, each family is informally responsible for reporting illegal tree cutting to the village council. The violator must pay a fine, half of which goes to the family that turned in the transgressor.

As vital as common properties are for the earth, they are equally important to the poor. Village studies in the dryland regions of India by N.S. Jodha, formerly of the International Crop Research Institute for the Semi-Arid Tropics in Hyderabad, India, reveal that wood, water, and fodder from common properties supply peasants with half their income during drought years.

Sadly, common properties are being besieged from all sides—by population growth, cultural changes, and state policies. First and foremost, however, the

resources themselves are shrinking from privatization and nationalization.

Privatization usurps grazing areas, especially those reserved for dry seasons. The Il Chamus herders of Kenya have seen one of their dry-season grazing areas reduced by 26,000 acres since the 1940s, as small formers encroached on their range. The hungry peasants, in turn, had been edged off land further south by the expansion of commercial farms. The Il Chamus have been forced to graze their herds in swamps, trampling the surrounding soil and vegetation.

Elsewhere in Africa where farms have seized dry-season grazing land, herders are pushed onto poorer soil when it is most susceptible to disruption. Multiplied across the globe, these local cases of livestock overcrowding have led to intense land degradation. According to the United Nations, overgrazing has degraded 7.7 billion acres—about 80 percent of the world's dry lands.

State-sponsored privatization also undermines common property regimes. The indigenous Indian community of Pasu Urcu in eastern Ecuador abandoned its fallow system in the 1970s after the land reform agency informed them that uncultivated land could be claimed by nearby peasants. Their sustainable cycle of shifting cultivation was severed.

In India, state land reforms have distributed traditional common properties, much of it to well-off farmers who had illegally encroached on the areas. Jodha's studies show that common property land has been nearly halved in size since 1950. More and more people foraging smaller areas for wood and fodder spell ruin for these ecologically marginal areas.

While privatization directly attacks common resources, nationalization sabotages the systems that manage them, obscuring lines of authority over the resource. In the Sudan, the Unregistered Land Act of 1970 gave the state title to rural land, undermining the power of village sheikhs to control tree cutting.

When people aren't answerable to a single authority, a common property can swiftly be opened to all—and the environment loses out.

Preserving common property systems can begin by protecting the resource. Since April 1988, the Colombian government has ceded nearly 30 million acres of the Amazon to indigenous tribes for collective and inalienable ownership. Jodha calls for a complete moratorium on conversion of common property, which would give users legal leverage to protect it. Careful research at the local level can determine how nationalization or privatization plans would hurt common property.

Ultimately, however, common property is more than a resource. Careful attention must be paid to the communities that manage such properties, and the forces undermining these communities.

the new income that beneficiaries earn can increase demand for goods and services that others might supply.

Contrary to what might be expected, reforms also increase agricultural output. Except for slips directly after land transfers, supported small farmers have proven themselves more productive than large farms. Small owner-operated farms in Taiwan produce 50 percent more than sugar plantations in the Philippines.

In the dozens of countries where land reforms have been undertaken, however, reality has seldom met the promise (see Table 1 on the following page). In most cases, a fraction of landless families have benefited. Measured against the enormous obstacles facing land reforms—resistant landowners, uncommitted leaders, unorganized peasants, and sketchy land records—these results are not surprising. Land reform is a risky proposition, and there is much room for error.

Imposing limits on farm size is a prime method for freeing private land for redistribution. Large landowners, however, can dodge such ceilings. In Mexico, estate owners held on to their property during land reforms in the 1930s by registering it under *prestanombres* (name lenders), who were either children or sympathetic neighbors. Incomplete rural land records are easily altered to this purpose.

Idle or "unproductive" estate lands are theoretically ripe for the taking. Almost invariably, farms use land in inverse proportion to their size: the larger they are, the more land is left alone. Although some land is fallow, more often estate owners let land lie because their incomes do not depend on agriculture. Their economic lifelines run to city businesses, while farms are mere investments against inflation. Brazil, with 9 million landless households, hoards an estimated 82 million idle acres of farmland.

When it comes to seizing this land, however, political opponents to reform have defined "unproductive" ambiguously in the law. Without a clear definition, land liable for expropriation cannot be taken. Landowners in Ecuador and Honduras have slipped through this loophole.

Then there are money questions. Crushing foreign debts and fear that farm productivity will plummet compel countries to exempt export cropland from reforms. Politicians opposed to the 1969 reform in Peru arranged generous compensations for former landowners, partially tying the hands of the government because of limited funds.

Even where landowners surrender land, they give up only their poorest acres. Of the 62 million acres of land parceled out under Mexico's reform in the 1960s, only 10 percent was arable.

"Land to the Tiller" programs, designed to give tenants title to their rented land, often complement legislation that limits farm size, but they present their own hurdles. The programs instead can compel owners to evict tenants preemptively. For victims of such practices, justice is often elusive. Bureaucratic red tape can also bog

Table 1. History of Land Reforms, Selected Countries

Taiwan	Prior to reform, United States and Japan conducted detailed land ownership survey. Reform (1949–1953) slashed rent, and sold public lands and farmland to tenants. Local Farm Tenancy Committees comprised of tenants, officials, and landlords settled disputes and enforced the law.
China	Post-revolution reform (1950) created cooperatives but allowed peasants small private plots. Since then, a legal roller coaster has formed communes and eliminated private plots (1958), reinstated private plots (1961), given peasants "use certificates" to land with no rights to sell or lease (1980), and in 1990 reclaimed property given to peasants.
Kenya	1954 Swynnerton Plan consolidated land fragments and gave title to farmers. By 1978, the reform had affected nearly half of the land.
Zimbabwe	From 1980 to 1989, the state settled 52,000 households onto farms abandoned at independence and public land. State legally owns settlement land (mostly of poor quality) and users cannot sell or inherit it.
Nicaragua	1979 reform seized land held by former ruler Anastasio Somoza and his cronies for state farms and established cooperatives from under-

utilized large farms. State gave credit, education, and health care to peasants. President Violeta Chamorra is trying to restore cooperative and state farmland to former owners.

Mexico Continual reform since 1917 has created group farms (ejidos), which cannot be sold or rented to non-heirs. After 1940s, state invested heavily in large commercial farms immune to reform, forcing the struggling ejido farmers to seek low-paying agricultural work elsewhere.

Chile A fairly successful reform was reversed after military coup in 1973. More than a quarter of reform land was restored to landowners, and reform cooperatives were divided into private holdings.

Sources: William Theisenhusen, ed., *Searching for Agrarian Reform in Latin America* (Winchester, MA: Unwin Hyman Press, 1989); Roy L. Prosterman, et al., eds., *Agrarian Reform and Grassroots Development: Ten Case Studies* (Boulder, CO: Lynne Reinner Publishers, 1990); John P. Powelson and Richard Stock, eds., *The Peasant Betrayed* (Washington, D.C.: CATO Institute, 1990).

down land titling, as in the case of El Salvador.

Since it is obviously easier to transfer land to those already living on it, the truly landless also lose out from "Land to the Tiller" programs. Peru's land reform of 1969 did little for seasonal workers and *minifundistas* (marginal farmers) of the highlands.

Land titling—giving formal deeds either to reform beneficiaries or illegal squatters—is another dimension of land reforms. Though often well-supported (the World Bank underwrites projects in northeast Brazil and Thailand), titling frequently excludes women, who shoulder 70 percent of the farming burden in Africa and 50 percent in Latin America. Women need title to obtain loans for seed and fertilizer. Titling also impinges on common properties.

Where all other obstacles are surmounted, supporting small-scale farmers with credit and advice is the final challenge. After doling out vast amounts of land in the 1930s, Mexico's government abandoned the struggling new landowners in the late 1940s, underwriting northern plantations producing for export instead. Peasants unable to survive on their land were forced into low-paying labor on these very plantations.

The fundamental issue that underlies all the barriers to land reform is summed up by Demetrios Christodoulou, formerly a researcher with the U.N. Food and Agriculture Organization: "Agrarian reform is about power." In rural societies, owning land means wielding power; surrendering it means sharing that power. Few landlords surrender willingly.

Yet despite the odds, some countries have succeeded at land reform. Japan, South Korea, Taiwan, and China all pushed through comprehensive reforms in the wake of wars or in the midst of political and social upheaval. In Korea, the landed aristocracy had been weakened during World War II and tenants were already refusing to pay rent before the reform. In Kerala, India, an organized, literate peasantry and a political party responsive to their demands pushed through a strong land reform in the 1970s against stiff landlord opposition.

Peasants today are pushing against similarly entrenched power bases opposed to land reform. It promises to be a long struggle.

Up from the Roots

Grass-roots efforts may be the best hope for putting land reform back on national agendas, and such movements appear to be increasing. Since 1989, landless peasants in Paraguay have undertaken about 90 land invasions—occupying and demanding rights to private and public land. Although the peasants are constantly threatened with military repression, invasions continue. In Brazil, which has a long, brutal history of peasant land struggles, demonstrations and land occupations persevere, spearheaded by the National Landless Workers Movement.

Although everywhere confronted with political intransigence and landlord violence, the poor are not fighting alone. In Tamil Nadu, a group called LAFTI (Land for the Tillers Freedom) is bringing land to the poor through bank loans, legal aid, and pressure on landlords. Land dividends are small, but as one woman said, "The one acre of land is precious for my family."

To Brazilian peasants, who have gained land through occupations and legal battles, the National Development Bank in Rio Grande do Sul is extending credit without demanding land as collateral. Thus, during the first uncertain years of farming, peasants are freed from worrying about foreclosure.

Since 1981, World Neighbors, a development group based in Oklahoma City, Oklahoma, has been teaching soil and water conservation methods to Filipino farmers working tiny plots of steep, rugged land on Cebu Island. These methods have eliminated the need to cut forests for fresh land. Also, in Guerrero state, Mexico, the peasant-run Coalition of Collective Ejidos (cooperative farms) provides a range of services from credit to women's workshops. More than 1,000 peasants have raised their incomes through this program.

By strengthening, educating, and empowering the poor, these efforts are critical to reform. But without support at the national and international level, they cannot succeed. Foreign donors can further set the stage for reform by buttressing the work of grass-roots groups and related outside organizations. With financial and technical support, governments or private groups also can gather data vital to implementing reforms: the amount of farmland available, beneficiary groups, acres-per-family ratios, costs, etc.

More directly, donors can earmark aid funds for land redistribution. Ensuring that targeted money is actually used to purchase land rather than just title beneficiaries of colonization, however, is essential if such efforts are to work. Typically, the World Bank and the U.S. Agency for International Development have supported the latter programs.

For the environment's sake, legal codes and their interpretation need changing. As Alvaro Umano, Costa Rica's former minister of natural resources, contends, "We need to address the problem of the law that says to get possession of land you have to show improvements, and to show improvements you have to remove the forest cover." In short, colonization schemes that level forests and destroy common property are not reform.

Finally, the end of the Cold War bodes well for land reform. Donors and developing states now may be less likely to perceive radical land reform as a Communist conspiracy and more as a policy capable of addressing the needs of both the environment and the people.

Still, the difficulties of reform cannot be glossed over. There are no quick fixes. Building the conditions and coalitions for reform carefully, and putting the issue back on the global agenda whenever possible, are the first steps. With these prerequisites in place, today's landless—and the world—may look forward to a jubilee year, and a healthier promised land.

3

FENNELL
KIDD
JUSTIN
15TH

When Brothers Share a Wife

Melvyn C. Goldstein

As you read:

1. Why have many Tibetans traditionally chosen fraternal polyandry as a marriage pattern?
2. Does this marriage pattern make good sense in this part of
   the world? Why or why not?

Eager to reach home, Dorje drives his yaks hard over the 17,000-foot mountain pass, stopping only once to rest. He and his two older brothers, Pema and Sonam, are jointly marrying a woman from the next village in a few weeks, and he has to help with the preparations.

Dorje, Pema, and Sonam are Tibetans living in Limi, a 200-square-mile area in the northwest corner of Nepal, across the border from Tibet. The form of marriage they are about to enter—fraternal polyandry in anthropological parlance—is one of the world's rarest forms of marriage but is not uncommon in Tibetan society, where it has been practiced from time immemorial. For many Tibetan social strata, it traditionally represented the ideal form of marriage and family.

The mechanics of fraternal polyandry are simple. Two, three, four, or more brothers jointly take a wife, who leaves her home to come and live with them. Traditionally, marriage was arranged by parents, with children, particularly females, having little or no say. This is changing somewhat nowadays, but it is still unusual for children to marry without their parents' consent. Marriage ceremonies vary by income and region and range from all the brothers sitting together as grooms to only the

eldest one formally doing so. The age of the brothers plays an important role in determining this: very young brothers almost never participate in actual marriage ceremonies, although they typically join the marriage when they reach their midteens.

The eldest brother is normally dominant in terms of authority, that is, in managing the household, but all the brothers share the work and participate as sexual partners. Tibetan males and females do not find the sexual aspect of sharing a spouse the least bit unusual, repulsive, or scandalous, and the norm is for the wife to treat all the brothers the same.

Offspring are treated similarly. There is no attempt to link children biologically to particular brothers, and a brother shows no favoritism toward his child even if he knows he is the real father because, for example, his older brothers were away at the time the wife became pregnant. The children, in turn, consider all of the brothers as their fathers and treat them equally, even if they also know who is their real father. In some regions children use the term "father" for the eldest brother and "father's brother" for the others, while in other areas they call all the brothers by one term, modifying this by the use of "elder" and "younger."

Unlike our own society, where monogamy is the only form of marriage permitted, Tibetan society allows a variety of marriage types, including monogamy, fraternal polyandry, and polygyny. Fraternal polyandry and monogamy are the most common forms of marriage, while polygyny typically occurs in cases where the first wife is barren. The widespread practice of fraternal polyandry, therefore, is not the outcome of a law requiring brothers to marry jointly. There is choice, and in fact, divorce traditionally was relatively simple in Tibetan society. If a brother in a polyandrous marriage became dissatisfied and wanted to separate, he simply left the main house and set up his own household. In such cases, all the children stayed in the main household with the remaining brother(s), even if the departing brother was known to be the real father of one or more of the children.

The Tibetans' own explanation for choosing fraternal polyandry is materialistic. For example, when I asked Dorje why he decided to marry with his two brothers rather than take his own wife, he thought for a moment, then said it prevented the division of his family's farm (and animals) and thus facilitated all of them achieving a higher standard of living. And when I later asked Dorje's bride whether it wasn't difficult for her to cope with three brothers as husbands, she laughed and echoed that rationale of avoiding fragmentation of the family land, adding that she expected to be better off economically, since she would have three husbands working for her and her children.

Exotic as it may seem to Westerners, Tibetan fraternal polyandry is thus in many ways analogous to the way primogeniture functioned in nineteenth-century England. Primogeniture dictated that the eldest son inherited the family estate, while younger sons had to leave home and seek their own employment—for example, in the military or the clergy. Primogeniture maintained family estates intact over generations by permitting only one heir per generation. Fraternal polyandry also accomplishes this

but does so by keeping all the brothers together with just one wife so that there is only one set of heirs per generation.

While Tibetans believe that in this way fraternal polyandry reduces the risk of family fission, monogamous marriages among brothers need not necessarily precipitate the division of the family estate: brothers could continue to live together, and the family land could continue to be worked jointly. When I asked Tibetans about this, however, they invariably responded that such joint families are unstable because each wife is primarily oriented to her own children and interested in their success and well-being over that of the children of other wives. For example, if the youngest brother's wife had three sons while the eldest brother's wife had only one daughter, the wife of the youngest brother might begin to demand more resources for her children since, as males, they represent the future of the family. Thus, the children from different wives in the same generation are competing sets of heirs, and this makes such families inherently unstable. Tibetans perceive that conflict will spread from the wives to their husbands and consider this likely to cause family fission. Consequently it is almost never done.

Although Tibetans see an economic advantage to fraternal polyandry, they do not value the sharing of a wife as an end in itself. On the contrary, they articulate a number of problems inherent in the practice. For example, because authority is customarily exercised by the eldest brother, his younger male siblings have to subordinate themselves with little hope of changing their status within the family. When these younger brothers are aggressive and individualistic, tensions and difficulties often occur despite there being only one set of heirs.

In addition, tension and conflict may arise in polyandrous families because of sexual favoritism. The bride normally sleeps with the eldest brother, and the two have the responsibility to see to it that the other

Monogamy		**Polyandry**
Brothers take wives and divide their inherited land		Brothers share a wife and work their inherited land together
3 brothers take 3 wives; Each bears 3 sons		3 brothers take 1 wife; She bears 3 sons

Generation 1

9 sons take 9 wives; Each bears 3 sons

3 sons take 1 wife; She bears 3 sons

Generation 2

27 grandsons take 27 wives

3 grandsons take 1 wife

Generation 3

Joe LeMonnier, Courtesy of *Natural History* Magazine.

males have opportunities for sexual access. Since the Tibetan subsistence economy requires males to travel a lot, the temporary absence of one or more brothers facilitates this, but there are also other rotation practices. The cultural ideal unambiguously calls for the wife to show equal affection and sexuality to each of the brothers (and vice versa), but deviations from this ideal occur, especially when there is a sizable difference in age between partners in the marriage.

Dorje's family represents just such a potential situation. He is fifteen years old and his two older brothers are twenty-five and twenty-two years old. The new bride is twenty-three years old, eight years Dorje's senior. Sometimes such a bride finds the youngest husband immature and adolescent and does not treat him with equal affection; alternatively, she may find his youth attractive and lavish special attention on him. Apart from this consideration, when a younger male like Dorje grows up,

he may consider his wife "ancient" and prefer the company of a woman his own age or younger. Consequently, although men and women do not find the idea of sharing a bride or a bridegroom repulsive, individual likes and dislikes can cause familial discord.

Two reasons have commonly been offered for the perpetuation of fraternal polyandry in Tibet: that Tibetans practice female infanticide and therefore have to marry polyandrously, owing to a shortage of females; and that Tibet, lying at extremely high altitudes, is so barren and bleak that Tibetans would starve without resort to this mechanism. A Jesuit who lived in Tibet in the eighteenth century articulated this second view: "One reason for this most odious custom is the sterility of the soil, and the small amount of land that can be cultivated owing to the lack of water. The crops may suffice if the brothers all live together, but if they form separate families they would be reduced to beggary."

Both explanations are wrong, however. Not only has there never been institutionalized female infanticide in Tibet, but Tibetan society gives females considerable rights, including inheriting the family estate in the absence of brothers. In such cases, the woman takes a bridegroom who comes to live in her family and adopts her family's name and identity. Moreover, there is no demographic evidence of a shortage of females. In Limi, for example, there were (in 1974) sixty females and fifty-three males in the fifteen- to thirty-five-year age category, and many adult females were unmarried.

The second reason is also incorrect. The climate in Tibet is extremely harsh, and ecological factors do play a major role perpetuating polyandry, but polandry is not a means of preventing starvation. It is characteristic, not of the poorest segments of the society, but rather of the peasant landowning families.

In the old society, the landless poor could not realistically aspire to prosperity, but they did not fear starvation. There was a persistent labor shortage throughout Tibet, and very poor families with little or no land and few animals could subsist through agricultural labor, tenant farming, craft occupations such as carpentry, or by working as servants. Although the per person family income could increase somewhat if brothers married polyandrously and pooled their wages, in the absence of inheritable land, the advantage of fraternal polyandry was not generally sufficient to prevent them from setting up their own households. A more skilled or energetic younger brother could do as well or better alone, since he would completely control his income and would not have to share it with his siblings. Consequently, while there was and is some polyandry among the poor, it is much less frequent and more prone to result in divorce and family fission.

An alternative reason for the persistence of fraternal polyandry is that it reduces population growth (and thereby reduces the pressure on resources) by relegating some females to lifetime spinsterhood. Fraternal polyandrous marriages in Limi (in 1974) averaged 2.35 men per woman, and not surprisingly, 31 percent of the females of child-bearing age (twenty to forty-nine) were unmarried. These spinsters either continued to live at home, set up their own households, or worked as servants for other families. They could also become Buddhist nuns. Being unmarried is not synonymous with exclusion from the reproductive pool. Discreet extramarital relationships are tolerated, and actually half of the adult unmarried women in Limi had one or more children. They raised these children as single mothers, working for wages or weaving cloth and blankets for sale. As a group, however, the unmarried woman had far fewer offspring than the married women, averaging only 0.7 children per woman, compared with 3.3 for married women, whether polyandrous, monogamous, or polygynous. While polyandry helps regulate population, this function of polyandry is not consciously perceived by Tibetans and is not the reason they consistently choose it.

If neither a shortage of females nor the fear of starvation perpetuates fraternal polyandry, what motivates brothers, particularly younger brothers, to opt for this system of marriage? From the perspective of the younger brother in a landholding family, the main incentive is the attainment or maintenance of the good life. With polyandry, he can expect a more secure and higher standard of living, with access not only to his family's land and animals, but also to its inherited collection of clothes, jewelry, rugs, saddles, and horses. In addition, he will experience less work pressure and much greater security because all responsibility does not fail on one "father." For Tibetan brothers, the question is whether to trade off the greater personal freedom inherent in monogamy for the real or potential economic security, affluence, and social prestige associated with life in a larger, labor-rich polyandrous family.

A brother thinking of separating from his polyandrous marriage and taking his own wife would face various disadvantages. Although in the majority of Tibetan regions all brothers theoretically have rights to their family's estate, in reality Tibetans are reluctant to divide their land into small fragments. Generally, a younger brother who insists on leaving the family will receive only a small plot of land, if that. Because of its power and wealth, the rest of the family usually can block any attempt of the younger brother to increase his share of land through litigation. Moreover, a younger brother may not even get a house and cannot expect to receive much above the minimum in terms of movable possessions, such as furniture, pots, and pans. Thus, a brother contemplating going it on his own must plan on achieving economic security and the good life not through inheritance but through his own work.

The obvious solution for younger brothers—creating new fields from virgin land—is generally not a feasible option. Most Tibetan populations live at high altitudes (above 12,000 feet), where arable land is extremely scarce. For example, in Dorje's village, agriculture ranges only from about 12,900 feet, the lowest point in the area, to 13,300 feet. Above that altitude, early frost and snow destroy the staple barley crop. Furthermore, because of the low rainfall caused by the Himalayan rain shadow, many areas in Tibet and northern Nepal that are within appropriate altitude range for agriculture have no reliable sources of irrigation. In the end, although there is plenty of unused land in such areas, most of it is either too high or too arid.

Even where unused land capable of being farmed exists, clearing the land and building the substantial terraces necessary for irrigation constitute a great undertaking. Each plot has to be completely dug out to a depth of two to two and a half feet so that the large rocks and boulders can be removed. At best, a man might be able to bring a few new fields under cultivation in the first years after separating from his brothers, but he could not expect to acquire substantial amounts of arable land this way.

In addition, because of the limited farmland, the Tibetan subsistence economy characteristically includes a strong emphasis on animal husbandry. Tibetan farmers regularly maintain cattle, yaks, goats, and sheep, grazing them in the areas too high for agriculture. These herds produce wool, milk, cheese, butter, meat, and skins. To obtain these resources, however, shepherds must accompany the animals on a daily basis. When first setting up a monogamous household, a younger brother like Dorje would find it difficult to both farm and manage animals.

In traditional Tibetan society, there was an even more critical factor that operated to perpetuate fraternal polyandry—a form of hereditary servitude somewhat analogous to serfdom in Europe. Peasants were tied to large estates held by aristocrats, monasteries, and the Lhasa government. They were allowed the use of some farmland to produce their own subsistence but were required to provide taxes in kind and corvée (free labor) to their lords. The corvée was a substantial hardship, since a peasant household was in many cases required to furnish the lord with one laborer daily for most of the year and more on specific occasions such as the harvest. This enforced labor, along with the lack of new land and the ecological pressure to pursue both agriculture and animal husbandry, made polyandrous families particularly beneficial. The polyandrous family allowed an internal division of adult labor, maximizing economic advantage. For example, while the wife worked the family fields, one brother could perform the lord's corvée, another could look after the animals, and a third could engage in trade.

Although social scientists often discount other people's explanations of why they do things, in the case of Tibetan fraternal polyandry, such explanations are very close to the truth. The custom, however, is very sensitive to changes in its political and economic milieu and, not surprisingly, is in decline in most Tibetan areas. Made less important by the elimination of the traditional serf-based economy, it is disparaged by the dominant non-Tibetan leaders of India, China, and Nepal. New opportunities for economic and social mobility in these countries, such as the tourist trade and government employment, are also eroding the rationale for polyandry, and so it may vanish within the next generation.

Oaxaca's Spiraling Race for Water

Susan H. Lees

As you read:
1. *How is traditional Oaxacan farming adapted to the environment?*
2. *How has the introduction of new technology affected the ability of farmers to survive in the long run?*
3. *How has traditional community social organization been affected by the introduction of new farming technology?*

In the hot sunlight of the Valley of Oaxaca, in Mexico's southern highlands, a Zapotec farmer peers into the hand-dug well in the center of his small plot of land. For several hours he has drawn up buckets of water and poured them over his pepper plants; now the well is dry, and he will have to wait until tomorrow to tend the last few rows—if they survive another day of desiccation in the heat.

Shading his eyes with his hand, the farmer looks across his plot to the fields of a neighbor who has drilled a deep well and bought a diesel-powered pump. Water flows wastefully in the furrows between his plants. The mechanized pump saves labor, but it lowers the water table more quickly, so that all the shallow wells in the area run dry within a few hours.

Hand irrigation of crops is a 3,000-year-old tradition in the Valley of Oaxaca. This ancient method indirectly regulated the use of water and maintained a long-term balance between farmers and their resources. But new irrigation practices, which have yet to come under general social or legal controls, require a new kind of response, a different social order.

For nearly 10,000 years there has been continuous occupation in the Valley of Oaxaca. The archeological sites at Monte Albán and Mitla are spectacular evidence of Oaxaca's leading role in the rise of Mesoamerica's ancient civilization. Based on a highly productive agricultural system, the civilization that created these monuments owed its success to the fertility of the valley's alluvial plain, the diversity of its environmental subzones, and the variety of techniques that were used to exploit them.

Water was then, and still is, the Oaxacan farmers' single most critical resource. Rainfall averages twenty to thirty inches each year, most of it coming during June, July, and August. But from one year to the next, the amount of rain and where it falls is unpredictable. In some parts of the valley the evaporation rate is four times the rate of precipitation, and farmers must use a variety of irrigation methods, depending on the local topography, to increase the water supply and meet the needs of their crops.

The Valley of Oaxaca is a region of contrasts. Steep, cool, and densely forested mountains surround the sixty-mile-long valley. But the narrow piedmont leading to the valley floor is barren and rocky, coming to life only in summer. For the most part, this zone is suitable only for growing maguey, a cactus from which alcoholic beverages and rope fibers are produced. Within this arid band, however, springs and streams, flowing throughout the year, support lush vegetation on their banks.

The Atoyac River, which divides the length of the valley floor, is joined by its main tributary, the Salado River, at the center of the valley. The two rivers give the valley the shape of a giant Y, with arms to the northeast, south, and southeast. Here, along the warm, wet valley floor, the rich alluvial soils grow a variety of crops during most of the year.

Farmers in this part of the valley have traditionally excavated ten- to twenty-foot-deep wells in their fields, from which they have drawn water by hand. Requiring intensive labor, this type of irrigation has been restricted to less than 10 percent of the cultivated land. But as a means of providing cash crops, such as green peppers and garlic, it still has considerable economic importance. Farmers can grow up to three crops each year using this technique.

In piedmont areas far from springs and streams, farmers use floodwater from rainfall for irrigation. After a heavy rainstorm, simple stone and brush dams block the water running off the mountains and down the piedmont slopes so that it flows more gently over the fields, briefly covering them. This is a difficult and unreliable undertaking; a strong current could sweep away the dams or uproot the plants. After each storm a farmer must carefully control the flow of water to his fields so that his crops get enough water but not too much: overflooding will kill them.

Farmers who cultivate near piedmont streams are more fortunate because their water supply lasts longer and is not as unpredictable. Placed at strategic points along a stream bed, brush, concrete, and stone dams—similar to those used for floodwater irrigation—channel the water through earthen canals to the fields. Where the ground is uneven, wood and stone aqueducts smooth out the canal bed.

The techniques of the canal system are quite simple, and farmers in the Valley of Oaxaca have been using them since 300 B.C. Their use can double or even quadruple crop yield, as they not only increase the water supply to the plants but also extend the growing season, permitting two crops to be planted in one year: one crop dependent partly on rainfall; the other, exclusively on canal irrigation.

Like their ancestors, Zapotec farmers today rely for subsistence primarily on corn, beans, and squash—plants well adapted to this arid climate. Although corn is the major crop in the valley, grown on 30 to 70 percent of the arable land, a certain proportion of the land has always been devoted to small-scale, cash-crop production for sale at weekly regional markets. In the northeastern arm of the valley, fruit and wheat were important cash crops in the central and southern areas of the valley, while the drier southeastern arm continues to specialize in maguey production.

The problem of seasonal water scarcity has been aggravated by the introduction of new cash crops, particularly alfalfa. With the recent growth of an urban market for milk products, farmers in the northern and central regions of the valley have found dairy farming a profitable source of income. To get the maximum amount of milk from their cows, dairy farmers prefer to stall feed their animals fresh alfalfa. This crop, now grown extensively for farm use and sale throughout the valley, has become Oaxaca's major irrigated cash crop. In some villages in the northern and central regions of the valley, nearly half the cultivated land is devoted to alfalfa.

Alfalfa may be profitable, but it requires a great deal of water: the more it is irrigated, the more it grows. Producing continuously for five to ten years, it needs water throughout the year. In the piedmont, alfalfa places heavy demands on stream water for canal irrigation; on the valley floor, farmers have installed diesel pumps in their wells to tap the water table with greater intensity than traditional techniques allow.

Unprecedented demands are now being made on the valley's water resources. Nine-foot-deep wells in the alluvium, which are still tapped by hand, dry up after two to four hours of use per day. Pump-drawn wells generally tap water at deeper levels—twelve to forty feet deep—but the increasing scarcity of water at these levels is now forcing some farmers to dig wells as deep as 90 to 180 feet. This usually requires government technical and financial assistance since villagers cannot carry out such a project using traditional methods.

In the upper piedmont zone, villages, assisted by government agencies, have built concrete dams and reservoirs in order to more efficiently tap stream waters and guarantee adequate year-round supplies for both irrigation and domestic use. But the intensive use of this water decreased the amount available in lower piedmont and alluvial villages, which formerly received a sufficient amount. These lower villages rely increasingly on deeper wells and more powerful pumps.

Even on the valley floor, where the water table is the highest, intensive pumping at higher altitudes makes hand-drawn water unreliable, and farmers turn, as much through necessity as through choice, to newer, more expensive technology. At the same time, they reduce the availability of their essential resource—water.

Not only does alfalfa use a great deal of water, but the method used to irrigate this crop is more wasteful, given the high evaporation rate, than the traditional hand-drawn technique. More water evaporates when it is spread on fields in furrows than when it is placed by hand only on the plants, not on the areas beside them. Storage dams, with extensive open water surfaces, also entail high water loss through evaporation. As a result, water shortages keep appear-

ing despite investments in ne' technology.

Because of their shift to alfal farmers depend more and more on technical assistance from the federal government, which frequently aids in the construction of new reservoirs and deep wells. As the farmers' dependence on technology grows, their interest and participation in national political institutions increases and their traditional isolation from the outside world rapidly disintegrates.

Government technicians who come to a rural community to help modernize irrigation facilities also attempt to modernize the organization of the village's water administration. Traditionally, the use and maintenance of community canals and wells varied from village to village according to local custom. Now, communities must alter their customs to conform to government standards and elect water committees responsible to the governmental agency that helped to construct the irrigation device. The government has also intervened in the allocation of water for urbanization and industry. Communities have thus lost control over their own resources.

Along with a change in the relationship of rural communities to the outside world has come a shift in attitudes and values within the community. Until ten or fifteen years ago, the accumulation of material wealth received little emphasis. Prestige and respect could be attained only by fulfilling community obligations. Among the most important of these was the personal sponsorship of a fiesta in celebration of one of the saints whose image was kept in the village church.

The member of the community sponsoring such a celebration had to buy fireworks, food, liquor, and the services of musicians, which sometimes required years of advance planning and saving. To raise money to pay for a fiesta, the sponsor was expected to use not only the profits from his good harvests but also to borrow goods and money from his friends and neighbors. Such loans would be repaid at a later date, perhaps when the lenders sponsored their own fiestas.

The continual flow of small surpluses within communities and the frequent borrowing and lending helped to mitigate the risks of crop failure in this uncertain environment. A farmer who had suffered a poor harvest always had some people in debt to him. And those who helped him did so with the realization that some day they, too, would have to seek help from a neighbor.

With this system of borrowing, lending, and ceremonial expenditures, there was little left over to invest in agricultural improvements, such as new equipment or chemical fertilizers. Partially because of this system, farmers did not attempt to produce the largest possible crops every year. Realizing that part of their profits would be drained away through loans and debt repayment, farmers geared production toward their own immediate but limited needs.

They adjusted the amount of land and seed they planted to the amount of rainfall they expected, basing their estimate on the spring rains. In years expected to be very dry, they planted more; in those expected to be wetter, they planted less. As a result, over the long run production remained fairly low and did not strain the environmental resources.

This traditional system depended for continuity on yet another factor: the isolation and relative autonomy of the local communities from the national governmental and economic institutions. Historically left to themselves, rural communities in an unpredictably varying environment devised social systems that spread the costs of community government and the risks of poverty. The result of this isolation and self-sufficiency was minimal participation in national and world markets, minimal aid on the part of the national

government in developing agriculture, low production levels, and a low standard of living for Oaxacan farmers.

The days of isolation have now ended. Federal and state governments, with some community support, are pressing for change. Increased schooling affects every household. Better transportation methods bring new products to the valley and make easier the exportation of crops to urban markets. Cities have increased the demand for agricultural products, and technology offers the means of providing them.

In traditional communities the individual's sole path to prestige lay in ceremonial sponsorship, but new cash crops, markets, and technological inventions are providing other alternatives. Today young Oaxacan farmers look to increased crop yields as a means of raising their standard of living and, hence, their social status according to values outside the local community.

Once farmers begin to base their prestige on material achievements, they intensify their use of local resources, particularly water. While traditional farmers decreased their acreage good years because they could satisfy their needs with limited effort, the goal of today's farmers is not just to satisfy their needs but to maximize their profits. In the effort to fulfill these new goals, farmers avoid—and then abandon—the former ideals of community and religious obligation.

When traditional values are undermined, community institutions lose their effectiveness in maintaining ecological equilibrium. Traditional farming, with its limited use of subsurface water, precluded overuse and, hence, scarcity of a vital resource. But now many farmers use all the water they have and thus contribute to conditions of scarcity for all.

In accepting the goals and the technology of the modernized world that surrounds them, Oaxacan farmers are burning their bridges behind them. They cannot reap the benefits of their new markets and cash crops without increasing their exploitation of ground and stream water. As they do so, the agricultural process becomes increasingly costly in terms of both resources and technology. To pay for continued provision of water, as well as new technology, they are obliged to become increasingly dependent on the outside world. More and more, farmers must abandon their community traditions that for centuries had maintaine between them and their enviror..... the ancient balance is lost, they will have little choice other than to continue to change as they move rapidly toward an uncertain future.

The Domestication of Wood in Haiti: A Case Study in Applied Evolution

Gerald F. Murray

As you read:

1. *What are the causes of deforestation in Haiti?*
2. *Why were government efforts to plant trees generally unsuccessful?*
3. *What skills and insights did Murray have as an anthropologist that enabled him to design a workable plan for reforestation?*
4. *How does thinking of wood as a crop offer a better solution to the environmental crisis of deforestation than do attempts to teach peasant farmers the ecological value of trees?*

Problem and Client

Expatriate tree lovers, whether tourists or developmental planners, often leave Haiti with an upset stomach. Though during precolonial times the island Arawaks had reached a compromise with the forest, their market-oriented colonial successors saw trees as something to be removed. The Spaniards specialized in exporting wood from the eastern side of the island, whereas the French on the western third found it more profitable to clear the wood and produce sugar cane, coffee, and indigo for European markets. During the nineteenth century, long after Haiti had become an independent republic, foreign lumber companies cut and exported most of the nation's precious hardwoods, leaving little for today's peasants.

The geometric increase in population since colonial times—from an earlier population of fewer than half a million former slaves to a contemporary population of more than six million—and the resulting shrinkage of average family holding size have led to the evolution of a land use system devoid of systematic fallow periods. A vicious cycle has set in—one that seems to have targeted the tree for ultimate destruction. Not only has land pressure eliminated a regenerative fallow phase in the local agricultural cycle; in addition the catastrophic declines in per hectare food yields have forced peasants into alternative income-generating strategies. Increasing numbers crowd into the capital city, Port-au-Prince, creating a market for construction wood and charcoal. Poorer sectors of the peasantry in the rural areas respond to this market by racing each other with axes and machetes to cut down the few natural tree stands remaining in remoter regions of the republic. The proverbial snowball in Hades is at less risk than a tree in Haiti.

Unable to halt the flows either of wood into the cities or of soil into the oceans, international development organizations finance studies to measure the volume of these flows (50 million trees cut per year is

Reprinted from: "The Domestication of Wood in Haiti: A Case Study in Applied Evolution" by Gerald F. Murray in *Anthropological Praxis*, © 1987, by permission of Westview Press, Boulder, Colorado.

one of the round figures being bandied about) and to predict when the last tree will be cut from Haiti. Reforestation projects have generally been entrusted by their well-meaning but short-sighted funders to Duvalier's Ministry of Agriculture, a kiss-of-death resource channeling strategy by which the Port-au-Prince jobs created frequently outnumber the seedlings produced. And even the few seedlings produced often died in the nurseries because the peasants were understandably reluctant to cover their scarce holdings with state-owned trees. Project managers had been forced to resort to "food for work" strategies to move seedlings out of nurseries onto hillsides. And peasants have endeavored where possible to plant the trees on somebody else's hillsides and to enlist their livestock as allies in the subsequent removal of this dangerous vegetation.

This generalized hostility to tree projects placed the U.S. Agency for International Development (AID)/Haiti mission in a bind. After several years of absence from Haiti in the wake of expulsion by Francois Duvalier, AID had reestablished its presence under the government of his son Jean Claude. But an ambitious Integrated Agricultural Development Project funded through the Ministry of Agriculture had already given clear signs of being a multimillion-dollar farce. And an influential congressman chairing the U.S. House Ways and Means Committee—consequently exercising strong control over AID funds worldwide—had taken a passionate interest in Haiti. In his worldwide travels this individual had become adept at detecting and exposing developmental charades. And he had been blunt in communicating his conviction that much of what he had seen in AID/ Haiti's program was precisely that. He had been touched by the plight of Haiti and communicated to the highest AID authorities his conviction about the salvific power of contraceptives and trees and his determination to have AID grace Haiti with an abundant flow of both. And he would

personally visit Haiti (a convenient plane ride from Washington, D.C.) to inspect for himself, threatening a worldwide funding freeze if no results were forthcoming. A chain reaction of nervous "yes sirs" speedily worked its way down from AID headquarters in Washington to a beleaguered Port-au-Prince mission.

The pills and condoms were less of a problem. Even the most cantankerous congressman was unlikely to insist on observing them in use and would probably settle for household distribution figures. Not so with the trees. He could (and did) pooh-pooh nursery production figures and asked to be taken to see the new AID forests, a most embarrassing request in a country where peasants creatively converted daytime reforestation projects into nocturnal goat forage projects. AID's reaction was twofold—first, to commission an immediate study to explain to the congressman and others why peasants refused to plant trees (for this they called down an AID economist); and second, to devise some program strategy that would achieve the apparently unachievable: to instill in cash-needy, defiant, pleasant charcoalmakers a love, honor, and respect for newly planted trees. For this attitudinal transformation, a task usually entrusted to the local armed forces, AID/Haiti invited an anthropologist to propose an alternative approach.

Process and Players

During these dynamics, I completed a doctoral dissertation on the manner in which Haitian peasant land tenure had evolved in response to internal population growth. The AID economist referred to above exhaustively reviewed the available literature, also focusing on the issue of Haitian peasant land tenure, and produced for the mission a well-argued monograph (Zuvekas 1978) documenting a lower rate of landlessness in Haiti than in many other Latin American settings but documenting as well the informal, extralegal character of the relationship between many peasant families and their landholdings. This latter observation was interpreted by some in the mission to mean that the principal determinant of the failure of tree planting projects was the absence among peasants of legally secure deeds over their plots. Peasants could not be expected to invest money on land improvements when at mildest the benefits could accrue to another and at worst the very improvements themselves could lead to expropriation from their land. In short, no massive tree planting could be expected, according to this model, until a nationwide cadastral reform granted plot-by-plot deeds to peasant families.

This hypothesis was reputable but programmatically paralyzing because nobody dreamed that the Duvalier regime was about to undertake a major cadastral reform for the benefit of peasants. Several AID officers in Haiti had read my dissertation on land tenure (Murray 1977), and I received an invitation to advise the mission. Was Haitian peasant land tenure compatible with tree planting? Zuvekas' study had captured the internally complex nature of Haitian peasant land tenure. But the subsequent extrapolations as to paralyzing insecurity simply did not seem to fit with ethnographic evidence. In two reports (Murray 1978a, 1978b) I indicated that peasants in general feel secure about their ownership rights over their land. Failure to secure plot-by-plot surveyed deeds is generally a cost-saving measure. Interclass evictions did occur, but they were statistically rare; instead most land disputes were intrafamilial. A series of extralegal tenure practices had evolved—preinheritance land grants to young adult dependents, informal inheritance subdivisions witnessed by community members, fictitious sales to favored children, complex community-internal share-cropping arrangements. And though these practices produced an internally heterogeneous system with its complexities, there was strong internal order.

Any chaos and insecurity tended to be more in the mind of observers external to the system than in the behavior of the peasants themselves. There was a danger that the complexities of Haitian peasant land tenure would generate an unintended smokescreen obscuring the genuine causes of failure in tree planting projects.

What then were these genuine causes? The mission, intent on devising programming strategies in this domain, invited me to explore further, under a contract aimed at identifying the "determinants of success and failure" in reforestation and soil conservation projects. My major conclusion was that the preexisting land tenure, cropping, and livestock systems in peasant Haiti were perfectly adequate for the undertaking of significant tree planting activities. Most projects had failed not because of land tenure or attitudinal barriers among peasants but because of fatal flaws in one or more key project components. Though my contract called principally for analysis of previous or existing projects, I used the recommendation section of the report to speculate on how a Haiti-wise anthropologist would program and manage reforestation activities if he or she had the authority. In verbal debriefings I jokingly challenged certain young program officers in the mission to give me a jeep and carte blanche access to a $50,000 checking account, and I would prove my anthropological assertions about peasant economic behavior and produce more trees in the ground than their current multimillion-dollar Ministry of Agriculture charade. We had a good laugh and shook hands, and I departed confident that the report would be as dutifully perused and as honorably filed and forgotten as similar reports I had done elsewhere.

To my great disbelief, as I was correcting Anthro 101 exams some two years later, one of the program officers still in Haiti called to say that an Agroforestry Outreach Project (AOP) had been approved chapter and verse as I had recommended it; and that if I was interested in placing my life where my mouth had been and would leave the ivory tower to direct the project, my project bank account would have not $50,000, but $4 million. After several weeks of hemming and hawing and vigorous negotiating for leave from my department, I accepted the offer and entered a new (to me) role of project director in a strange upside-down world in which the project anthropologist was not a powerless cranky voice from the bleachers but the chief of party with substantial authority over general project policy and the allocation of project resources. My elation at commanding resources to implement anthropological ideas was dampened by the nervousness of knowing exactly who would be targeted for flak and ridicule if these ideas bombed out, as most tended to do in the Haiti of Duvalier.

The basic structural design of AOP followed a tripartite conceptual framework that I proposed for analyzing projects. Within this framework a project is composed of three essential systemic elements: a technical base, a benefit flow strategy, and an institutional delivery strategy. Planning had to focus equally on all three, I argued that defects in one would sabotage the entire project.

Technical Strategy

The basic technical strategy was to make available to peasants fast-growing wood trees (*Leucaena leucocephala, Cassia siamea, Azadirachta indica, Casuarina equisetifolia, Eucalyptus camaldulensis*) that were not only drought resistant but also rapid growing, producing possible four-year harvest rotations in humid lowland areas (and slower rotations and lower survival rates in arid areas) and that were good for charcoal and basic construction needs. Most of the species mentioned also restore nutrients to the soil, and some of them coppice from a carefully harvested stump, producing several rotations before the need for replanting.

Of equally critical technical importance was the use of a nursery system that produced light-weight microseedlings. A project pickup truck could transport over 15,000 of these microseedlings (as opposed to 250 traditional bag seedlings), and the average peasant could easily carry over 500 transportable seedlings at one time, planting them with a fraction of the ground preparation time and labor required for bulkier bagged seedlings. The anthropological implications of this nursery system were critical. It constituted a technical breakthrough that reduced to a fraction the fossil-fuel and human energy expenditure required to transport and plant trees.

But the technical component of the project incorporated yet another element: the physical juxtaposition of trees and crops. In traditional reforestation models, the trees are planted in large unbroken monocropped stands. Such forests or woodlots presuppose local land tenure and economic arrangements not found in Haiti. For the tree to make its way as a cultivate into the economy of Haitian peasants and most other tropical cultivators, reforestation models would have to be replaced by agroforestry models that entail spatial or temporal juxtaposition of crops and trees. Guided by prior ethnographic knowledge of Haitian cropping patterns, AOP worked out with peasants various border planting and intercropping strategies to make tree planting feasible even for small holding cultivators.

Benefit Flow Strategies

With respect to the second systemic component, the programming of benefit flows to participants, earlier projects had often committed the fatal flaw of defining project trees planted as *pyebwa leta* (the state's trees). Authoritarian assertions by project staff concerning sanctions for cutting newly planted trees created fears among peasants that even trees planted on their own land would be government property. And several peasants were frank in reporting fears that the trees might eventually be used as a pretext by the government or the "Company" (the most common local lexeme used to refer to projects) for eventually expropriating the land on which peasants had planted project trees.

Such ambiguities and fears surrounding benefit flows paralyze even the technically soundest project. A major anthropological feature of AOP was a radical frontal attack on the issue of property and usufruct rights over project trees. Whereas other projects had criticized tree cutting, AOP promulgated the heretical message that trees were meant to be cut, processed, and sold. The only problem with the present system, according to project messages, was that peasants were cutting nature's trees. But once the landowner "mete fos li deyo" (expends his resources) and plants and cares for his or her own wood trees on his or her own land, the landowner has the same right to harvest and sell wood as corn or beans.

I was inevitably impressed at the impact that this blunt message had when I delivered it to groups of prospective peasant tree planters. Haitian peasants are inveterate and aggressive cash-croppers; many of the crops and livestock that they produce are destined for immediate consignment to local markets. For the first time in their lives, they were hearing a concrete proposal to make the wood tree itself one more marketable crop in their inventory.

But the message would ring true only if three barriers were smashed.

1. The first concerned the feared delay in benefits. Most wood trees with which the peasants were familiar took an impractically long time to mature. There fortunately existed in Haiti four-year-old stands of leucaena, cassia, eucalyptus, and other project trees to which we could take peasant groups to demonstrate the growth speed of these trees.

2. But could they be planted on their scanty holdings without interfering with crops? Border and row planting techniques were demonstrated, as well as intercropping. The average peasant holding was about a hectare and a half. If a cultivator planted a field in the usual crops and then planted 500 seedlings in the same field at 2 meters by 2 meters, the seedlings would occupy only a fifth of a hectare. And they would be far enough apart to permit continued cropping for two or three cycles before shade competition became too fierce. That is, trees would be planted on only a fraction of the peasant's holdings and planted in such a way that they would be compatible with continued food growing even on the plots where they stood. We would then calculate with peasants the potential income to be derived from these 500 trees through sale as charcoal, polewood, or boards. In a best-case scenario, the gross take from the charcoal of these trees (the least lucrative use of the wood) might equal the current annual income of an average rural family. The income potential of these wood trees clearly would far offset any potential loss from decreased food production. Though it had taken AID two years to decide on the project, it took about twenty minutes with any group of skeptical but economically rational peasants to generate a list of enthusiastic potential tree planters.

3. But there was yet a third barrier. All this speculation about income generation presupposed that the peasants themselves, and not the government or the project, would be the sole owners of the trees and that the peasants would have unlimited rights to the harvest of the wood whenever they wished. To deal with this issue, I presented the matter as an agreement

between cultivator and the project: We would furnish the free seedlings and technical assistance; the cultivators would agree to plant 500 of these seedlings on their own land and permit project personnel to carry out periodic survival counts. We would, of course, pay no wages or "Food for Work" for this planting. But we would guarantee to the planters complete and exclusive ownership of the trees. They did not need to ask for permission from the project to harvest the trees whenever their needs might dictate, nor would there be any penalties associated with early cutting or low survival. If peasants changed their minds, they could rip out their seedlings six months after planting. They would never get any more free seedlings from us, but they would not be subject to any penalties. There are preexisting local forestry laws, rarely enforced, concerning permissions and minor taxes for tree cutting. Peasants would have to deal with these as they had skillfully done in the past. But from our project's point of view, we relinquish all tree ownership rights to the peasants who accept and plant the trees on their property.

Cash-flow dialogues and ownership assurances such as these were a far cry from the finger-wagging ecological sermons to which many peasant groups had been subjected on the topic of trees. Our project technicians developed their own messages; but central to all was the principle of peasant ownership and usufruct of AOP trees. The goal was to capitalize on the preexisting fuel and lumber markets, to make the wood tree one more crop in the income-generating repertoire of the Haitian peasant.

Institutional Strategy

The major potential fly in the ointment was the third component, the institutional component. To whom would AID entrust its funds to carry out this project? My own research had indicated clearly that Haitian governmental involvement condemned a project to certain paralysis and possible death, and my report phrased that conclusion as diplomatically as possible. The diplomacy was required to head off possible rage, less from Haitian officials than from certain senior officers in the AID mission who were politically and philosophically wedded to an institution-building strategy. Having equated the term "institution" with "government bureaucracy," and having defined their own career success in terms, not of village-level resource flows, but of voluminous and timely bureaucracy-to-bureaucracy cash transfers, such officials were in effect marshaling U.S. resources into the service of extractive ministries with unparalleled track records of squandering and/or pilfering expatriate donor funds.

To the regime's paradoxical credit, however, the blatant openness and arrogance of Duvalierist predation had engendered an angry willingness in much of Haiti's development community to explore other resource flow channels. Though the nongovernmental character of the proposal provoked violent reaction, the reactionaries in the Haiti mission were overridden by their superiors in Washington, and a completely nongovernmental implementing mode was adopted for this project.

The system, based on private voluntary organizations (PVOs), worked as follows.

1. AID made a macrogrant to a Washington-based PVO (the Pan American Development Foundation, PADF) to run a tree-planting project based on the principles that had emerged in my research. At the Haiti mission's urging, PADF invited me to be chief of party for the project and located an experienced accountant in Haiti to be financial administrator. PADF in addition recruited three American agroforesters

who, in addition to MA-level professional training, had several years of overseas village field experience under their belts. Early in the project they were supplemented by two other expatriates, a Belgian and a French Canadian. We opened a central office in Port-au-Prince and assigned a major region of Haiti to each of the agroforesters, who lived in their field regions.

2. These agroforesters were responsible for contacting the many village-based PVOs working in their regions to explain the project, to emphasize its microeconomic focus and its difference from traditional reforestation models, to discuss the conditions of entry therein, and to make technical suggestions as to the trees that would be appropriate for the region.

3. If the PVO was interested, we drafted an agreement in which our mutual contributions and spheres of responsibility were specified. The agreements were not drafted in French (Haiti's official language) but in Creole, the only language spoken by most peasants.

4. The local PVO selected *animateurs* (village organizers) who themselves were peasants who lived and worked in the village where trees would be planted. After receiving training from us, they contacted their neighbors and kin, generated lists of peasants interested in planting a specified number of trees, and informed us when the local rains began to fall. At the proper moment we packed the seedlings in boxes customized to the particular region and shipped them on our trucks to the farmers, who would be waiting at specified drop-off points at a specified time. The trees were to be planted within twenty-four hours of delivery.

5. The animateurs were provided with Creole language data forms by which to gather ecological, land use, and land tenure data on each plot where trees would be planted and certain bits of information on each peasant participant. These forms were used to follow up, at periodic intervals, the survival of trees, the incidence of any problems (such as livestock depredation, burning, disease), and—above all—the manner in which the farmer integrated the trees into cropping and livestock patterns, to detect and head off any unintended substitution of food for wood.

Results and Evaluation

The project was funded for four years from October 1981 through November 1985. During the writing of the project paper we were asked by an AID economist to estimate how many trees would be planted. Not knowing if the peasants would in fact plant any trees, we nervously proposed to reach two thousand peasant families with a million trees as a project goal. Fiddling with his programmed calculator, the economist informed us that that output would produce a negative internal rate of return. We would need at least two million trees to make the project worth AID's institutional while. We shrugged and told him cavalierly to up the figure and to promise three million trees on the land of six thousand peasants. (At that time I thought someone else would be directing the project.)

Numbers of Trees and Beneficiaries

Though I doubted that we could reach this higher goal, the response of the Haitian peasants to this new approach to tree planting left everyone, including myself, open mouthed. Within the first year of the project, one million trees had been planted by some 2,500 peasant households all over Haiti. My fears of peasant indifference were now transformed into nervousness that we could not supply seedlings fast enough to meet the demand triggered by our wood-as-a-cash-crop strategy. Apologetic village animateurs informed us that some cultivators who had not signed up on the first lists were actually stealing newly planted seedlings from their neighbors' fields at night. They promised to catch the scoundrels. If they did, I told them, give the scoundrels a hug. Their pilfering was dramatic proof of the bull's-eye nature of the anthropological predictions that underlie the project.

By the end of the second year (when I left the project), we had reached the four-year goal of three million seedlings and the project had geared up and decentralized its nursery capacity to produce several million seedlings per season (each year having two planting seasons). Under the new director, a fellow anthropologist, the geometric increase continued. By the end of the fourth year, the project had planted, not its originally agreed-upon three million trees, but twenty million trees. Stated more accurately, some 75,000 Haitian peasants had enthusiastically planted trees on their own land. In terms of its quantitative outreach, AOP had more than quintupled its original goals.

Wood Harvesting and Wood Banking

By the end of its fourth year the project had already received an unusual amount of professional research attention by anthropologists, economists, and foresters. In addition to AID evaluations, six studies had been released on one or another aspect of the project (Ashley 1986; Balzano 1986; Buffum and King 1985; Conway 1986; Grosenick 1985; McGowan 1986). As predicted, many peasants were harvesting trees by the end of the fourth year. The most lucrative sale of the wood was as polewood in local markets, though much charcoal was also being made from project trees.

Interestingly, however, the harvesting was proceeding much more slowly than I had predicted. Peasants were "clinging" to their trees and not engaging in the clear cutting that I hoped would occur, as a prelude to the emergence of a rotational system in which peasants would alternate crops with tree cover that they themselves had planted. This technique would have been a revival, under a "domesticated" mode, of the ancient swidden sequence that had long since disappeared from Haiti. Though such a revival would have warmed anthropological hearts, the peasants had a different agenda. Though they had long ago removed nature's tree cover, they were extremely cautious about removing the tree cover that they had planted. Their economic logic was unassailable. Crop failure is so frequent throughout most of Haiti, and the market for wood and charcoal so secure, that peasants prefer to leave the tree as a "bank" against future emergencies. This arboreal bank makes particular sense in the context of the recent disappearance from Haiti of the peasant's traditional bank, the pig. A governmentally mandated (and U.S. financed) slaughter of all pigs because of fears of African swine fever created a peasant banking gap that AOP trees have now started to fill.

The Anthropological Difference

Anthropological findings, methods, and theories clearly have heavily influenced this project at all stages. We are dealing, not with an ongoing project affected by anthropological input, but with a project whose very existence was rooted in anthropological research and whose very character was determined by ongoing anthropological direction and anthropologically informed managerial prodding.

My own involvement with the project spanned several phases and tasks:

1. Proposal of a theoretical and conceptual base of AOP, and concept of "wood as a cash crop."

2. Preliminary contacting of local PVOs to assess preproject interest.

3. Identification of specific program measures during project design.

4. Preparation of social soundness analysis for the AID project paper.

5. Participation as an outside expert at the meetings in AID Washington at which the fate of the project was decided.

6. Participation in the selection and in-country linguistic and cultural training of the agroforesters who worked for the project.

7. Direction and supervision of field operations.

8. Formative evaluation of preliminary results and the identification of needed midcourse corrections.

9. Generation of several hundred thousand dollars of supplemental funding from Canadian and Swiss sources and internationalization of the project team.

10. Preparation of publications about the project (Murray 1984, 1986).

In addition to my own participation in the AOP, four other anthropologists have been involved in long-term commitments to the project. Fred Conway did a preliminary study of firewood use in Haiti (Conway 1979). He subsequently served for two years as overall project coordinator within AID/ Haiti. More recently he has carried out revealing case study research on the harvesting of project trees (Conway 1986). Glenn Smucker likewise did an early feasibility study in the northwest (Smucker 1981) and eventually joined the project as my successor in the directorship. Under his leadership, many of the crucial midcourse corrections were introduced. Ira Lowenthall took over the AID coordination of the project at a critical transitional period and has been instrumental in forging plans for its institutional future. And Anthony Balzano has carried out several years of case study fieldwork on the possible impact of the tree-planting activities on the land tenure in participating villages. All these individuals have PhDs, or are PhD candidates, in anthropology. And another anthropologist in the Haiti mission, John Lewis, succeeded in adapting the privatized umbrella agency outreach model for use in a swine repopulation project. With the possible exception of Vicos, it would be hard to imagine a project that has been as heavily influenced by anthropologists.

But how specifically has anthropology influenced the content of the project? There are at least three major levels at which anthropology has impinged on the content of AOP.

1. *The Application of Substantive Findings.* The very choice of "wood as a marketable crop" as the fundamental theme of the project stemmed from ethnographic knowledge of the cash-oriented foundations of Haitian peasant horticulture and knowledge of current conditions in the internal marketing system. Because of ethnographic knowledge I was able to avoid succumbing to the common-sense inclination to emphasize fruit trees (whose perishability and tendency to glut markets make them commercially vulnerable) and to choose instead a fast-growing wood tree. There is a feverishly escalating market for charcoal and construction wood that cannot be dampened even by the most successful project. And there are no spoilage problems with wood. The peasants can harvest it when they want. Furthermore, ethnographic knowledge of Haitian peasant land tenure—which is highly individualistic—guided me away from the community forest schemes that so many development philosophers

seem to delight in but that are completely inappropriate to the social reality of Caribbean peasantries.

2. *Anthropological Methods.* The basic research that led up to the project employed participant observation along with intensive interviewing with small groups of informants to compare current cost/benefit ratios of traditional farming with projected cash yields from plots in which trees are intercropped with food on four-year rotation cycles. A critical part of the project design stage was to establish the likelihood of increased revenues from altered land use behaviors. During project design I also applied ethnographic techniques to the behavior of institutional personnel. The application of anthropological notetaking on 3-by-5 slips, not only with peasants but also with technicians, managers, and officials, exposed the institutional roots of earlier project failures and stimulated the proposal of alternative institutional routes. Furthermore, ethno-scientific elicitation of folk taxonomies led to the realization that whereas fruit trees are classified as a crop by Haitian peasants, wood trees are not so classified. This discovery exposed the need for the creation of explicit messages saying that wood can be a crop, just as coffee, manioc, and corn can. Finally, prior experience in Creole-language instrument design and computer analysis permitted me to design a baseline data gathering system.

3. *Anthropological Theory.* My own thinking about tree planting was heavily guided by cultural-evolutionary insights into the origins of agriculture. The global tree problem is often erroneously conceptualized in a conservationist or ecological framework. Such a perspective is very short-sighted for anthropologists. We are aware of an ancient food crisis, when humans still hunted and gathered, that was solved, not by the adoption of conservationist practices, but rather by the shift into a domesticated mode of production. From hunting and gathering we turned to cropping and harvesting. I found the analogy with the present tree crisis conceptually overpowering. Trees will emerge when and only when human beings start planting them aggressively as a harvestable crop, not when human consciousness is raised regarding their ecological importance. This anthropological insight (or bias), nourished by the aggressive creativity of the Haitian peasants among whom I had lived, swayed me toward the adoption of a dynamic "domestication" paradigm in proposing a solution to the tree problem in Haiti. This evolutionary perspective also permitted me to see that the cashcropping of wood was in reality a small evolutionary step, not a quantum leap. The Haitian peasants already cut and sell natural stands of wood. They already plant and sell traditional food crops. It is but a small evolutionary step to join these two unconnected streams of Haitian peasant behavior, and this linkage is the core purpose of the Agroforestry Outreach Project.

Broader anthropological theory also motivated and justified a nongovernmental implementing mode for AOP. Not only AID but also most international development agencies tend to operate on a service model of the state. This idealized model views the basic character of the state as that of a provider of services to its population. Adherence to this theoretically naive service model has led to the squandering of untold millions of dollars in the support of extractive public bureaucracies. This waste is justified under the rubric of institution building—assisting public entities to provide the services that they are supposed to be providing.

But my anthropological insights into the origins of the state as a mechanism of extraction and control led me to pose the somewhat heretical position that the predatory behavior of Duvalier's regime was in fact not misbehavior. Duvalier was merely doing openly and blatantly what other state leaders camouflage under rhetoric. AID's search of nongovernmental implementing channels for AOP, then, was not seen as a simple emergency measure to be employed under a misbehaving regime but rather as an avenue of activity that might be valid as an option under many or most regimes. There is little justification in either ethnology or anthropological theory for viewing the state as the proper recipient of developmental funds. This theoretical insight permitted us to argue for a radically nongovernmental mode of tree-planting support in AOP. In short, sensitivity to issues in anthropological theory played a profound role in the shaping of the project.

Would AOP have taken the form it did without these varied types of anthropological input? Almost certainly not. Had there been no anthropological input, a radically different scenario would almost certainly have unfolded with the following elements.

1. AID would probably have undertaken a reforestation project—congressional pressure alone would have ensured that. But the project would have been based, not on the theme of "wood as a peasant cash-crop," but on the more traditional approach to trees as a vehicle of soil conservation. Ponderous educational programs would have been launched to teach the peasants about the value of trees. Emphasis would have been placed on educating the ignorant and on trying to induce peasants to plant commercially marginal (and nutritionally tangential) fruit trees instead of cash-generating wood trees.

2. The project would have been managed by technicians. The emphasis would probably have been on carrying out lengthy technical research concerning optimal planting strategies and the combination of trees with optimally effective bench terraces and other soil conservation devices. The outreach problem would have been given second priority. Throughout Haiti hundreds of thousands of dollars have been spent on numerous demonstration projects to create terraced, forested hillsides, but only a handful of cooperative local peasants have been induced to undertake the same activities on their own land.

3. The project would almost certainly have been run through the Haitian government. When after several hundred thousand dollars of expenditures few trees were visible, frustrated young AID program officers would have gotten finger-wagging lectures about the sovereign right of local officials to use donor money as they see fit. And the few trees planted would have been defined as *pyebwa leta* (the government's trees), and peasants would have been sternly warned against ever cutting these trees, even the ones planted on their own land. And the peasants would soon turn the problem over to their most effective ally in such matters, the free-ranging omnivorous goat, who would soon remove this alien vegetation from the peasant's land.

Because of anthropology, the Agroforestry Outreach Project has unfolded to a different scenario. It was a moving experience for me to return to the village where I had done my original fieldwork (and which I of course tried to involve in the tree-planting activities) to find several houses built using the wood from leucaena trees planted during the project's earliest phases. Poles were beginning to be sold, although the prices had not yet stabilized for these still unknown wood types. Charcoal made from project trees was being sold in local markets. For the first time in the history of this village, people were "growing" part of their house structures and their cooking fuel. I felt as though I were observing (and had been a participant in) a replay of an ancient anthropological drama, the shift from an extractive to a domesticated mode of resource procurement. Though their sources of food energy had been domesticated millennia ago, my former village neighbors had now begun replicating this transition in the domain of wood and wood-based energy. I felt a satisfaction at having chosen a discipline that could give me the privilege of participating, even marginally, in this very ancient cultural-evolutionary transition.

References

Ashley, Marshall D. 1986. *A Study of Traditional Agroforestry Systems in Haiti and Implications for the USAID/Haiti Agroforestry Outreach Project.* Port-au-Prince: University of Maine Agroforestry Outreach Research Project.

Balzano, Anthony. 1986. *Socioeconomic Aspects of Agroforestry in Rural Haiti.* Port-au-Prince: University of Maine Agroforestry Outreach Research Project.

Buffum, William, and Wendy King. 1985. *Small Farmer Decision Making and Tree Planting: Agroforestry Extension Recommendations.* Port-au-Prince: Haiti Agroforestry Outreach Project.

Conway, Frederick. 1979. *A Study of the Fuelwood Situation in Haiti.* Port-au-Prince: USAID.

———. 1986. *The Decision Making Framework for Tree Planting Within the Agroforestry Outreach Project.* Port-au-Prince: University of Maine Agroforestry Outreach Research Project.

Grosenick, Gerald. 1985. *Economic Evaluation of the Agroforestry Outreach Project.* Port-au-Prince: University of Maine Agroforestry Outreach Research Project.

McGowan, Lisa A. 1986. *Potential Marketability of Charcoal, Poles, and Planks Produced by Participants in the Agroforestry Outreach Project.* Port-au-Prince: University of Maine Agroforestry Outreach Research Project.

Murray, Gerald F. 1977. *The Evolution of Haitian Peasant Land Tenure: A Case Study in Agrarian Adaptation to Population Growth.* Ph.D. dissertation, Columbia University, New York.

———. 1978a. *Hillside Units, Wage Labor, and Haitian Peasant Land Tenure: A Strategy for the Organization of Erosion Control.* Port-au-Prince: USAID.

———. 1978b. *Informal Subdivisions and Land Insecurity: An Analysis of Haitian Peasant Land Tenure.* Port-au-Prince: USAID.

———. 1979. *Terraces, Trees, and the Haitian Peasant: An Assessment of 25 Years of Erosion Control in Rural Haiti.* Port-au-Prince: USAID.

———. 1984. "The Wood Tree as a Peasant Cash-Crop: An Anthropological Strategy for the Domestication of Energy." In A. Valdman and R. Foster, eds., *Haiti—Today and Tomorrow: An Interdisciplinary Study.* New York: University Press of America.

———. 1986. "Seeing the Forest While Planting the Trees: An Anthropological Approach to Agroforestry in Rural Haiti." In D.W. Brinkerhoff and J.C. Garcia-Zamor, eds., *Politics, Projects, and Peasants: Institutional Development in Haiti.* New York: Praeger, pp. 193-226.

Smucker, Glenn R. 1981. *Trees and Charcoal in Haitian Peasant Economy: A Feasibility Study.* Port-au-Prince: USAID.

Zuvekas, Clarence. 1978. *Agricultural Development in Haiti: An Assessment of Sector Problems, Policies, and Prospects under Conditions of Severe Soil Erosion.* Washington, D.C.: USAID.

THE WORLD'S CHANGING CULTURES

All people today face the problem of keeping up with the rapid cultural changes that occur during their lifetime. The pace of cultural change is the most rapid in many traditional societies that are being assimilated into the modern global economy. Many of these societies are undergoing a process known as acculturation—the adoption of aspects of other cultures.

European culture has had a particularly widespread impact on societies around the world in the last few centuries as European nations have expanded their economic colonization to most areas of the world. Anthropologists are concerned that the world's cultures will become increasingly homogeneous as they adopt Western culture. The problem with this, from an anthropological perspective, is that cultural diversity is as important to human survival as ecological diversity is to the survival of ecosystems. Differences in culture allow modern humans to have a broad range of knowledge and diverse world views through which to approach problems. The loss of our cultural diversity would, therefore, impair our ability to solve many of the problems we face as a species.

Unfortunately, many aspects of traditional cultures around the world are in danger of becoming extinct. In Jared Diamond's article, "Speaking with a Single Tongue," the tragedy of the loss of an important aspect of humanity's cultural diversity—our many languages and all of the cultural knowledge that is imbedded in them—is highlighted.

On a more positive note, however, there is strong evidence that even though many societies are adopting elements of Western technology and culture, they are still maintaining their unique cultural traditions. Many of the things that people in other cultures adopt from the West are interpreted through their own culture instead of being substituted for it. In "Confucius and the VCR," Jesse W. Nash describes the way in which television and movies help to reinforce traditional values in Vietnamese-

American culture. In "Tech in the Jungle," Carl Zimmer examines the use of modern technology by people in an Amazonian society as they attempt to pursue their own political survival in the face of acculturation into Brazilian society. Emilienne Ireland also describes attempts by Amazonian peoples to unite politically and gain control of their political and social future in her article, "Neither Warriors nor Victims: The Wauja Peacefully Organize to Defend Their Land." The social, economic, and political problems that the San People of Africa face and their attempts to solve these problems is the topic of "The Bushmen of Today" by Megan Biesele.

The articles in this section, therefore, provide us with a picture of not only the acculturation problems people face in many areas of the world, but also of the solutions they are devising to these problems through the knowledge afforded them by their own culture.

4

Speaking with a Single Tongue

Jared Diamond

As you read:

1. *Why, according to Diamond, are human languages disappearing?*
2. *What are the consequences of the extinction of most of the world's languages?*

"Kópipi! Kópipi" In jungle on the Pacific island of Bougainville, a man from the village of Rotokas was excitedly pointing out the most beautiful birdsong I had ever heard. It consisted of silver-clear whistled tones and trills, grouped in slowly rising phrases of two or three notes, each phrase different from the next. The effect was like one of Schubert's deceptively simple songs. I never succeeded in glimpsing the singer, nor have any of the other ornithologists who have subsequently visited Bougainville and listened spellbound to its song. All we know of the kópipi bird is that name for it in the Rotokas language and descriptions of it by Rotokas villagers. As I talked with my guide, I gradually realized that the extraordinary music of Bougainville's mountains included not only the kópipi's song but also the sounds of the Rotokas language. My guide named one bird after another: *kópipi, kurupi, vokupi, kopikau, kororo, keravo, kurue, vikuroi. . . .* The only consonant sounds in those names are *k, p, r,* and *v.* Later I learned that the Rotokas language has only six consonant sounds, the fewest of any known language in the world. English, by comparison, has 24, while other languages have 80 or more. Somehow the people of Rotokas, living in a tropical rain forest on one of the highest mountains of the southwest Pacific, have

managed to build a rich vocabulary and communicate clearly while relying on fewer basic sounds than any other people. But the music of their language is now disappearing from Bougainville's mountains, and from the world. The Rotokas language is just one of 18 languages spoken on an island roughly three-quarters the size of Connecticut. At last count it was spoken by only 4,320 people, and the number is declining. With its vanishing, a 30,000-year history of human communication and cultural development is coming to an end.

That vanishing exemplifies a little-noticed tragedy looming over us: the possible loss of 90 percent of our creative heritage, linked with the loss of 90 percent of our languages. We hear much anguished discussion about the accelerating disappearance of indigenous cultures as our Coca-Cola civilization spreads over the world. Much less attention has been paid to the disappearance of languages themselves and to their essential role in the survival of those indigenous cultures. Each language is the vehicle for a unique way of thinking, a unique literature, and a unique view of the world. Only now are linguists starting seriously to estimate the world's rate of language loss and to debate what to do about it.

If the present rate of disappearance continues, our 6,000 modern languages could be reduced within a century or two to just a few hundred. Time is running out even to

Jared Diamond/© 1993 Discover Magazine

study the others. Hence linguists face a race against time similar to that faced by biologists, now aware that many of the world's plant and animal species are in danger of extinction.

To begin to understand the problem, we should take a look at how the world's languages are divvied up. If the global population of about 5.5 billion humans were equally distributed among its 6,000 tongues, then each language would have roughly 900,000 speakers—enough to give each language a fair chance of survival. Of course, the vast majority of people use only one of a few "big" languages, such as Mandarin Chinese, English, or Spanish, each with hundreds of millions of native speakers. The vast majority of languages are "little" ones, with a median number of perhaps only 5,000 speakers.

Our 6,000 languages are also unevenly distributed over the globe. Western Europe is especially poorly endowed, with about 45 native languages. In 1788, when European settlement of Australia began, aboriginal Australia was considerably richer: it had 250 languages, despite having far fewer people than Western Europe. The Americas at the time of Columbus's arrival were richer yet: more than 1,000 languages. But the richest region of the globe, then and now, is New Guinea and other Pacific islands, with only 8 million people, or less than .2 percent of the world's population, but about 1,400 languages, or almost 25 percent of the world's total! While New Guinea itself stands out with about 1,000 of those languages, other neighboring archipelagoes are also well endowed—Vanuatu, for example, with about 105, and the Philippines with 160.

Many New Guinea languages are so distinctive that they have no proven relationship with any other language in the world, not even with any other New Guinea language. As I travel across New Guinea, every 10 or 20 miles I pass between tribes with languages as different as English is from Chinese. And most of those languages are "tiny" ones, with fewer than 1,000 speakers.

How did these enormous geographic differences in linguistic diversity arise? Partly, of course, from differences in topography and human population density. But there's another reason as well: the original linguistic diversity of many areas has been homogenized by expansions of political states in the last several thousand years, and by expansions of farmers in the last 10,000 years. New Guinea, Vanuatu, the Philippines, and aboriginal Australia were exceptional in never having been unified by a native empire. To us, the British and Spanish empires may be the most familiar examples of centralized states that imposed their state language on conquered peoples. However, the Inca and Aztec empires similarly imposed Quechua and Nahuatl on their Indian subjects before A.D. 1500. Long before the rise of political states, expansions of farmers must have wiped out thousands of hunter-gatherer languages. For instance, the expansion of Indo-European farmers and herders that began around 4000 B.C. eradicated all preexisting Western European languages except Basque.

I'd guess that before expansions of farmers began in earnest around 6000 B.C. the world harbored tens of thousands of languages. If so, then we may *already* have lost much of the world's linguistic diversity. Of those vanished languages, a few—such as Etruscan, Hittite, and Sumerian—lingered long enough to be written down and preserved for us. Far more languages, though, have vanished without a trace. Who knows what the speech of the Huns and the Picts, and of uncounted nameless peoples, sounded like?

As linguists have begun surveying the status of our surviving languages, it has become clear that prognoses for future survival vary enormously. Here are some calculations made by linguist Michael Krauss of the University of Alaska at Fairbanks. Presumably among the languages with the most secure futures are the official national languages of the world's sovereign states, which now number 170 or so. However, most states have officially adopted English, French, Spanish, Arabic, or Portuguese, leaving only about 70 states to opt for other languages. Even if one counts regional languages, such as the 15 specified in India's constitution, that yields at best a few hundred languages officially protected anywhere in the world. Alternatively, one might consider languages with over a million speakers as secure, regardless of their official status, but that definition also yields only 200 or so secure languages, many of which duplicate the list of official languages. What's happening to the other 5,800 of the world's 6,000?

As an illustration of their fates, consider Alaska's 20 native Eskimo and Indian languages. The Eyak language, formerly spoken by a few hundred Indians on Alaska's south coast, had declined by 1982 to two native speakers, Marie Smith (age 72) and her sister Sophie Borodkin. Their children speak only English. With Sophie Borodkin's death last year at the age of 80, the language world of the Eyak people reached its final silence—except when Marie Smith speaks Eyak with Michael Krauss. Seventeen other native Alaskan languages are moribund, in that not a single child is learning them. Although they are still being spoken by older people, they too will meet the fate of Eyak when the last of those speakers dies; in addition, almost all of them have fewer than 1,000 speakers each. That leaves only two native Alaskan languages still being learned by children and thus not yet doomed: Siberian Yupik, with 1,000 speakers, and Central Yupik, with a grand total of 10,000 speakers.

The situation is similar for the 187 Indian languages surviving in North America outside Alaska, such as Chickasaw, Navajo, and Nootka. Krauss estimates that 149 of these are already moribund. Even Navajo, the language with by far the largest number of speakers (around 100,000), has a doubtful future, as many or most Navajo

children now speak only English. Language extinction is even further advanced in aboriginal Australia, where only 100 of the original 250 languages are still spoken or even remembered, and only 7 have more than 1,000 speakers. At best, only 2 or 3 of those aboriginal languages will retain their vitality throughout our lifetime.

In monographs summarizing the current status of languages, one encounters the same types of phrase monotonously repeated. "Ubykh [a language of the northwest Caucasus] . . . one speaker definitely still alive, perhaps two or thee more." "Vilela [sole surviving language of a group of Indian languages in Argentina] . . . spoken by only two individuals." "The last speaker of Cupeño [an Indian language of southern California], Roscinda Nolasquez of Pala, California, died in 1987 at the age of 94." Putting these status reports together, it appears that up to half of the world's surviving languages are no longer being learned by children. By some time in the coming century, Krauss estimates, all but perhaps a few hundred languages could be dead or moribund.

Why is the rate of language disappearance accelerating so steeply now, when so many languages used to be able to persist with only a few hundred speakers in places like traditional New Guinea? Why do declining languages include not only small ones but also ones with many speakers, including Breton (around 100,000) and even Quechua (8.5 million)? Just as there are different ways of killing people—by a quick blow to the head, slow strangulation, or prolonged neglect—so too are there different ways of eradicating a language.

The most direct way, of course, is to kill almost all its speakers. This was how white Californians eliminated the Yahi Indian language between 1853 and 1870, and how British colonists eliminated all the native languages of Tasmania between 1803 and 1835. Another direct way is for governments to forbid and punish use of minority languages. If you wondered why 149 out of

187 North American Indian languages are now moribund, just consider the policy practiced until recently by the U.S. government regarding those languages. For several centuries we insisted that Indians could be "civilized" and taught English only by removing children from the "barbarous" atmosphere of their parents' homes to English-language-only boarding schools, where use of Indian languages was absolutely forbidden and punished with physical abuse and humiliation.

But in most cases language loss proceeds by the more insidious process now underway at Rotokas. With political unification of an area formerly occupied by sedentary warring tribes comes peace, mobility, intermarriage, and schools. Mixed couples may have no common language except the majority language (for example, English or Pidgin English in Papua New Guinea, the nation to which Bougainville belongs). Young people in search of economic opportunity abandon their native-speaking villages and move to mixed urban centers, where again they have no option except to speak the majority language. Their children's schools speak the majority language. Even their parents remaining in the village learn the majority language for its access to prestige, trade, and power. Newspapers, radio, and TV overwhelmingly use majority languages understood by most consumers, advertisers, and subscribers. (In the United States, the only native languages regularly broadcast are Navajo and Yupik.)

The usual result is that minority young adults tend to become bilingual, then their children become monolingual in the majority language. Eventually the minority language is spoken only by older people, until the last of them dies. Long before that end is reached, the minority language has degenerated through loss of its grammatical complexities, loss of forgotten native words, and incorporation of foreign vocabulary and grammatical features.

Those are the overwhelming facts of worldwide language extinction. But now let's play devil's advocate and ask, So what? Are we really so sure this loss is a terrible thing? Isn't the existence of thousands of languages positively harmful, first because they impede communication, and second because they promote strife? Perhaps we should actually *encourage* language loss.

The devil's first objection is that we need a common language to understand each other, to conduct commerce, and to get along in peace. Perhaps it's no accident that the countries most advanced technologically are ones with few languages. Multiple languages are just an impediment to communication and progress—at least that's how the devil would argue.

To which I answer: Of course different people need some common language to understand each other! But that doesn't require eliminating minority languages; it only requires bilingualism. We Americans forget how exceptional our monolingualism is by world standards. People elsewhere routinely learn two or more languages as children, with little effort. For example, Denmark is one of the wealthiest and most contented nations in the world. Danes have no problem doing business profitably with other countries, even though practically no one except the 5 million Danes speaks Danish. That's because almost all Danes also speak English, and many speak other foreign languages as well. Still, Danes have no thought of abandoning their tongue. The Danish language, combined with polylingualism, remains indispensable to Danes being happily Danish.

Perhaps you're thinking now, All right, so communication doesn't absolutely require us all to have a single language. Still, though, bilingualism is a pain in the neck that you yourself would rather be spared.

But remember that bilingualism is practiced especially by minority language speakers, who learn majority languages. If they choose to do that extra work, that's their business; monolingual speakers of majority languages have no right or need to prevent them. Minorities struggling to preserve their language ask only for the freedom to decide for themselves—without being excluded, humiliated, punished, or killed for exercising that freedom. Inuits (Eskimos) aren't asking U.S. whites to learn Inuit; they're just asking that Inuit schoolchildren be permitted to learn Inuit along with English.

The devil's second objection is that multiple languages promote strife by encouraging people to view other peoples as different. The civil wars tearing apart so many countries today are determined by linguistic lines. Whatever the value of multiple languages, getting rid of them may be the price we have to pay if we're to halt the killing around the globe. Wouldn't the world be a much more peaceful place if the Kurds would just agree to speak Arabic or Turkish, if Sri Lanka's Tamils would consent to speak Sinhalese, and if the Armenians would switch to Azerbaijani (or vice versa)?

That seems like a very strong argument. But pause and consider: language differences aren't the sole cause, or even the most important cause, of strife. Prejudiced people will seize on any difference to dislike others, including differences of religion, politics, ethnicity, and dress. One of the world's most vicious civil wars today, that in the land that once was Yugoslavia, pits peoples unified by language but divided by religion and ethnicity: Orthodox Serbs against Catholic Croats and Muslim Bosnians, all speaking Serbo-Croatian. The bloodiest genocide of history was that carried out under Stalin, when Russians killed mostly other Russians over supposed political differences. In the world's bloodiest genocide since World War II, Khmer-speaking Cambodians under Pol Pot killed millions of other Khmer-speaking Cambodians.

If you believe that minorities should give up their languages in order to promote peace, ask yourself whether you believe that minorities should also promote peace by giving up their religions, their ethnicities, their political views. If you believe that freedom of religion but not of language is an inalienable human right, how would you explain your inconsistency to a Kurd or an Inuit? Innumerable examples besides those of Stalin and Pol Pot warn us that monolingualism is no safeguard of peace. Even if the suppression of differences of language, religion, and ethnicity did promote peace (which I doubt), it would exact a huge price in human suffering.

Given that people do differ in language, religion, and ethnicity, the only alternative to tyranny or genocide is for people to learn to live together in mutual respect and tolerance. That's not at all an idle hope. Despite all the past wars over religion, people of different religions do coexist peacefully in the United States, Indonesia, and many other countries. Similarly, many countries that practice linguistic tolerance find that they can accommodate people of different languages in harmony: for example, three languages in Finland (Finnish, Swedish, and Lapp), four in Switzerland (German, French, Italian, and Romansh), and nearly a thousand in Papua New Guinea.

All right, so there's nothing inevitably harmful about minority languages, except the nuisance of bilingualism for the minority speakers. What are the positive advantages of linguistic diversity, to justify that minor nuisance?

One answer is that languages are the most complex products of the human mind, each differing enormously in its sounds, structure, and pattern of thought. But a language itself isn't the only thing lost when a language goes extinct. Each language is indissolubly tied up with a unique culture, literature (whether written or not), and worldview, all of which also represent

Indian Education:

A Government View

(Excerpts from a report by J.D.C. Atkins,
U.S. Commissioner of Indian Affairs from 1885 to 1888.)

"The instruction of Indians in the vernacular [that is, in Indian language] is not only of no use to them, but is detrimental to the cause of their education and civilization, and it will not be permitted in any Indian school over which the Government has any control. . . . This [English] language, which is good enough for a white man and a black man, ought to be good enough for the red man. It is also believed that teaching an Indian youth in his own barbarous dialect is a positive detriment to him. The first step to be taken toward civilization, toward teaching the Indians the mischief and folly of continuing in their barbarous practices, is to teach them the English language."

Indian Education:

An Indian View

(Excerpts from interviews with Indian adults in British Columbia
about their experiences as children forced to attend missionary schools,
quoted in a report by Robert Levine and Freda Cooper.)

INTERVIEWER: "Were you allowed to speak your own language?"
INDIAN MAN: "We wasn't allowed to speak our language in the open."
INTERVIEWER: "What would happen if you did?"
INDIAN MAN: "Well, they punish us for anything we do . . . go without supper or whatever . . . and that was a big punishment, if you missed a meal, 'cause he feed us very little anyway. You go hungry all the time in there."
INDIAN WOMAN: "They said, no more—you don't talk your own language anymore; that's finished. And if we were caught talking our own language we would get punished."
INTERVIEWER: "How would they punish you?"
INDIAN WOMAN: "Well, they had these straps, these thick straps that the Sisters carried under their aprons."
INTERVIEWER, to another Indian woman: "What were the punishments you saw; how severe were they?"
INDIAN WOMAN: "Sometimes the worst punishment was to scrub I don't know how many flights of stairs, or do a large amount of work, where you're working all day— or else most of the punishment was done by straps on the hand."
INTERVIEWER: "When you got out of boarding school, did you find that you had difficulty communicating with other people . . . when you tried to talk with them in your own language?'
INDIAN WOMAN: "Oh, yeah, I had a real difficulty, mostly in pronouncing the words, thinking in Indian again, that sort of thing."

the end point of thousands of years of human inventiveness. Lose the language and you lose much of that as well. Thus the eradication of most of the world's accumulation of languages would be an overwhelming tragedy, just as would be the destruction of most of the world's accumulated art or literature. We English-speakers would regard the loss of Shakespeare's language and culture as a loss to humanity; Rotokas villagers feel a similar bond to their own language and culture. We are putting millions of dollars into the effort to save one of the world's 8,600 bird species, the California condor. Why do we care so little about most of the world's 6,000 languages, or even desire their disappearance? What makes condors more wonderful than the Eyak language?

A second answer addresses two often-expressed attitudes: "One language is really as good as another," or conversely, "English is much better than any of those fiendishly complicated Indian languages." In reality, languages aren't equivalent or interchangeable, and there's no all-purpose "best language." Instead, as everyone fluent in more than one language knows, different languages have different advantages, such that it's easier to discuss or think about certain things, or to think and feel in certain ways, in one language than another. Language loss doesn't only curtail the freedom of minorities, it also curtails the options of majorities.

Now perhaps you're thinking, Enough of all this vague talk about linguistic freedom, unique cultural inheritance, and different options for thinking and expressing. Those are luxuries that rate low priority amid the crises of the modern world. Until we solve the world's desperate socioecionomic problems, we can't waste our time on bagatelles like obscure Indian languages.

But think again about the socioeconomic problems of the people speaking all those obscure Indian languages (and thousands of other obscure languages around the world). Their problems aren't just narrow ones of jobs and job skills, but broad ones of cultural disintegration. They've been told for so long that their language and everything else about their culture are worthless that they believe it. The costs to our government, in the form of welfare benefits and health care, are enormous. At the same time, other impoverished groups with strong intact cultures—like some recent groups of immigrants—are already managing to contribute to society rather than take from it.

Programs to reverse Indian cultural disintegration would be far better than welfare programs, for Indian minorities and for majority taxpayers alike. Similarly, those foreign countries now wracked by civil wars along linguistic lines would have found it cheaper to emulate countries based on partnerships between proud intact groups than to seek to crush minority languages and cultures.

Those seem to me compelling cultural and practical benefits of sustaining our inherited linguistic diversity. But if you're still unconvinced, let me instead try to persuade you of another proposition: that we should at least record as much information as possible about each endangered language, lest all knowledge of it be lost. For hundreds, perhaps thousands, of the world's 6,000 languages, we have either no written information at all, or just brief word lists. If many of those languages do indeed vanish, at least we'd have preserved as much knowledge as possible from irreversible loss.

What is the value of such knowledge? As one example, consider that relationships of the languages that survive today serve to trace the history of human development and migrations, just as relationships of existing animal and plant species trace the history of biological evolution. All linguists agree, for instance, that we can trace existing Indo-European languages back to an ancestral Proto-Indo-European language spoken somewhere in Europe or western Asia around 6,000 years ago. Now some linguists are trying to trace languages and peoples back much further in time, possibly even back to the origin of all human language. Many tiny modern languages, the ones now most at risk of vanishing unrecorded, have proved disproportionately important in answering that question that never fails to interest each of us: Where did I come from?

Lithuanian, for example, is an Indo-European language with only 3 million speakers, and until recently it struggled against Russian for survival. It's dwarfed by the combined total of 2 billion speakers of the approximately 140 other Indo-European languages. Yet Lithuanian has proved especially important in understanding Indo-European language origins because in some respects it has changed the least and preserved many archaic features over the past several thousand years.

Of course, dictionaries and grammars of Lithuanian are readily available. If the Lithuanian language were to go extinct, at least we'd already know enough about it to use it in reconstructing Indo-European language origins. But other equally important languages are at risk of vanishing with much less information about them recorded. Why should anyone care whether four tiny languages, Kanakanabu, Saaroa, Rukai, and Tsou, spoken by 11,000 aborigines in the mountains of Taiwan, survive? Other Asians may eventually come to care a lot, because these languages may constitute one of the four main branches of the giant Austronesian language family. That family, consisting of some 1,000 languages with a total of 200 million speakers, includes Indonesian and Tagalog, two of Asia's most important languages today. Lose those four tiny aboriginal languages and these numerous Asian peoples may lose one-quarter of the linguistic data base for reconstructing their own history.

If you now at last agree that linguistic diversity isn't evil, and might even be interesting and good, what can you do about the present situation? Are we helpless in the face of the seemingly overwhelming forces tending to eradicate all but a few big languages from the modern world?

No, we're not helpless. First, professional linguists themselves could do a lot more than most of them are now doing. Most place little value on the study of vanishing languages. Only recently have a few linguists, such as Michael Krauss, called our attention to our impending loss. At minimum, society needs to train more linguists and offer incentives to those studying the languages most at risk of disappearing.

As for the rest of us, we can do something individually, by fostering sympathetic awareness of the problem and by helping our children become bilingual in any second language that we choose. Through government, we can also support the use of native languages. The 1990 Native American Languages Act actually *encourages* the use of those languages. And at least as a start, Senate Bill 2044, signed by former President Bush last October, allocates a small amount of money—$2 million a year—for Native American language studies. There's also a lot that minority speakers themselves can do to promote their languages, as the Welsh, New Zealand Maori, and other groups have been doing with some success.

But these minority efforts will be in vain if strongly opposed by the majority, as has happened all too often. Should some of us English-speakers not choose actively to promote Native American languages, we can at least remain neutral and avoid crushing them. Our grounds for doing so are ultimately selfish: to pass on a rich, rather than a drastically impoverished, world to our children.

Confucius and the VCR

Jesse W. Nash

𝄞𝄞𝄞𝄞𝄞

As you read:
1. *What cultural values are reinforced in Vietnamese and Chinese movies?*
2. *What are the "concentric circles of conflict" portrayed in these movies?*

Vietnamese immigrants in the United States are intensely curious about almost all movies or television shows, aptly referring to themselves as "movie addicts." The TV set and videocassette recorder have become common features of their homes and are the focus of much conversation concerning what it means to be an American and what it means to be Vietnamese in the United States.

American television and movies worry many Vietnamese, especially parents and elders, who see them as glorifying the individual and his or her war with the family, social institutions, the community, and even the state. Reflecting the individualism of American culture, conflict resolution typically occurs at the expense of the family or community (except in situation comedies usually panned as being "saccharine" or "unrealistic" by television critics). American movies and television, many Vietnamese assert, are most effective in imagining worlds of mistrust, promoting self-righteous rebellion, and legitimizing the desires of the individual.

The antiauthoritarianism of much of American television and movies disturbs Vietnamese, but there are also offerings they commend, such as "The Cosby Show," which explores and promotes val-ues they themselves prize: familial loyalty, togetherness, and a resolution of conflicts within the established social structures. Such shows, I've been told, remind the Vietnamese of their Confucian education and heritage.

Because the language of the immigrant community is still primarily Vietnamese, movies on videotapes imported from Taiwan and Hong Kong and dubbed in Vietnamese form a significant portion of the entertainment diet. The movies most favored are long, multitape epics that run from five to more than twenty hours. These include contemporary crime stories, soap operas, and romantic comedies, but the clear favorites are the medieval-military-romance cum kung fu extravaganzas.

There is a steady stream of customers at the various local shops that rent imported videotapes. Neighbors, friends, and relatives compare notes on favorite films and stars. Posters and pocket photos of heroes and heroines are eagerly bought. Entire families will sit through the night eating up the latest kung fu romance, their reddened eyes a testimony of devotion to the genre and quality of the film.

Atop nearly every TV set in the community rests a tape. While babysitting, grandmothers and aunts will place toddlers in front of the tube and play a Chinese film. (Depending on the time of day, little boys will cut in to watch "The Transformers,"

"Thundercats," or "G.I. Joe.") Young women confess that they would like to visit Hong Kong, where their favorite movies are made and their favorite stars live. Young men with a definite tendency to hesitancy and the doldrums are not so much reacting to a harsh social and familial atmosphere as modeling their behavior on the beloved melancholic hero of the Chinese movie. Older, more mature men are not immune to the wiles of the films either. I have observed formerly impassive faces creased with emotion and dampened by tears during the viewing of a particularly sad movie, the dialogue of which is punctuated by sniffling sounds and a periodic blowing of noses.

The plots of these films are complicated and try the patience of outside audiences to whom I have introduced these films. Their broad outline can best be described as a series of concentric circles of conflict. At the outer edge, there is a general global conflict, such as a war between the Chinese and the Mongols (the latter sure to bring heated boos from the audience). Moving toward the center, the scope of the conflict—but not its intensity—narrows to two families or two different kung fu schools. Judging either side is a difficult endeavor; the conflict is not merely a matter of an obvious good versus an obvious evil, as in American movies. Conflict is inherent in the human desire to form groups, whether the group is a family unit or a kung fu school. And beneath this umbrella of intergroup conflict, there is intragroup conflict. This kind of conflict is generally romantically induced when someone falls in love with a member of an opposing family or school.

While Western media are filled with conflict, they have nothing over the conflict-fraught Chinese film. Take, for example, *The Mighty Sword* (Than Chau Kiem Khach). Bac Phi, the hero, is a promising kung fu artist, whose master has high hopes of elevating him to take his own place upon retirement. To belong to a kung

fu school is to belong to a family, with all that that entails in Oriental culture. The master is the father, and the other members are brothers and sisters. The school's members generally marry members of other schools to form alliances. As in any real family, there is considerable conflict and dissent, but the ideal of remaining faithful and obedient to the master is stressed.

Bac Phi's troubles begin when he helps a damsel, Lady Tuyet, who is being besieged by ruffians. She herself is an incredibly gifted kung fu fighter and, as fate would have it, perhaps the most beautiful woman in the world. They immediately fall in love—love at first sight being the rule in the world of Chinese film.

In the film one gets a feel for the Chinese and, by derivation, the Vietnamese way of romance. The hero and heroine do not touch; most certainly, they do not fondle or kiss. With a particularly sad melody in the background, they look into each other's eyes. The viewers all sigh and point; they know that the two are in love by "reading their eyes." Traditionally in Vietnam, lovers communicated with their eyes. Folklore, proverbs, and songs all depict a romance of the eyes: "Like a knife cutting the yellow betel leaf,/His eyes glance, her eyes dart back and forth." The stage is set for what appears to be a romance made in Heaven. Our two lovers vow to marry and to love each other forever.

After this moment, the meaning of the sad melody becomes apparent. The hero and heroine have pledged their love in ignorance of certain facts ruling the social reality around them. The lovers learn that their two schools are mortal enemies. Bac Phi's school and master are held to be responsible for the murder of Tuyet's father, and neither Bac Phi's master nor Tuyet's mother will countenance the marriage. The intragroup relationships of both lovers are strained. Tuyet and her mother are at odds and come to blows. Bac Phi's relationship with his best friend is strained, and he learns that his master is planning to have him marry another girl.

At this point in American television and movies, we would expect an easy solution to the problem. (To the dismay of the audience, I counseled "Elope!") The Chinese and Vietnamese solution is much more complicated. To decide between Tuyet and his school is not a simple matter, and characteristically for the Chinese hero, Bac Phi is paralyzed by the situation, torn between his lover and his quasi family, his desire and his duty. He becomes lovesick and pines away for Tuyet but never decides once and for all to choose her over his school.

To make matters worse, there are forces behind the scenes manipulating all involved as if they were puppets. Unseen powers are seeking to deepen the rift between Bac Phi's school and that of Tuyet. These powers attempt to undermine Bac Phi's love for and trust in Tuyet by posing one of their own as Tuyet and having him/her murder one of Bac Phi's schoolmates. An already impossible situation is raised to the nth degree. Bac Phi, because of his position in his school, must now avenge the death.

The conflict and its resolution are characteristic of the Vietnamese community. When I asked why the couple simply didn't run away and elope, the Vietnamese audience laughed. "That is the American way," I was told. "But we have a Confucian tradition." The Vietnamese were trained in Confucian values at school and at home. Confucianism, in a Vietnamese context, is a tradition of loyalty to one's family, superiors, and prior obligations. "We were always taught to love our parents more than life itself," one woman observed. "Parents were more important than the man or woman you loved."

The conflict would not actually be resolved by Bac Phi and Tuyet eloping and abandoning the social units to which they belong. As the Vietnamese themselves ask,

"Could Tuyet trust Bac Phi if he were to fudge on his obligations to his school?" If Bac Phi will sever the bonds of previously established relationships, such as those with friends and superiors, what guarantee does Tuyet have that, when she has lost her figure and taken on wrinkles, he won't abandon her and chase after a younger, more nubile woman? There is a logic of trust in the films and the community that forbids them to take advantage of a simplistic formula, namely, "If you want it, go for it." The Vietnamese, ever moralistic, will ask, "Is it right for you to want it?"

The conflict, in the case of *The Mighty Sword*, is eventually resolved by the defeat of the powers behind the scenes, by a change of heart and character on the part of Tuyet's mother and Bac Phi's master, and by the two lovers working to break the endless cycle of revenge and misunderstanding. The conflict is resolved within the social structures, not by their destruction. Despite the mazelike layers of deceit, fear, and manipulation, the movie ends affirming the ultimate worthwhileness of living in society, of being a social animal and not merely a lover.

Unlike most American television shows and movies, the Chinese hero does not always get the girl. A happy ending cannot be predicted. Although most Vietnamese I have talked to prefer a happy ending to their Chinese films, they appreciate and approve of the ethical message of a melancholic ending. "Love doesn't conquer all," one viewer told me, tears in his eyes. "Sometimes we have to pay for our mistakes. Sometimes we don't get what we want just because we want it." One woman recommended a particularly touching Chinese soap opera to me. "It has a very sad ending. It is very beautiful. It is very Confucian." She explained that the movie, which I later watched with a lump in my jaded throat, tried to teach that romance must be accompanied by ethics. One cannot simply be a lover. One also has to be a good son or daughter and citizen.

In America, where films and television shows tend to glorify the individual and romance, the Chinese films the Vietnamese adore reaffirm traditional values and help educate their children in the art of being Confucian. Traditional Vietnamese Confucianism has sneaked in through the back door, so to speak, through the VCR. American pluralism and technology have made this possible. They also may have let in a Trojan horse that promises to offer a venerable critique of certain American values. The Vietnamese may do American culture a favor by offering a countervision of what it means to be a social animal, and not merely an animal.

½
70

Tech in the Jungle

Carl Zimmer

As you read:
1. *How is the camcorder "mightier than the war club"?*
2. *What is the political goal of the Kayapó? How are they using modern technology to achieve this goal?*

The Kayapó chiefs had come to see the damage. The Tucuruí hydroelectric dam, recently built on the Tocantins River in eastern Brazil, had flooded 800 square miles of rain forest that had once been the home of the Parakanan and Gavioes Indians. Now Electronorte, the regional power company, was planning to build a whole series of dams in the middle of Kayapó territory, including one that would flood an area more than twice as large as the Tucuruí reservoir. Wearing full ceremonial costume, with brilliantly feathered headdresses and black body paint and, in some cases, enormous disks in their lower lips, the Kayapó chiefs toured the Tucuruí dam. They took a boat trip on the new lake. They looked out at the dead trees that still rose, bleached and bare, above the water, and they wanted all their kin to see what a dam could do. So they videotaped it.

That was in January 1989. In the months that followed the videotape was seen by hundreds of Kayapó on a videocassette recorder hooked up to a gasoline-powered generator. The dramatic footage helped unite the factious Kayapó, who number no more than 3,000 and live in villages scattered across hundreds of miles of central Brazilian jungle. They staged demonstrations at the site of the largest of the proposed dams and in the nearby town of Altamira. And for the moment, at least, they won: within two months of the chiefs' visit to Tucuruí, the Altamira dam project was put on hold, perhaps for good.

The Kayapó experience isn't unique. Throughout the Amazon, Indian tribes are turning to modern communications and computer technology to help them protect the rain forest and, more paradoxically, to help them protect a thoroughly unmodern way of life. The sight of a man in body paint and a loincloth toting a camcorder seems incongruous to someone in the United States. But with 2,500 acres of Amazonian rain forest being lost every day, the Indians themselves are interested in whatever tools work. "The hard truth of the matter is that Amazonian Indians have to play with fire," says anthropologist Jason Clay, director of research at Cultural Survival, a human rights group that has helped Indians acquire modern technology, "because everything around them is burning."

The fight over the Altamira project makes it clear how differently Indians and many other Brazilians view the rain forest. Altamira was the centerpiece of a huge program of dam building in the Amazon that Electronorte predicted would add 20 gigawatts to Brazil's power supply—enough power to satisfy all of New England—by the turn of the century. Brazil certainly needs more power; at present many towns get their electricity from diesel-fired generators, and that fuel has to be hauled in over poor roads or by barge. The shaky energy supply could end up throttling

Carl Zimmer/© 1990 Discover Magazine

Brazil's effort to develop the Amazon and to move part of its rapidly growing population out of its clogged cities.

Hydroelectric projects, which provide large amounts of cheap, clean power, might be the solution for Brazil—as they were for the American West earlier in this century. According to Electronorte, the reservoirs from the 11 dams it still has planned for the Amazon region (not including the Altamira project) will cover a total of 3,800 square miles. That's twice the size of Delaware, but it represents only two-tenths of one percent of the Brazilian Amazon. To Electronorte, the loss of that land and the cost of relocating a few thousand Indians is a reasonable price to pay for a reliable energy supply.

Not surprisingly, the Kayapó didn't agree with that logic, which is why they wanted the Altamira project canceled. It wasn't just a question of not wanting to move their villages. Their lives are intertwined with the rain forest around them to an extent that is difficult for citizens of industrialized societies to appreciate. The Kayapó garden, hunt, fish, and forage in the rain forest. Its plants and animals figure heavily in their shamanistic rituals. At a Washington press conference, a Kayapó chief named Paiakan tried to dissuade the World Bank from funding the Altamira project. "The forest is our salvation," he said. "We need to preserve our forests, and within our forests we need to preserve our cultures. Without our cultures, there is no reason to live."

As the venue for Paiakan's remarks indicates, not all Kayapó shun contact with the outside world. To be sure, there are still villages whose residents are willing to kill any whites who trespass on their land. But other villages believe in some interaction with white society. Some of the chiefs of Gorotire, for instance, were educated in cities, and the village makes $2 million a year from the proceeds of gold mines on its territory. Even before the Altamira conflict, the villagers had decided to invest in a television, videocassette recorder, video

camera, satellite dish, and an airplane and pilot. Modern technology is not a new concept to the Kayapó.

It was Paiakan who realized that such technology could be used to unite the diverse Kayapó against the dam project—and also to focus the rising power of the international environmental movement on what might seem a purely local dispute. All he had to do was get the word out. Video images of the Tucuruí dam galvanized the Kayapó, and Paiakan used two-way radios to communicate with chiefs in distant villages and plan a joint demonstration. With the help of a fax machine, he cooperated with outside groups who were trying to get the international media interested.

The efforts paid off. In February 1989, 500 Kayapó—a sixth of the tribe—demonstrated in Altamira. Some of them had traveled through hundreds of miles of jungle to get there. For several days they met with Electronorte officials, and the meetings were heavily covered by the world press. According to Terence Turner, a University of Chicago anthropologist who documented the protest, the global attention was crucial in forcing bankers to pull back from the Altamira dam project; the project became a symbol of the mismanagement of the rain forest. That success, says Turner, illustrates how far the Kayapó have come in the 28 years that he has been studying them: "They've become media manipulators—perhaps the best in Brazil." He is now trying to get them video editing equipment, so they can turn their uncut footage into more polished movies.

Their struggle is far from over, though, and media manipulation alone won't win it. The territory they claim is large—the size of Great Britain, for 3,000 people—and the incursions on it are many. White settlers burn the rain forest and convert it to ranch land; miners stake claims for gold and pay the Kayapó a pittance. According to Clay, over the years Brazilian government officials have made and broken many verbal promises to stop such incursions and to help the Kayapó organize to defend their interests. Now, with the help of modern technology (and modern anthropologists), the Kayapó are organizing themselves.

Elsewhere in the Amazon modern technology is catching on as well. On the eastern flank of the Ecuadorian Andes, the Runa Indians are learning land management on a 386 AT personal computer with a 60-megabyte hard drive, having traded up from a small laptop. The Runa face some of the same problems as the Kayapó—notably land-grabbing by white settlers—but also some different ones. Having been encouraged by the Ecuadorian government to abandon their traditional crops in favor of cattle ranching and cash crops such as coffee and cacao, they now find themselves overwhelmed by the capital costs of those operations and desperately in debt. At the same time they are importuned by lumber companies, which would like to log Runa land for two or three dollars per tree.

To get out of this predicament the Runa are trying, with the help of Dominique Irvine of Cultural Survival, to find outside markets for traditional crops such as manioc (an edible root) and peach palm and to develop their own lumbering operation at a level that the forest can sustain. They are compiling an inventory of the trees in their forests, and they are studying their land holdings to determine the best locations for planting crops. The computer will allow them to organize all these data on a spreadsheet. It also allows them to use land-management software, provided by Irvine.

From the start, says Irvine, the Runa were completely unfazed by the computer. "The Runa see Western technology as a power that they wouldn't mind getting control over," she says. "But they want to get control over it for their own purposes. There's no fear or intimidation involved— I'm convinced that Americans are far more frightened of computers than are most Ecuadorian Indians."

Cultural Survival hopes to make software similar to what the Runa now use available to Indians throughout the Amazon Basin. And recently it received funding for an even more ambitious project. Starting this year, says Clay, he and his colleagues will begin distributing computers to villages around the Brazilian Amazon. The idea is to eventually create a sophisticated network linking the villages to the outside world and to one another. The 180 Brazilian tribes, now separated by cultural differences as well as by vast stretches of rain forest, will begin to share information on their common concerns, and, as Clay sees it, begin to collaborate in a common struggle for survival.

Clearly, though, Indian cultures that do manage to survive with the help of computers, fax machines, and video cameras will not be the same ones that existed just 30 years ago, when many Amazonian Indians had not yet seen their first white man. And just as clearly the role of anthropologists in the Amazon has changed, from studying cultures as they found them to helping them evolve along a particular path. But Clay, for one, has no qualms about his part in the technology transfer. "We can't just say, 'We won't let you have this because you'll change'," he says. "We all change, Indians included. It's a myth of ours that Indians have no history, that they're not a dynamic society. We can't insulate Indians from technology, as if we were God. Our obligation is to let them know what their choices are, supplying them with the best information possible."

Neither Warriors nor Victims: The Wauja Peacefully Organize to Defend Their Land

Emilienne Ireland

As you read:
1. *What is the significance of Kamukuaka to the Wauja?*
2. *Why did the Wauja request a government survey of land outside Xingu National Park? What did they do when this request was not fulfilled?*

An idea is spreading in the rain forests of central Brazil, perhaps even more rapidly than the fires of deforestation: that Indians as a group are politically powerful. Indians living in isolated rainforest villages throughout Amazonia are coming to think of themselves as sharing an identity as Indian people.

In February 1989, the Kayapó and their allies staged a historic peaceful demonstration against a proposed hydroelectric project at Altamira, Brazil. The project, to be funded by the World Bank, would have flooded vast areas of Kayapó land and destroyed most of their rivers for fishing. Outraged that they had not even been consulted, the Kayapó organized themselves and mounted a spectacular media event in protest. Their campaign was so creative and well-executed that the ensuing international outcry caused the World Bank to withdraw its support for the dam project. The success of this initiative at Altamira profoundly changed political reality and expectations for Indian people in Brazil and beyond. The stereotype of Indian as victim was broken.

One example of this legacy is the current effort of the Wauja of the Upper Xingu to reclaim peacefully, under Brazilian law, traditional fishing grounds and a sacred ceremonial site, Kamukuaka. Both are currently being invaded or occupied by ranchers and poachers.

The Wauja are a community of about 200 relatively traditional Arawak-speaking Indians who live by fishing and swidden horticulture in the Xingu National Park in Northern Mato Grosso. Although during the past generation their economy has become dependent on steel tools, fishhooks, and other manufactured goods, their involvement in the cash economy is still minimal and sporadic, limited mainly to sale of handicrafts.

Like virtually all Indian people, during the early period of contact they suffered horrific population losses due to recurrent epidemics of introduced disease. Unlike most other Indians, however, much of their traditional land was reserved for them under law soon after regular contact began in the 1940s. Despite this measure of protection, an essential part of their traditional territory was left out of the park. This unprotected area includes fishing grounds; agricultural land; and, most important, Kamukuaka, the most sacred Wauja ceremonial site.

By Emilienne Ireland, "Neither Warriors nor Victims: The Wauja Peacefully Organize to Defend Their Land." From *Cultural Survival Quarterly* 15, No. 1 (1991): 54-59. Reprinted by permission of Cultural Survival, 215 First Street, Cambridge, MA 02142, USA.

When the Wauja first began to understand that only part of their traditional territory fell within park boundaries, they protested to the government Indian agency, FUNAI, saying that the excluded area was essential to their survival as an Indian people. In response to the Wauja's most recent protests on the matter, FUNAI stated that a five-year study is needed before action can be taken.

The Wauja say that if nothing is done, in five years their ancestral land will be overrun and lost to them forever. Ranchers already occupy Kamukuaka, which is situated on the upper Batovi-Tamitatoala River. Atamai, political chief of the Wauja, describes the site as an extraordinary place, a great stone cavern beside a waterfall. At the mouth of the cavern are rock carvings made by ancestors of the Wauja, images of the parts of women that create life. The Wauja say the carvings have power to make living things increase and become abundant.

In addition, the Wauja revere Kamukuaka as the dwelling place of spirits. These spirits are respectfully addressed as kin, and referred to in the Wauja language as *inyákánáu,* "those who teach." The spirits guide the elders, appearing to them in visions and helping them heal the sick and maintain harmony within the village. To honor these spirits, the Wauja and their neighbors the Bacari have performed ceremonies at Kamukuaka for many generations. Wauja elders emphasize their most sacred ceremony, *kawika,* was performed at that place, and can proudly list deceased relatives who played kawika flutes at Kamukuaka. Mayaya, brother of Atamai and ceremonial leader of the Wauja, once sought to express his attachment to Kamukuaka without reducing it to words. An accomplished musician, he softly sang the melody of the sacred flute ceremony, concluding, "therefore that land means everything to us." In Wauja oral tradition, Kamukuaka has existed since the beginning of the world, before human beings

were created. Chief Atamai says his late father took his children there before he died and told them the sacred story linked to that place, of how the Sun dwelt in the great stone house when he still walked the earth in human form. Atamai himself has seen the gaping hole in the side of the cavern where, according to the ancestors, the Sun tried to tear the house apart in those ancient times.

Today, the ranchers keep the Wauja out. The ancient ceremonies cannot be performed, and young people know Kamukuaka only through the stories of their elders. Even worse, the Wauja say, is the desecration the ranchers have brought:

> They have turned Kamukuaka into a cattle pasture. There used to be giant trees all around the stone cavern, right up to the waterfall, but the ranchers have ripped them all out, leaving the earth bare and pitiful. They graze cattle there now. Our ceremonial ground is covered with stinking cattle droppings. The whiteman has covered the dust of our ancestors with shit.

The loss of Kamukuaka has had economic consequences for the Wauja as well, since the area along the Batovi near Kamukuaka is the only source for certain essential raw materials, including ceramic pigments, medicinal plants, and shells used in trade.

But Kamukuaka is not the only area where outsiders are invading the Wauja's ancestral land. In 1988 and again in 1989, Atamai complained to government officials that poachers were penetrating deep into Wauja territory and taking commercial quantities of fish to sell in Brazilian towns along the upper Batovi River. The poachers enter Wauja waters in boats filled with heavily armed men, and transport the fish to small trucks waiting at designated locations outside Wauja territory.

Wauja attempts to keep poachers out have led to violent confrontations in which poachers have shot at Wauja fishermen without provocation. Because of poachers, ordinary overnight fishing trips have suddenly become dangerous. Parents now discourage their adolescent boys from going on fishing trips unless accompanied by an elder who can be trusted to handle a threatening situation.

In addition to the physical danger posed by armed invaders, the sheer loss of fish is a serious problem, since the Wauja depend on fish for most of the protein in their diet. The areas currently being invaded by poachers are some of the best traditional fishing grounds. Generations of Wauja have relied on these areas to provide the large numbers of fish needed for ceremonial feasts. As a result of the continuing depredation by poachers, the Wauja say these areas are becoming "fished out." Poaching therefore threatens traditional Wauja economy, which is based in large part on communal sharing and ceremonial redistribution, not private profit and accumulated wealth.

The incident in early 1989, when the chief and other elders were shot at by poachers, was a turning point for the Wauja. That summer they decided the government would not defend their land and resources, and that they would have to do it themselves. They built a new village, Aldeia Batovi, within the park but near the area where the poachers and ranchers were penetrating. Gardens were cleared and planted; three large, traditional houses were built; and several families took up permanent residence there, maintaining contact with the main village at Lake Piyulaga by radio.

In June 1990, this new village was burned to the ground by an employee of a local rancher. The three houses were lost, along with all they contained: tools, stores of food, and medical supplies. Responding to letters of protest from abroad, the Brazilian government tried to minimize this incident, alleging the ranchers merely torched a makeshift campsite the Wauja had used overnight and abandoned. This is not the case. No temporary Wauja campsite has first-year gardens; the village was inhab-

ited. Confrontation was avoided only because the occupants were away attending a ceremony at the main village during the attack.

The Brazilian government insists these incidents were not violent, even though shots were fired and houses burned. The Wauja do not agree. They consider themselves under attack, and blame the escalating violence on faulty demarcation of their territory years ago, when the Xingu National Park was created. To correct the situation, the Wauja say park boundaries must be moved south a distance of 30-40 km, to include critical parts of their traditional territory. The area of land is not large, but it is crucial to the Wauja and to peace in the region. Though it forms the outer margin of their territory, it is at the center of their traditions and their identity as Indian people.

The Wauja have already rebuilt their burned village and renamed it Aldeia Ulupuene. To maintain an increased presence in the area, they are adding an airstrip at the site of the attack. Soon after their village was burned, the Wauja asked the government to survey the land officially outside the park in order to have it included in the park and thereby protected. Officials replied that they lacked funds for such a project. In response, the Wauja, together with members of other indigenous communities, decided to survey the land themselves.

In August, a volunteer force of about 50 men drawn from Kayapó, Kajabi, Soya, Trumai, Yawalapiti, and Wauja communities assembled at the burned village site to survey the land. This in itself is a major achievement by the Wauja, and a credit to the volunteers. In the first half of this century, some of these communities fought pitched battles against each other, and in several well-remembered instances inflicted heavy casualties and took women and children captive. The men in this volunteer group are working close beside traditional enemies of their fathers and grandfathers.

That they all are united in a common purpose bespeaks their determination to protect their shared future as Indian people.

The volunteers have begun clearing surveying sightlines and building the airstrip. The project is expected to take three to six months, depending on support from outside sources. Since the new village is six days' journey from the main village by dugout canoe, the Wauja need motorboats to transport people and supplies, as well as food to feed the volunteers.

The Rainforest Foundation, founded in 1988 by Kayapó chief Raoni and rock musician Sting to support Indian-initiated efforts to protect the rainforest, has taken on the Wauja project as a top priority. Olympio Serra, formerly director of the Xingu National Park and now working on the Rainforest Foundation's Brazilian board, Fundáçao Mata Virgem, reports that 4,000 liters of gasoline and food for the volunteers were shipped to the Wauja the first week of October 1990. These supplies should enable the Wauja to finish the job before the heavy rains arrive in December.

José Carlos Libânio at the Nucleus for Indigenous Rights (NDI) in Brasilia explains that surveying the area is an important step in protecting it for Indian people under Brazilian law. He says the Wauja's legal case, currently under preparation, stands to set a legal precedent on behalf of all Brazilian Indians. To expand the Xingu National Park boundaries, the Wauja's lawyers must challenge an administrative decree that currently prohibits altering existing boundaries of indigenous reserves. This decree works against Indians, denying them redress against boundary decisions made without their knowledge or consent.

Libânio says the Wauja case is strong, and he expects them to win it. However, it will take at least a year for the case to proceed through the Brazilian courts. During that time, the Wauja will need support from the international community. A public information and letter-writing campaign is currently being organized to help create a climate of opinion in Brazil favorable to a just resolution of the Wauja's legal case.

Although all Amazonian Indians are facing serious threats to their survival, the Wauja's case is crucial in several respects. First, their legal case stands to set a major precedent on behalf of all Brazilian Indians. If the Wauja win the right to reclaim traditional territory under law, all Brazilian Indians benefit.

Second, the Wauja campaign for nonviolent, legal reclamation of territory is setting a historical precedent as well. The Wauja have never attacked or killed Brazilian settlers. If they are successful in reclaiming their territory through entirely nonviolent means, it will be a landmark victory for both Indian rights and rainforest conservation.

Third, the Wauja's case presents a unique opportunity simply because they stand a good chance of winning. The Yanomami situation is currently receiving worldwide attention; Survival International rightly calls it one of the great humanitarian campaigns of the late twentieth century. Both in numbers of people affected, and in severity of human rights violations, the Yanomami case outweighs the Wauja case. But the Yanomami campaign faces great odds, and will be very difficult to win. The gold miners are organized and determined; the political situation is complex and entrenched. The suffering of the Yanomami is so intense and unrelenting that it is a public relations problem to maintain enough optimism to keep the international community actively involved.

The Wauja case, on the other hand, is relatively straightforward and easy to win. A win for the Wauja will help the Yanomami as well, because success attracts optimism and support. The Yanomami situation seems almost hopeless, and this is a great part of the problem. If the Wauja create a well-publicized victory for indigenous rights in Brazil, the cause of the Yanomami and other Brazilian Indians will be advanced, just as the Wauja's own cause was advanced by the Kayapó victory at Altamira.

It is difficult to convey to members of an international community that is increasingly mobile and secular how the Wauja, and other people in traditional small-scale societies, are connected to their ancestral lands not only by economic necessity, but by far deeper bonds. The Wauja's land provides far more than food, tools, and shelter. It is the dwelling place of the spirits who guide them, the birthplace of their children, and the resting place of their ancestors. It is the sacred landscape of all their poetry, stories, songs, and prayers; it is their one place upon the earth. Everything needed for human life, everything sacred and precious, flows from that land. If it is ripped away from the Wauja, if they lose it, they lose their future as Indian people, a danger of which they are keenly aware.

The Bushmen of Today

Megan Biesele

As you read:
1. *What is n!ore? Why is the legal institutionalization of the n!ore system important to the people of Nyae Nyae?*
2. *What is the Nyae Nyae Farmers' Cooperative?*
3. *Describe Bushman democracy.*

Until the 1950's several thousand Bushman people were still hunting large game with poisoned arrows and gathering wild food in the westward extension of the Kalahari basin in Namibia. This area provided a last refuge for the Bushman people, hunted as vermin since the first arrival of Dutch settlers at the Cape in 1652. In the Kalahari basin they were able to continue their ancient way of life, living in small, mobile bands of about 40 people, each one centered on and supported by the resources of a *n!ore*, the Ju/'hoan Bushman word meaning "the place to which you belong," or "the place which gives you food and water." Bushmen have lived around these *n!ores* for as long as 40,000 years, practicing one of the most ancient and simple human technologies on earth.

In the past 40 years, however, life has changed drastically for Namibia's Bushmen. In the mid-1960's the Odendaal Commission recommended to the South West African government that the West Caprivi and Bushmanland be designated as "homelands" for all the people classified as "Bushman" in Namibia. Ironically the proclamation of "homelands" has meant the loss of vast areas of land traditionally used by the Bushmen. The process of "legal"

dispossession, which predates the decision to establish homelands, signalled the end of the hunter-gatherer way of life for the vast majority of Namibian Bushmen. Beginning in the 1950's the Department of Nature Conservation began to expropriate large sections of the traditional hunting lands for game and nature reserves. The process began with the Hai//'om Bushmen being driven from their lands to make way for the Etosha Game Reserve. Around the same time the Kxoe Bushmen lost their land on the Kavango River when it was proclaimed a nature reserve. In 1968 the Department of Nature Conservation expropriated the West Caprivi for a game reserve. About 6000 Ju/'hoan people were evicted from the land they had lived on for centuries.

In 1970 Bushmanland was established. For the Ju/'hoan Bushmen it meant the loss of 90% of their traditional land of Nyae Nyae, and all but one of their permanent waterholes. Southern Nyae Nyae, about 32,000 sq km, was expropriated by the administration and given to the Herero as Hereroland East.

Northern Nyae Nyae, about 11,000 sq km was first incorporated into the Kavango homeland and then proclaimed the !Kaudum Game Reserve in 1982. One of the last acts of the Interim Government of

National Unity was to confirm the expropriation of the !Kaudum Game Reserve.

Today 33,000 people classified as "Bushman" in Namibia have no land on which to hunt, gather or produce food and are increasingly without work. Without land they have resorted to employment in the army or to ill-paid work for white and black farmers. The vast majority who have been unable to get employment squat near places of work, dependent on the wage earners. This has been the pattern for so long now that new generations have grown up without the skills to hunt and gather. Malnutrition and disease led to a 5% decline in the population classified as "Bushman" in the 1970's. . . .

The Ju/'hoan people of Eastern Bushmanland, called Nyae Nyae, have been more fortunate. Some 3,000 out of the total population of 33,000 Bushmen have retained ties to a fragment of their land. For the past generation they have been the only people in Namibia who have hunted and gathered for their living while learning new farming skills. They are also the only people classed as "Bushman" who still have real residential ties to their foraging territory.

Nyae Nyae stretches north to south along the Namibia-Botswana border between the Kavango River and the Eiseb Valley. Originally it extended over approximately 50,000 sq km. Hunter-gatherers need more than 37 sq km per person to sustain a stable population in this area. An uplift in the rock formation brings water to the surface in Nyae Nyae. Clearly visible on a geological map, the uplift makes Eastern Bushmanland rise like an island in a sea of sand. Twelve permanent and nine semi-permanent waterholes make the communal land habitable. . . .

In contrast to Nyae Nyae, Western Bushmanland—two thirds of the homeland created in 1970—lies in the deep sand sea. Water must come from deep boreholes requiring expensive pumping engines. The cost of fuel for pumping makes subsistence farming impossible. Bush foods and game are scarce. *Gifblaar*, a plant poisonous to cattle, is very common.

It was in Western Bushmanland that the South African Defense Force (SADF) chose to locate its "Bushman" battalion headquarters and bases. Bushmen from Namibia and those displaced by the Angolan civil war were recruited into the army as trackers and infantrymen for the offensive against Swapo in Angola. Thousands of Bushman people lived in Western Bushmanland until the elections in November 1989, supported by the relatively high salaries of war. Now with the war over, people have nowhere to turn. Some are reportedly trying to eat grass in a desperate struggle to survive. . . .

Most of the Bushmen who made a career of army life over the last decade are Barakwengo, Hai//'om and Vasekela people from the northern areas and from Angola. Now, as the wages of war dry up the soldiers and their families squat in a kind of numbness. They have no land and no homes.

"My future?" one man said, "I don't see a future."

Other ex-soldiers are more fortunate. Ju/'hoan Bushmen from Eastern Bushmanland around Tium!kui have land to return to, and families who have stayed on the land to develop and possess it. /Kaece /Kunta, whose people live at the permanent waterhole at /Aotcha settled by ≠Oma Stump, welcomed the end of life in the army when the war ended. /Kaece /Kunta has no regrets as he recalls his war experiences.

"They told us we would be getting on a plane in Rundu. We had to fly at night because when you fly into Angola in the daytime they shoot you down. The flight is about 1000 km. When we arrived there, they told us to be very careful of going out in the open, because planes were flying over and shooting from the air. It was here that we saw fighter planes for the first time in our lives. The white people lined us up and we stood there and looked at them. Then the white people said, 'Hey, Bushmen, you must watch out for those planes: if they see you they'll shoot you dead—' and after that we knew.

"When we were on the ground later, we were very much afraid, because the planes were searching for us up in the sky above. They shot at us terribly, pursuing us relentlessly. . . .

"People were also throwing hand grenades. These bombs are certain death and even to speak of them is to speak badly. The only reason we lived through it is we were taught how to be careful. If this had not happened, none of us Bushmen would have returned. All our thoughts were put to living through it.

"We saw the villages of the dead, those who had been killed, and their dead children. We saw the skulls of dead people, and those of children who had died. When you walked through these villages, you were stepping on death, the corpses of dead people. It was horrible. You had to step on them and they just crumbled to dust.

"If hunger gripped your middle while you were on these 'ops' and you hadn't seen food for three days, and then you had a chance to eat, you couldn't eat the food because it all tasted like death. If you were too weak to work, they'd prick your one shoulder with a needle, then prick your other shoulder, so you'd have strength to work well. . . .

"My parents didn't agree when I first wanted to go into the army. But I went in anyway—I thought it was just plain work. It was only later that they began killing people. The whole time I was in Angola, all I thought about was staying alive long enough to get back to my family."

Death by Myth

There are two kinds of films. One kind shows us as people like other people, who have things to do and plans to make.

This kind helps us. The other kind shows us as if we were animals, and plays right into the hands of people who want to take our land.

—Tsamkxao ≠Oma

One of many pernicious myths about Bushman people, exacerbated by films like "The Gods Must Be Crazy," is that they still live in a desert never-never land without unfulfilled desires. The reality is that all but about 3% of the Bushman people in Namibia are completely dispossessed and must struggle unremittingly to survive. Whether they do so on white-owned farms, on Herero or Kavango cattle posts, squatting at the edges of towns, or living in dependence on police or the army, their ability to control their own lives is very limited. As a people with a long history as hunter-gatherers, everything in their background conditions them for dependency on people they perceive as stronger.

Traditionally, the Bushmen had no leaders, believing that a person who set himself up as better than another was without shame and harmful to group life. Nurturant and undemanding of their children, they promoted tolerance and downplayed ambition. Thus they suffer today not only from exploitation at the hands of more arrogant peoples, but also from the social legacy of a life that once worked when land was limitless and competing people few. Bushman people can be fairly characterized as those who have again and again stood aside as stronger forces muscled in. . . .

A n!ore Is a Place You Do Not Leave

The trees are ours, and the elephants are ours. This is our land. Our things we make and wear come from it—our ostrich beads, our bows and arrows.

We Ju/'hoansi are people who have lived in our n!oresi for a long time. We didn't know the thing called a horse, and we made fires and did all our work without burning the tortoises and other tiny things. There were no white people's trucks driving around in our n!ore, here on our land. When these things came, their people saw us as nothing-things. So they shut off the land with fences and the eland died against the fences so that today our children are dying of hunger. There are no eland left, the wire has killed them all. And that fence between here and Botswana has also killed many animals. This was the work of governments. We once had our own government which kept us alive but this new government which has come in has killed us.

—/Kaece Kxao, N//haru≠'han, Eastern Bushmanland

Isolation from the outside world ended abruptly for the Ju/'hoansi when Native Administration of their area began in 1960. There was a migration of all bands to a single administrative centre called Tjum!kui, where they were given a school, a clinic, a church, a large jail, and some small jobs.

Some 900 Ju/'hoan people believed the administration's promises to teach them gardening and subsidize stock-raising, and an area which once supported 25 people by hunting and gathering was overwhelmed. A government-subsidized bottle store, unemployment, and the local disappearance of bush foods under heavy human pressure combined to turn Tjum!kui into a rural slum. The Ju/'hoansi called it "the place of death."

In the late 1970's a movement began among some families in Tjum!kui to return to the *n!oresi* from which they came. Tsamkxao ≠Oma and his father ≠Oma "Stump" took their people back to /Aotcha, location of the only permanent waterhole now left within the shrunken borders of Bushmanland. Black /Ui took his family to N≠aqmtjoha, and Kxao "Tekening," the artist, took his to N≠anemh. They began to work in earnest to hold onto their land. Now 25 new communities have returned to their families' old places. "We must lift ourselves up, or die!" people tell each other.

The Ju/'hoansi in Nyae Nyae have started a new life as farmers. They still rely a great deal upon hunting and gathering as they make the difficult transition to small-scale stock-raising. But they know the land left to them does not permit a return to hunting and gathering alone. Life in such a transition is not easy and they struggle against many things: against lions that kill their cattle, and elephants that trample their gardens and wreck their water pumps; against unhelpful or hostile officials who believe them incapable of development. They also struggle within themselves to adapt the cultural rules and values that underwrote the old foraging way of life to the very different one of agriculture.

Ju/'hoansi know that without more intensive food production they are doomed to remain wards of some government, dependent and vulnerable. Tsamkxao ≠Oma is the chairperson of the newly-formed Nyae Nyae Farmers' Cooperative, a body which ties all the communities together to support the farming effort. Since 1986 Tsamkxao and the representatives from the 25 new communities have worked to make the cooperative a democratic organization responsible for many decisions about development. But as Tsamkxao said, "The Farmers' Coop is coming into government things much later than everyone else: the Boers took hold of things first. Now it's very late and we have to get going.". . .

At the time of the November 1989 election in Namibia, the Nyae Nyae Farmers' Cooperative was ratifying its first constitution, ≠*Hanu a N!an!a'an.* Representatives from the 25 villages travelled the rutted dirt tracks of Eastern Bushmanland to hold informational meetings and explain the new document. Written by a committee of Ju/'hoansi and hired scribes in English and the Ju/'hoan language, the constitution is intended to inject legal strength into ancient Ju/'hoan concepts of communal land holding. . . .

Representatives of the Farmers' Cooperative know that media coverage of what they are now trying to do is essential. They want to make the point in Southern Africa that there are similar groups of people in other parts of the world. Australian Aborigines, and North and South American Indians are also struggling for land rights and self-determination. Tsamkxao ≠Oma, the coop chairman welcomed a journalist recently saying, "We're glad you're here because newspapers are very important to us. I went to a conference in Cape Town last year and I found that many people there had never even heard about us. Newspapers will help us inform people, and they may be a way to help end discrimination. These days we cannot accept that our children have to hear words like 'bobbejaan' and 'kaffir'."

Easily mythologized, Bushman people have captured the interest of popular media like film, TV, and glossy magazines. But their real voices have been obscured by the loud clamor of the myths in which they are enshrined. Silenced by the voice-overs, not only of film narrators, but also of neighbors and governments and even of well-meaning friends, they have gone on communicating to each other but not to the world outside. Bushmen have been seen both as a sort of fairyfolk, floating over the landscape with no concept of property and no need for solid resources, and as bloodthirsty poachers with a killer instinct. Romanticisation and denigration can amount to the same thing in the end, a kind of death by myth . . . or by misinformation.

The Nature Conservation forces of what was once the South West African government were succeeding in taking Bushman land right up until the last days before N Resolution 435 was implemented. Dreaming of a future revenue-generating tourist industry, the conservationists have sequestered huge swatches of what once was the well-known and reliably productive *n!lores* of the Ju/'hoan and Kxoe Bushmen. Tsamkxao spoke of an area of Nyae Nyae where Ju/'hoansi have lived for as long as anyone can remember, the permanent

waterhole of Gura, where Nature Conservation and the Department of Government Affairs have joined forces to promote safaris and trophy hunting at the expense of Farmers' Coop plans for the area.

"Something we've known for a long time is that the antelopes of Gura were ours, our fathers' fathers' sustenance. And the water there has been our source of life. Even I, when I was small, washed myself at Gura and drank the water there when I was thirsty. At that time I didn't know of a single European or Afrikaner who had been there. This government which calls itself 'Bushmanland' is talking about my things! Why should other people make money here from our animals? We have been here a long time: don't the Nature Conservation officials know they are just small children?"

Officials do seem to be neglecting an important source of information about the environment by not listening to the Ju/'hoan hunters. These people, with their long history of stability in the area have a great deal to contribute to conservation planning. Many generations of information about animal and plant species and their interactions should not be discounted simply because they have been passed on orally. The written tradition of scientific study in this area is young by comparison, and could profit from an infusion of older wisdom. Bushman folklore and religion contain evidence of a very ancient and healthy respect for natural resources, and an ethic of conservation which is thoroughgoing and socially sound. In fact, seeing these people as natural conservators may be a good way to appreciate what they can contribute. As a /Gwi Bushman, Compass Matsoma, of neighboring Botswana said recently, "We are the only ones who can live with animals without killing them all."

Not only tourists and hunters but also eager pastoral peoples now wait at the shrunken borders of "Bushmanland" for opportunities to move in. Descendants of survivors of the German Herero Wars at the beginning of this century, when General Von Trotha issued his famous genocide order to kill all men, women and children, have been living as refugees in Botswana. With the coming of independence, many now hope to return across the border and settle on the rich pastures and relatively abundant waters of the Nyae Nyae area, one of the last areas not yet overgrazed in Namibia.

But the Nyae Nyae people say "People shouldn't think they can ruin one area by grazing too many cattle and then move onto someone else's land and ruin that too. We will keep the numbers of our cattle small. We think not only of today but of tomorrow and the day after that."

As new cattle herders, Ju/'hoansi face many challenges. The primary one is the confrontation with their own tried-and-true means of organizing their work. While hunting with poisoned arrows is a most individualistic pursuit, sharing of all food was customary. Keeping cattle and planting dryland gardens involves a new negotiation of labor processes and products. Ju/'hoansi spend a lot of time talking about this.

A dark side coexists with the exultation and excitement of new beginnings. Alcohol undermines Ju/'hoan spirit as it does that of so many African communities. People in Eastern Bushmanland do not seem to be chronic alcoholics at this stage. Distance from bottle stores and poverty have protected most of them. But many brew beer from sugar and yeast on pension day, and when the bottle store was still open in Tjum!kui it caused immense social disruption.

Just after the independence election, Ju/'hoan people took their first public stand acknowledging that excessive drinking is a community problem. At a meeting of the Nyae Nyae Farmers' Cooperative, strong feeling arose over the issue of the social disruption caused by home-brewed beer.

"Those who drink are the ones who cause anger and fighting. Those who don't drink just sit quietly. . . . We're not saying don't drink at all, but just drink slowly and wisely. . . . I think we should say to ourselves, I have work to do before I drink. First I'm going to do my work.

"When you drink, you shouldn't go around thinking like a Boer and telling people that you are a big shot. If you do that, someday people will become angry with you and their hearts will grow big against you. You don't go saying you're a chief. Instead, you sit together and understand each other. None of us is a chief, we're all alike and have our little farms. So when you drink, just think clearly about it and talk to each other about being careful. We've been told now, so let's be smart about drinking. Let's not fight. Let's start today to talk to each other about drinking and help each other." (Dabe Dahm.)

The bottle store at Tjum!kui, which once did big business on army pay day, has been closed.

Back on their land after living in town with the problems of alcoholism and unemployment, Ju/'hoansi can once more be dignified examples for their children. "We are people who have our work," they say. Children see their mothers and fathers engaged again in productive activities they know well.

A sense of purpose again pervades life in Eastern Bushmanland. Enthusiasm to take part in building a new Namibia runs through the meetings of the Nyae Nyae Farmers' Coop. . . .

Not Knowing Things Is Death

The importance of knowledge in obtaining a living is very much present in the minds of the Ju/'hoan Bushmen. Once they had to be able reliably to tell the difference between poisonous and nonpoisonous plants and to judge the likelihood of crossing paths with a worthwhile animal at a given season of the year. They had to know how to make riems, rope, string, sinew thread, carrying bags and nets, stamping blocks, aerodynamically effective arrows, and much more, all from natural materials. The word for "owner" (*kxao*) in Ju/'hoan most deeply means "master," in the sense of one who knows, or knows how to use. To own property is to be its steward; to own an area of land, a *n!ore*, is not to possess it exclusively but to use it well.

"A big thing is that my food is here and my father taught me about it. I know where I can drink water here. My father said to me, 'These are your foods and the foods of your children's children.' If you stay in your *n!ore* you have strength. You have water and food and a place.". . .

When things change greatly in one generation, sometimes older people teach children, and sometimes children are in a position to teach adults. Kxao/Ai!ae of N≠anemh says to his boys that the way to keep your *n!ore* is to develop it.

"I hold my cattle in my left hand, and my garden in my right hand, and together they give me life.". . .

New ideas and new concepts have flooded into Nyae Nyae in one generation. Has there been enough time for Ju/'hoansi themselves to change sufficiently to participate in the coming independence? Events like UN Resolution 435 and free elections and the final end of apartheid have suddenly overtaken them with many of them not knowing what is really in store.

Like other Namibians, Ju/'hoan Bushmen have had their geographical isolation deepened by the apartheid policies of South Africa and before that, as long as a century ago, by the original German colonial administration of *Südwest*. They have lived through decades of administrations whose communications have somehow missed them because, being egalitarian, they did not have identifiable chiefs. . . .

Suddenly, now, Ju/'hoansi face both the challenge and the opportunity of taking part in a political process watched eagerly by the eyes of the world. But can a small minority with a hunting and gathering heritage, a recent history of isolation and exclusion from affairs that concern them, and a problematic present situation of economic underdevelopment and militarization transform itself quickly enough? Can the Ju/'hoansi hold on to what remains of their ancient territory and also take advantage of the new opportunities of freedom? An egalitarian culture which has always underplayed leadership is faced with the necessity of selecting leaders to participate in the new politics. As at the South African Cape three centuries ago, when leaders were called into being among Bushman groups warring for their lives with the Dutch colonists, Ju/'hoansi are now creating leaders to meet the challenges of the present. . . .

In 1988, news of the implementation of UN Resolution 435 and the promise of free elections in 1989 startled the Ju/'hoansi into a realization of the magnitude of possible changes. Since September of 1988 the Nyae Nyae Farmers' Cooperative, a grassroots community organization in Eastern Bushmanland, has been holding informational meetings about Namibian independence at far-flung villages. Black /Ui at N≠aqmtjoha welcomed the arrival of the discussion team: "I thank you all. I thank you for this talk which comes from far away to us. But one thing that gives me pain is that long ago I never heard anything like this, but only today am hearing it. Today my heart is happy with what I have heard. News is life."

Before the effects of the UN election information process were felt in Bushmanland, the Farmers' Coop tried to explain elections to people who had no word for them in their language. Many had never even heard the Afrikaans word *verkiesing*.

"An election means to come to an understanding about a *n!ore*."

"An election means that you give praise to the person who will sit in the chair of leading, the head person."

"An election is where you plant your feet and stop."

The talks about elections and other democratic concepts were held in villages of grass or mud houses with no protected public gathering place. The sun beat down at the edges of whatever patch of shade could be found large enough to shelter the village people and the bakkie-load of travellers. Children bounced on their mothers' laps and people of all ages sat close together, often with their legs crossing those of their neighbors. The chairperson of the Farmers' Cooperative, Tsamkxao ≠Oma, constantly encouraged others besides himself to speak.

Issues as small as how to keep tourists from swimming in the drinking water dams to ones as large as securing legal title to their land have been under long discussion at these meetings.

The Nyae Nyae area communities are preoccupied with how to ensure that they are included in talks about conservation and other issues concerning them. Great resentment is felt toward government officials who travel all the way from Windhoek to Tjum!kui, a distance of 750 kilometers, ostensibly to consult with the Ju/'hoan communities, but actually only to meet with the white officials at the comfortable Nature Conservation rest camp, and then go home. The public nature of communication has become a vital issue, and it came to a head in early March 1989 with the arrival of an SADF public relations team at /Aotcha.

Huge armored vehicles swept into the tiny village of mud houses. Uniformed men with submachine guns silenced the usual hubbub. The army was pulling out of northern Namibia, campaigning as it went for the Democratic Turnhalle Alliance (DTA), Swapo's main opposition. "Watch out for the Hyena" (Swapo) and "Vote for the Eland" (DTA) were the condescending folktale slogans the soldiers offered. "The eland is the animal without deceit: you are the eland."

The Ju/'hoan hunters' sign for eland antelope horns is a "V" made with the first and second fingers. This also happens to be the adopted hand sign for the DTA. In a further twist of irony, which the soldiers couldn't have known about, but which made an even harder puzzle for the Ju/'hoansi to unravel, "Eland" is an ancient clan name for many Ju/'hoansi in the area. Hyenas, on the other hand, are thought of as outcast animals who are always up to no good. Some people were taken in by this overwhelming symbolism, but others remained skeptical. "Swapo has never done anything to us; why should anyone call them hyenas before hearing what they have to say?" said one man.

Ultimately, the public relations meeting at /Aotcha was a bit of a rout because the officer in charge refused the people's request to tape the session. The message brought by the SADF that day was hardly secret, but since it could not be taped, the people regarded the communication as a "theft." Unfortunately for the army it didn't know that the Ju/'hoansi call tape cassettes ≠xusi, their word for oracle disks. Oracle disks are thrown down on the ground like dice and are said to reveal the future by the pattern they make. These disks are traditionally made from eland hide and are thus associated with the eland's herd sociability and supposed guilelessness.

Playing with strong symbolism can ultimately backfire, as it did resoundingly during the last feverish days of election campaigning in Bushmanland. Dabe Dahm, a Farmers' Cooperative representative at the village of //Auru, had thought for a year about the DTA's use of the eland to represent its party. Having observed violent drunkenness and clear intimidation of potential voters by the DTA campaigners, he said, "Today my shame is piled high. My people's name from long ago, 'the people of the eland,' has been rubbed in the dirt and stolen by politicians who will never do anything for us. All they want is to give other people our land."

The same day at Dabe Dahm's village people spoke of the loss of the actual eland on which they once depended. Many adults remembered a time when eland were abundant in their area.

Most Ju/'hoansi believe that the drastic reduction in eland numbers is due to the game fences. . . . Regardless of their decline in numbers, eland live in folklore and inhabit people's minds and a move to try eland domestication in Nyae Nyae is gaining support. Ju/ 'hoansi see eland farming as a sensible alternative to the kind of abuse of grazing resources they have seen destroy the productivity of adjacent areas such as Eastern Hereroland. The eland is adapted to the area, it does not suffer from the effects of *gifblaar*, and it can sustain itself on water-bearing plants such as desert cucumbers and juicy roots when water is scarce. Some Ju/'hoan people have worked on the farms of Afrikaner people in the Grootfontein area who keep eland and other game on their farms, and they know what a fine candidate the eland is for management as a herd animal. . . .

"Trucks with hunters shooting from them have chased away the animals we had here, trucks and the fences that have been built. Long ago you saw all the animals here, even eland. But today there's not a single eland. Even ostrich eggs you don't see, because the ostriches too are stopped by the fences. We don't want this, we want the fences taken down so that wild animals will come back and be close to us as before."

"If Ju/'hoansi had strength, maybe they could think of catching lots of eland, and maybe roan antelopes, and farming with them. But until after the election we will have no strength. The white people still have all the strength in this land. Maybe after the election we could do it. . . . Long ago the eland used to cross Nyae Nyae according to the season, but one season the fence was closed on them and on their calves, and they haven't returned."

It's clear that the policies of the South West African state with their paternalism and emphasis on separation have angered the Ju/'hoansi for a long time. In particular they resent being left out of communications. Ju/'hoansi call themselves "the owners of argument," and "the people who talk too much." For them, it's important that issues be discussed and debated by everyone so that ill-will doesn't fester in someone left out of the talk. . . .

The idea of representation for their voices in government is catching on among the Ju/'hoansi at the same time as they are realizing the power of the printed word. As Tsamkxao told one group meeting under a thorn tree, "One problem is that we have no scribe. We have no-one who is the 'owner of the mail.' So let the children help us. Let the children go to school, learn, and know. Let's make a plan. Let's let everyone know that we have someone with a writing-stick. Let's have a scribe, a writer, a translator. Let's not be without these."

None of the language of democracy, in fact, seems terribly new among the Ju/'hoansi, rather it is age-old. These are the people who gravely said to anthropologist Richard Lee over a decade ago: "We have no headman, each one of us is a headman over himself." The concept of "one person, one vote" fits right in with Ju/'hoan ideology, and among these sexually egalitarian people one doesn't even have to add, as would be necessary in many parts of the world, "and a woman's vote is just like a man's."

Tsamkxao illustrated democracy at one meeting, at a place called //Xa/oba, talking about collective strength and the responsibilities of the people's representatives: "I thank the old people who have spoken, but we also need to begin to hear from the young people about their *n!ores*. Everyone must work together. Do you see these sticks in my hand? If you pick up lots of sticks, you can't break them. But one stick alone breaks easily. So we want things from now on to be done on paper, legally, beginning with meetings where everyone comes together to listen. We don't want a Ju/'hoan representative who just stuffs news into his own ears and doesn't speak to us. If you speak for a group of people to a government, and if you speak badly, it doesn't just affect one person. It affects everyone. When you do something, all your people should have a way of learning about it. Political parties are for letting people know things."

One of the things Ju/'hoansi are letting people know now is that they suggest legal institutionalization of something like their old *n!ore* system. They know it has been successful over a long span of time, and see it as the basis for something that could work in Namibia's future. It would mean a new kind of survival for them, too, not the traditional one, but a creative one, their own special contribution to nation-building.

In 1989 Namibia had good rains. By March, Bushmanland was lush and green. One evening, as lilac-breasted rollers tumbled after insects against cumulus clouds lit with a pink glow by the setting sun, an historic meeting began at Nyae Nyae. After generations without meaningful talk with outside political forces, representatives of the Nyae Nyae Farmers' Coop met with officials of Swapo, the party which will construct the Namibian land tenure systems to come. With the two groups sitting on the grass in a rough circle of about forty people, including onlookers, the Coop presented a document stating its goals with regard to land and representation. Written in the Ju/'hoan language and translated into English, the statement calls for a democratic national system with regional autonomous government in Nyae Nyae based on current and long-term residence.

Ju/'hoansi know they are the last Bushman people in Namibia to have an unbroken contact with even the small fragment of land that is still theirs. And they know these ties to land are their main resource: "Where your mother and father are buried is where you have your strength."

The Ju/'hoansi of Eastern Bushmanland are the lucky ones. But they are planning carefully to share their land and a chance to make an independent living with other Bushmen in Namibia. The election and the talk that preceded it has begun to give these isolated people a sense of the altruism needed to create a nation.

"I said to the Administrator General, 'Will you help us since our *n!ore* is small? Hereros have taken part of it and !Kaudum is another part gone.'

"I also told him, 'The people who once worked in the army today have no work and no other strength. How will we help those people?'

"I said, 'The people called Vasekela—we still haven't met together to talk with them. I understand that they may be allowed to stay in Western Bushmanland and make gardens. We must ask how they are going to do that without water.'

"We want to help everyone we can. It's important that we who are the Ju/'hoansi have our own government and do our own work. We have only a small place, but we want to go to the Gobabis farms and find our people who long ago were taken away. We want to get them and bring them here. Can we find a way to help everyone?

"We have received money from the owners of helping' [aid funds] and we have dug boreholes for more water in our small land. The !Kaudum people are many, and many others are on police-posts that will now die, or in Gobabis. We who are representatives of the Nyae Nyae Farmers' Cooperative are like people planting a tree. We should realize that we are not just one small thing but are starting something big. The work will go on, even beyond our deaths. The boreholes will be there." (Tsamkxao ≠Oma.)

GLOSSARY

Acculturation   Culture change which occurs when societies with different cultures come into prolonged contact with one another.

Agriculture   A subsistence pattern based upon the cultivation of plants and/or the raising of livestock. TRADITIONAL AGRICULTURE involves the use of human labor and draft animals to produce food. INDUSTRIAL AGRICULTURE involves the use of machinery and chemicals to produce large quantities of food.

Band Societies   Societies in which people exist in small groups which lack any formalized system of political leadership. Kinship is generally the basic unit of organization in these egalitarian groups.

Bride Price   Money or items of value given to the bride's family as part of the marriage arrangement.

Comparative Research   Research focusing on the analysis of similarities and differences among peoples.

Cultural Anthropology   That branch of anthropology which studies people who define themselves as a social group. Cultural anthropologists attempt to describe and analyze how the culture of a people affects their behavior.

Cultural Relativism   An approach to understanding the behavior of a group of people by analyzing that behavior within the context of their particular culture.

Culture   The shared knowledge that a group of people use to construct their own behavior and to interpret the behavior of others.

Enculturation   The process of learning a culture that occurs as a child grows

Ethnocentrism   The belief that one's own culture is superior to all others.

Fieldwork   The anthropological method of studying another culture by going to the place where the people being studied live.

Fraternal Polyandry   The marriage pattern wherein a woman is married to two or more men who are brothers.

Genotype   The genetic make-up of an individual.

Holism   The notion that culture is composed of a variety of elements, including subsistence pattern, kinship system, political organization, belief system, etc. and that all of these elements must be considered together.

Homo Erectus   Category of fossil hominid that preceded *Homo sapiens* in the fossil record.

Horticulture   A system of food production which involves the clearing of relatively small portions of forest to prepare the land for gardening.

Hunting and Gathering   A system of food production which involves the hunting of animals and the collecting of wild plant foods.

Longhouse   Type of house built by the Iroquois Indians of northeastern North America. It was a long, rectangular building which housed an extended family composed of related females and their husbands and children.

Matrilineal   A system of kinship in which descent is traced through females.

Multicultural Society   A society within which are found a number of separate cultures.

Participant Observation   A fieldwork method used by cultural anthropologists. It involves participating in the daily life of the people being studied.

Pastoralism   A system of food production based upon the herding of domesticated animals. It often involves at least seasonal nomadic shifting of herds and associated human camps.

Patrilateral Parallel Cousin Marriage   A form of marriage in which a man marries his father's brother's daughter.

Phenotype   Outward physical appearance of an individual.

Physical Anthropology   That branch of anthropology which focuses upon the biological aspect of humanity.

Polyandry   The marriage pattern whereby one woman is married to two or more men. See also FRATERNAL POLYANDRY.

Polygyny   The marriage pattern whereby one man is married to two or more women.

Race   A population within a species that differs genetically from other populations of the same species.

Racism   A notion that some races are "superior" or "inferior" to others.

Shaman   An individual who is believed to have special abilities to communicate with and/or control supernatural forces. Shamans are most often associated with less technologically complex cultures as hunter-gatherers and horticulturalists.

Subculture   An identifiably separate cultural group existing within a larger society. A society containing several subcultures would be called a multicultural society.

Subsistence Pattern   The technology, behaviors, and beliefs associated with a particular method of making a living. Examples include hunting and gathering, horticulture, and pastoralism.

INDEX